D1547334

Composition's Roots in English Education

Edited by Patricia Lambert Stock

Boynton/Cook Publishers
HEINEMANN
Portsmouth, NH

Boynton/Cook Publishers, Inc.
361 Hanover Street
Portsmouth, NH 03801–3912
www.boyntoncook.com

Offices and agents throughout the world

The editor and publisher wish to thank those who have generously given permission to reprint borrowed material:

Figure 5.1: Scale of Intellectual Ascent for Discourse from "Invisible Writing: Investigating Cognitive Processes in Composition" by Sheridan Blau, *College Composition and Communication* (Vol. 34, No. 3). Copyright © 1983 by the National Council of Teachers of English. Reprinted with permission of the publisher.

Excerpt from "Friends' caring and sharing shows the way" by Donald M. Murray, *Boston Globe* (January 2, 2007). Donald M. Murray's work is reprinted with the permission of The Rosenberg Group on behalf of the Author's estate.

"On My Disciplinary Birth" from *True to the Language Game* by Keith Gilyard. Copyright © 2011 by Routledge, Taylor & Francis Group. Reprinted with permission of the publisher.

Library of Congress Cataloging-in-Publication Data
Composition's roots in English education / edited by Patricia Lambert Stock.
    p. cm.
  ISBN-13: 978-0-86709-610-1
  ISBN-10: 0-86709-610-1
    1. English language—Study and teaching.   2. Language arts.   3. English language—Composition and exercises—Study and teaching.   I. Stock, Patricia L.

LB1576.C5795   2011
372.6'044—dc23   2011032363

Editor: Charles I. Schuster
Production: Abigail M. Heim
Typesetter: Val Levy, Drawing Board Studios
Cover design: Monica Crigler
Manufacturing: Steve Bernier

Printed in the United States of America on acid-free paper

T & C Digital

For Richard

Contents

Acknowledgments

Although it was unplanned, it is fitting that this collection of essays appears on the hundredth anniversary of the founding of the National Council of Teachers of English, the colloquy within which the fields of English education and composition studies were conceived and established in America. For more than a century, the scholars who have contributed essays to this collection and those about whom they write have beneficially influenced education in the English language arts from kindergarten through the university level. Their work has developed the fields of English education and composition studies in council meetings and publications and beyond. For this reason, I thank the countless English language arts educators who have come together in NCTE over the years to teach and learn from one another for the benefit of students at all levels of instruction and who have insisted from the outset that learning to write by writing to learn is central to every student's education. Among them, there are those to whom I offer particular thanks.

Lisa Luedeke and Charles Schuster, Boynton/Cook–Heinemann acquisitions and series editors, thank you for embracing and encouraging this project from the beginning. Chuck, thank you for wise advice and guidance, all along the way. Abby Heim, Sarah Fournier, and Anita Gildea, Boynton/Cook–Heinemann production editors, thank you for your steadfast and creative attention to small details and the larger project, and thank you Monica Crigler, for a cover design that reflects so well the books contents.

Sheridan Blau, Lil Brannon, Janet Emig, Cathy Fleischer, Anne Gere, Keith Gilyard, Cy Knoblauch, Charlie Moran, Tom Newkirk, Bonnie Sunstein, Kathi Yancey, and Jim Zebroski—teacher scholars I admire—thank you for joining me to tell an important chapter of the story of composition's roots in English education.

Sheridan Blau, Cathy Fleischer, Dixie Goswami, Joe Harris, and Duane Roen, thank you for discussing the project with me over the years to its benefit.

Carl Berger, Anne Gere, Jay Robinson, Homer Rose, and Bernard Van't Hul, thank you for helping me to learn more fully the roles the University of Michigan played in the establishment of English education and composition studies in America.

Up close and personal: Thank you, Richard, for encouraging me to do this work in the first place; thank you, Heidi, Andrew, and Theresa, for your genuinely thoughtful interest in a mother's work; and thank you, Maddie, David, Rachel, and Henry, for reminding me—every day—of why living and learning and loving are gifts. "I lucky to you!"

Patricia Lambert Stock
East Lansing, Michigan

Preface

The Backstory

This book, a history of the roots of composition studies in the field of English education—composed in the form of representative memoirs, case studies, and analytical narratives—has its own history. Over coffee at the 2002 meeting of the Conference on College Composition and Communication (CCCC), I asked Lisa Luedeke and Charles Schuster if Boynton/Cook–Heinemann might be interested in doing a twentieth-anniversary edition of *fforum: Essays on Theory and Practice in the Teaching of Writing*, a book I edited that Boynton/ Cook–Heinemann published in 1983. Like other collections of essays at the time, *fforum* was designed to offer a conceptual overview of the emerging field of composition studies: in this case, a view that focused attention on how the scholarship of English educators was shaping the field. I proposed this second collection of essays to Lisa and Chuck because I believed that at the turn of the twenty-first century, a new generation of compositionists was largely unaware of the role that English educators—who worked across the twentieth century and most influentially in the 1960s, 1970s, and 1980s—played in establishing the field of composition studies. Lisa and Chuck were interested.

Hours later, at the same CCCC meeting, the imperative for this collection became more striking. Sitting in a session that was described as speaking to the role composition studies might play in improving English education, I was surprised that none of the panelists referred to the work of English educators who had been founders of the field of composition studies. In the question-and-answer session that followed presentations, discussion confirmed my concern. Almost no one, in a crowded room, knew the story of composition's roots in English education—a story vital to understanding the origins and early development of the field of composition studies.

Certainly this history may be found—a piece here, a bit there—in books and articles written over the years by teachers and scholars in English education and composition, but not in one comprehensive text aimed at identifying and discussing in some depth the rootedness of the field of composition studies in the works and lives of scholars in the field of English education. To address this gap in the histories of both composition and English education, I turned to a group of teacher-scholars—highly regarded in both fields—whose academic preparation or first area of academic specialization was English education. I asked them if they would consider writing personally inflected histories for this collection, essays that would directly recount or evocatively reveal the larger transpersonal story of composition's roots in English education. I

ix

made this request hoping that collectively we would compose a history that animated names and publications and dates with portraits and scenes, a history that would invite readers into the times and commitments of dedicated teacher-scholars who were as generously supportive of one another as they were determined to learn how best to teach their students to write effectively at all levels of instruction.

Personal and professional demands on its authors' lives have taken this project a decade to complete. To name a few of the commitments that have occupied the authors whose essays are collected here, let me note that six have been presidents of the National Council of Teachers of English; four, chairs of CCCC; ten, directors of writing project sites; four, editors of national journals and book series; twelve, department chairs or program directors or both. The authors of hundreds of books and articles in the fields of English education and composition studies, Sheridan Blau, Lil Brannon, Janet Emig, Cathy Fleischer, Anne Ruggles Gere, Keith Gilyard, Cy Knoblauch, Charles Moran, Thomas Newkirk, Patricia Lambert Stock, Bonnie Sunstein, Kathleen Blake Yancey, and James Zebroski are scholars and professional citizens, working in the tradition of the teacher-scholars whose work we aim to document here.

I invite you to sit back and see our fields through our eyes, perhaps newly.

Patricia Lambert Stock
East Lansing, Michigan

Foreword

Remembering Composition

> . . . the *rhetoric and composition* designation glosses
> over the deep roots of its work in these fields [of education and linguistics]
> . . . despite the fact that many figures whose work has historically
> been key to rhetoric and composition, and many figures active
> in the field so designated, are most closely affiliated with
> these fields; . . . and despite the fact that many others in rhetoric and composition
> bring substantial experience in education and linguistics, including experience teaching
> high school and English as a second language, to their work in what is nonetheless
> simply called *rhetoric and composition.*
>
> —Horner and Lu (487–88)

It's a sign of the maturing of a discipline/field, or perhaps its success, that scholars want to write its history. Initially, of course, academics—scholars and teachers—are too busy *creating* the history that will then be documented to concern themselves very much about how they or others might represent it. But that changes when a field or discipline reaches a certain status, which rhetoric and composition has surely achieved. It's no surprise, then, that histories are now accumu-

> *A commonplace circulates that rhetoric is the mother of composition.*
>
> —*Keith Gilyard*

lating, adding to ones that have near canonical status—for instance, Berlin's *Rhetoric and Reality: Writing Instruction in American Colleges, 1900–1985*; Connors' *Composition-Rhetoric: Backgrounds, Theory, and Pedagogy*; and Goggin's *Authoring a Discipline: Scholarly Journals and the Post-World War II Emergence of Rhetoric and Composition*—newer volumes like Hawk's *A Counter-History of Composition: Toward Methodologies of Complexity* and Dobrin's *Postcomposition*, the latter of which looks backward largely to look forward. And of course, we have histories of composition, writing, and literacy

> *Clearly the forgetting of English education has much to do with the forgetting of women's work: teaching, like cooking, seems to leave no history.*
>
> —*Charles Moran*

that focus largely on the K–12 world; again we have a canon there as well, with Arthur Applebee's *Tradition and Reform in the Teaching of English: A History* likely being first on the list. What we haven't had is a history that brings together the multiple traditions suggested here, one that would quite intentionally and specifically speak to language and rhetoric, to composition and writing, to education and English, to K–12 and college. Until now.

We have many reasons to be pleased about this new volume, and although I suspect they will be obvious to readers, please allow me to try your patience as I think aloud about five of them.

One is that this volume speaks in many voices to the question about the genesis of composition studies—and it's a fair question: When did composition studies begin? It's also fair enough to say, "That depends," suggesting that the frame of reference influences the answer one composes. At the same time, too often we neglect the frame and generalize a specific beginning as *the* beginning, as though there were a Magna Carta for rhetoric and composition. Put differently, as we see here, it's valuable to have a historical volume that articulates the question and frames the answer so that we can see what has previously been largely invisible and unarticulated—and what has been available has been dispersed across sites and platforms. There is, in fact, another history. And all this is particularly important in an era when offhand references, accurate or not and whether in a conference hallway or on a listserv, become accepted as fact in a field where our work ethic is admirable but our memories are remarkably short.

Like many of us who represent the previous generations of academic specialists in English education and composition, James Moffett never had a graduate course in either composition or English education and came to both fields by stumbling into a secondary school teaching job.

—Sheridan Blau

As our field matures and those who remember the contributions of Richard Braddock fade from view, we lose a portion of our history. And it is not just the history of an individual; it is a portion of our collective identity that is at risk of disappearing from our concept of the field and its work.

—Anne Ruggles Gere

Two is that the history here, like other histories, is composed of many materials, including the memories of many—first-person accounts as well as remembrances of others—that in this case are the material of *our* history. We are fortunate in that this history was lived by teachers and scholars who are still alive and who can thus share with us information about their own experiences as well as their memories of scholar-leaders like James Moffett and Richard Braddock, of editors like Bob

Boynton, and of foundational events like Project English and the Dartmouth Conference. The wealth of material here—including memories, accounts, information, and analyses of major figures, events, publishers, and individual programs—helps us understand the roles that each of these plays, individually and collectively, in forming any discipline and that helped form ours.

Like autumn in New England, a time of contextual convergence—sea and air, soil and leaf, foggy unreality and crisp reality— our profession has experienced a season of shifting understandings and companion ironies.

—Bonnie Sunstein

Three is that the volume before us is composed of many voices. Perhaps one hundred years from now, a scholar of the history of composition studies can visit archives, read journal articles, and access transcripts of interviews in an effort to construct the contingent definitive history. And again, perhaps not. If history is lived by a group of people, it's a good question as to why they shouldn't at least help compose this history. Other institutions are beginning to make this assumption: The Smithsonian's African American History Museum, for example, only recently received approval for the design of its new building, but for years citizens have been invited to "tell us your history, share a family photograph, and connect with others by contributing to the Museum's Memory Book." For a history to be authentic as well as accurate, a multiplicity of voices is required,

Indeed, for all of those writing for Boynton/ Cook, their ethos was that of a philosopher, constructing their classrooms as a site for reflection, action, and change. They wrote as teachers for an audience of teachers, their work with students their driving force.

—Lil Brannon and Cy Knoblauch

we now believe. And here, we hear from such a multiplicity, spread across differing periods of time, institutions, and genres.

Four is the twofold way that the volume demonstrates our relationship to schools and to students. On the one hand, looking backward, it's a mantra in the field that composition is unique in its attention to students; here we see how that played out, from the very beginning, with a foundational assumption that students aren't merely the beneficiaries of our intellectual and pedagogical largesse, but rather that they are participants with much to share with us, not least of which is what they already know about composing. On the other hand, looking forward, this volume will allow us to share a very different view of the field with our students, who, like mine this term in a grad-

Many of us who experienced this shift there would inhabit two worlds: spending a morning in an East Austin high school supervising student teachers, and an afternoon in a Kinneavy seminar (the only graduate course in rhetoric) struggling to see how Merleau-Ponty provided the rationale for Kinneavy's view of expressive discourse.

—Thomas Newkirk

We took writing seriously again, after an unhappy hiatus, rescuing it from being regarded simply as a skill and a domestic drudgery. Instead, we honored it as a central symbolic process worthy of being a subject and an object of inquiry, possibly constituting a unique field, perhaps even a discipline. We took children and adolescents seriously as learners. We took schools, especially public schools, seriously, noting how they both form and deform learning.

—*Janet Emig*

uate class in composition theory, include English education students working with rhetoric and composition students. Together, they are building a future; it will be good for them, and for us, to know how that future carries forward the past.

Five is the provocative nature of the volume, and by provocative, I don't mean unpleasant or agonistic, but rather thought-provoking and surprising: here, some of our cherished beliefs are called into question. Some of the questions are historical in nature. What, for example, was the role of education in the formation of composition studies? What was the role of gender in its formation? Class—defined in a variety of ways—is certainly another important element, but in what ways and to what effect? Other questions are more future-oriented and inferential. Are there certain sites, physical sites like the state of Michigan and organizational sites like the National Council of Teachers of English itself, that were especially hospitable for the development of composition, why, and what does that mean for us today? What especially might that mean today as an increasing number of writing programs leave English departments and create their own programs and departments and design their own writing majors? As composition continues to thrive, will our students remain at the center of the field, and if that's important, how do we ensure that this centrality continues?

What we saw was that the intersections are natural ones and that the end results—when we take care to recognize and celebrate these intersections—can be vitally important for literacy teaching and learning.

—*Cathy Fleischer*

As I develop my argument, I am going to refer to the early informal, unstable, often antidisciplinary collectives of people interested in composition, especially at the college level, as a social formation. Composition "within" English was antidisciplinary because it was not literary study or New Critical. It often drew on social science research. For the most part, this social formation only occurred in the late 1960s and during the 1970s. Composition as a social formation began to gather in the years 1968–1973.

—*James Zebroski*

Here, then, is a new history of composition studies, one that complements, complicates, and, in many ways, challenges what we think we know about our own history. Located in rich memories and diverse genres, this history points us toward a future for the field as it asks us if we will continue our dual commitment to students and to social justice. And not least, in its specifics of the early days of the field, it provides a human account that engages us— as readers and as human beings— precisely because of its humanity.

The discipline—composition studies— would not have come to be and come to be recognized had it not been for the scholars in English education about whom you will read here.

—Patti Stock

Works Cited

Applebee, Arthur N. 1974. *Tradition and Reform in the Teaching of English: A History.* Urbana, IL: NCTE.

Berlin, James A. 1987. *Rhetoric and Reality: Writing Instruction in American Colleges, 1900–1985.* Carbondale, IL: Southern Illinois University Press.

Connors, Robert J. 1997. *Composition-Rhetoric: Backgrounds, Theory, and Pedagogy.* Pittsburgh, PA: University of Pittsburgh Press.

Dobrin, Sid. 2011. *Postcomposition.* Carbondale, IL: Southern Illinois UP.

Goggin, Maureen. 2000. *Authoring a Discipline: Scholarly Journals and the Post-World War II Emergence of Rhetoric and Composition.* London: Routledge.

Hawk, Byron. 2007. *A Counter-History of Composition: Toward Methodologies of Complexity.* Pittsburgh, PA: University of Pittsburgh Press.

Horner, Bruce, and Min Zhan Lu. 2010. "Working Rhetoric and Composition." *College English* 72.5 (May): 470–94.

Kathleen Blake Yancey
Florida State University

Introduction

The Intertwined Roots of English Education and Composition Studies

Patricia Lambert Stock

In recent years, a number of histories of composition studies have added substantially to the field's self-knowledge. These histories have also contributed to
the enhanced status that composition studies has experienced in the academy,
in part because they have uncovered and interpreted what the new historicists
might call an impressive body of overlooked and undervalued texts that invite
rereading and reevaluation of earlier histories of English studies, particularly
of the teaching and learning of English composition in America. However, as
James Zebroski reminds us in his essay in this collection, both the more traditional and the more radical of these histories (e.g., Berlin 1996, 1987, 1984;
Connors 1997; Crowley 1998; Harris 1997; Miller 1998, 1991; Miller 1997,
to name a few) have almost completely overlooked modern composition studies' roots in the field of English education. This collection of essays was conceived to address that oversight. In preparation for composing the collection, I
learned what I had not known before: Just as the field of composition studies'
roots are deeply imbedded in English education, so too are the field of English
education's roots deeply imbedded in composition studies. Just as histories
of composition studies have almost completely overlooked that field's roots
in English education, histories of English education have almost completely
overlooked that field's roots in composition studies.

In light of this discovery, I decided to introduce the essays collected here,
written by outstanding scholars who have made significant contributions to
both the fields of English education and composition studies, with two telling stories that shed light on the larger narrative of composition studies' and
English education's intertwined roots. The first expands the generally accepted
understanding that the National Council of Teachers of English (NCTE) was
established to counteract uniform reading lists and their constraints on secondary school English curricula in the early years of the twentieth century. This
story accounts for how concern about the teaching of writing played a significant role in the establishment of NCTE. The second, that flows easily out of

1

the first, illustrates how English education and composition studies developed and interanimated one another across the twentieth century in one American university: the University of Michigan. This case study is one of many that might be offered to demonstrate how English education and composition studies developed interdependently in America.

Establishing the Field of English Education in America

The scholarly discipline and the school subject English are relative newcomers to the academic scene. Harvard, Oxford, and Cambridge universities did not establish professorships of English until 1876, 1904, and 1911, respectively (Parker 1967); and it is generally understood that the school subject English was defined and established as a required part of the secondary school curriculum in America as a result of the work of the 1892 Committee of Ten appointed by the National Education Association (NEA). As I see it, the founding of the NCTE in December 1911 and the publication of *English Journal (EJ)*, beginning in January 1912, staked claim in America to a corner of the developing field of English studies that we call English education. Although the term *English education* has come—over the years—to denote particularly the work of English teacher educators, I am using the term in this essay to refer to the work of teacher-scholars who formed themselves into a professional community for the purpose of shaping curriculum and instruction in subject English and for the preparation of those who would teach it.

Although the ground for the platting of English education had been stirred in emerging city, state, and regional associations of teachers of English, the Modern Language Association of America (MLA), the English Round Table of the Secondary Section of the NEA, and books and articles about the teaching of English that began to appear in the final years of the nineteenth century, it was not until NCTE's meetings and publications that issues and investigations of concern to English educators across all levels of instruction became systematically available for peer review and community use, for a scholarship of English education to be developed.

In his highly regarded history of the field of English education, Arthur Applebee (1974) tells us that two movements, begun in the Northeast, led to the founding of NCTE. One was aimed at the general reorganization of secondary education to better suit the needs of the increasing numbers of increasingly diverse students who were entering the nation's secondary schools, most of whom were not college bound. The second was a protest against Uniform Reading Lists—designed to prepare students for college entrance examinations—that were shaping and constraining the secondary school teaching of literature. When NEA was approached to lodge a formal protest against these lists, the association's Secondary Roundtable asked James Fleming Hosic of Chicago Normal School to chair a committee to study the issue.

Acting on his charge, in December 1911 at the Great Northern Hotel in Chicago, Hosic, who would become the first executive secretary of the council, convened a meeting of representatives of twelve states, most of whom were secondary school teachers. Hosic came prepared to this meeting with the draft of a constitution for a National Council of Teachers of English and an offer to found—at his own expense—a journal that would serve as the official organ of the council. Among the charter members of the council who joined him at the meeting were Fred Newton Scott, Professor of Rhetoric in the University of Michigan, who served as the NCTE's first and second president and about whom I will have more to say later in this essay, and Edwin Mortimer Hopkins, Professor of English in the University of Kansas, who would become the council's fifth president. Hopkins' contributions to the meeting provide me a starting place to add to the generally known history of the founding of NCTE and the field of English education in America and to contribute a new chapter to the history of modern composition studies, one that draws attention to that discipline's roots in English education.

The first number of *EJ*, published in January 1912, reveals that in addition to the protest movements that originated in the Northeast, a third movement precipitated the founding of NCTE. In the lead piece in the "Round Table," a feature that Hosic intended to encourage discussion of "lively" issues, Hopkins put into writing remarks he had made the month before in Chicago. Introducing his remarks with reference to the general topic Hosic posed for the "Round Table"—"What Problems Should the Council First Attempt to Solve?" (1912, 49), Hopkins wrote:

> I am glad that the question put the word problems in the plural, for the Council is certainly large enough in membership to do more than one thing at a time, and it seems to me that four things need early attention. First are the two discussed today: We may well aid the eastern teachers to secure needed revision of college-entrance requirements, if they will join us to secure an adequate number of persons for teaching English composition. (49)

By opening "The Roundtable" with Hopkins' statement, I suspect Hosic meant to document the range of forces that brought NCTE into being: the well-known movement to counteract the constraining effects of book lists and entrance requirements on the secondary school English curriculum and the less well-known movement to counteract working conditions constraining the effective teaching of writing. Articles in the early issues of *EJ* demonstrate that Hopkins was not playing sandbox politics when he asked, in return for his and others' support of Northeastern teachers' protest movements, reciprocal support of Midwestern teachers' efforts to put into place labor-intensive strategies for teaching writing that they were moving from the extracurriculum to the formal curriculum (see, for example, Carino 1995; Gere 1987, 1994). The fifty-three articles published in the first ten issues of *EJ* (1912) demonstrate the widespread interest of English teachers at all levels of instruction in the teaching of writing: twelve of the articles were about the teaching of written composition; seven, about speaking (oral composition); six, about drama; five, about poetry; four, about school-college relationships, objectives, and curriculum; three, about the teaching of literature and the English language; two each, about college English and professional problems; one each, about financial support of English, fiction, course organization, the school library, evaluation, principles of methods, use of magazines, and the teaching of composition and literature (Hook 1979, 27).[1] More than a third of the articles published in the first year's issues of *EJ* were about the teaching of writing.

If the movement in the Northeast that led to the establishment of NCTE can be traced to meetings in New York City and New York State, the movement in the Midwest can be traced to a meeting of the Central Division of the MLA in Iowa City in 1909 in which English educators expressed their collective concern about working conditions that constrained composition teachers from offering the writing workshop ("laboratory") courses they were persuaded were the best means of teaching students to write effectively. At that meeting, a committee of five, with Hopkins as its chair, was charged to determine and report on "the conditions of English composition teaching with especial reference to the amount of written work necessarily required, the proper disposal of it, and the necessary equipment" (*PMLA* 1910, xxxiv).[2]

The committee began its work, as concerned teachers in the Northeast had, with a survey study. A year later, at the 1910 MLA meeting, Hopkins reported on what the committee learned from more than one thousand teachers' responses to the questionnaire they circulated (*PMLA* 1911):

> That English composition is not only a fundamental and necessary subject but is also a laboratory subject, requiring besides oral training much practice in writing, which should average about 400 words a week for high school pupils and 650 for college freshmen; and for proper attention from instructors should take not less than an hour of time for each 2000 words in high schools and 2200 in colleges, under average conditions.
>
> That while eye and brain and nervous system can endure on the average barely two hours a day of theme reading with continued maintenance of health and efficiency, under present average conditions composition teachers must either spend from 20 to 30 hours a week (reported maximum 75 hours) in reading themes, and take the physical consequence often ending in permanent and serious injury, or else slight their work or leave it in proportionate part undone.
>
> That under these conditions a majority of composition teachers either regret their choice of profession or hold it through resolve to sacrifice health and personal ambition to the interests of their pupils.
>
> That the principal reasons for their discouragement are these: (a) It is physically impossible to secure reasonably satisfactory results, since their work is from 50 to 150 percent greater than that required of other instructors.

[handwritten margin note: Poor teaching conditions]

(b) In 25 per cent of the schools reporting, their pay is less. (c) The drain upon mental and physical vitality rapidly depreciates efficiency. (d) Adequate reading and scholarship and maintenance of professional standing are commonly impossible. (e) The facts herein stated are commonly disbelieved or disregarded by school officers and administrators, when brought to their attention.

That the work of a composition teacher should be measured by the number of students in his classes, only incidentally by the number of his class recitation hours; and that under favorable conditions this number should not exceed eighty for high schools and sixty for college freshman classes. (xliii–xliv)

It appears that those who heard Hopkins' report in 1910 asked the Committee on Teaching English Composition to make specific recommendations about action that should be taken in view of the facts the committee had learned because, a year later in his report at the 1911 meeting of MLA, Hopkins indicated that making the facts of composition teachers' working conditions public "with the utmost possible weight of emphasis and authority" was the only way to realize change (*PMLA* 1912, xxviii). He reported further that he had already begun work to accomplish this goal: He had prepared a pamphlet for that purpose and distributed it in seven states (usually at state expense, since the committee did not have funds of its own). In addition, and significantly in the history of English education and composition studies' intertwined roots, he published in the founding issue of *EJ* an interim report of his committee's findings and another survey questionnaire designed to collect additional information. The interim report, "Can Good Composition Teaching Be Done Under Present Conditions?"[3] appeared as the lead article in the first issue of the first journal published in the field of English education in America.

Hopkins begins the article as he began his report to the MLA in 1910 with a description of composition teachers' difficult working conditions. But this time, instead of letting a description of those conditions stand as an argument for the need to change them as he had in his 1910 MLA report, Hopkins shapes his argument in terms that would be familiar and potentially persuasive in the discourse developing in the field of education at the time:

powerful)
dramatic

Every year teachers resign, break down, perhaps become permanently invalided, having sacrificed ambition, health, and in not a few instances even life, in the struggle to do all the work expected of them. Every year thousands of pupils drift through the schools, half-cared for in English classes where they should have constant and encouraging personal attention, and neglected in other classes where their English should be watched over as least incidentally, to emerge in a more or less damaged linguistic condition, incapable of meeting satisfactorily the simplest practical demand upon their powers of expression. Much money is spent, valuable teachers are worn out at an inhumanly rapid rate, and results are inadequate or wholly lacking. From any point of view—that of taxpayer, teacher, or pupil—such a situation is intolerable. (1912, 1)

When Hopkins suggests that composition teachers' working conditions—too few teachers for too many students—shortchange students and taxpayers, he casts his argument in language and practices that characterized an influential strand of the discourse and discursive practices that education had borrowed from business and industry.[4] The per-pupil cost of staffing courses in public schools was widely used to determine curricular offerings at the time. To make his case persuasive to educational administrators and policy makers—to argue for those changes in composition teachers' working conditions that he and his colleagues wanted to see come to pass because of instructional practices valued by teachers of English, Hopkins also drew upon the discourse and discursive practices of English studies at the time:

> A single statement will explain the fundamental trouble [facing teachers of composition]. Not very many years ago, when effort was made to apply the principle that pupils should learn to write by writing, English composition, previously known as rhetoric, became ostensibly a laboratory subject, but without any material addition to the personnel of its teaching force; there was merely a gratuitous increase in the labor of teachers who were already doing full duty. . . .
>
> Probably no other laboratory subject has ever been introduced into any school till space enough and apparatus enough and teachers enough had been provided to insure to each pupil that degree of individual attention necessary to his individual development. But the laboratory teaching of English during all these years has had so little provision made for it that it has been for the most part, little more than a travesty. (1912, 2)

Articles published in the early issues of the *EJ* reveal that the "laboratory" method of teaching writing was a topic of frequent discussion among composition teachers associated with NCTE. In an essay written some years later, in which he traces roots of contemporary writing center practices, Peter Carino (1995) speculates that Philo Buck, a high school teacher from St. Louis, may have coined the term *laboratory method* in a talk he offered in 1904 during the Forty-third Annual Meeting of the NEA. In his talk, Buck described how he taught students to write. In his classroom, students wrote about topics of interest to them and both he and their peers read and critiqued students' work in progress. Carino also speculates that Philo Buck was probably using the term, as Hopkins did in his MLA reports and his 1912 essay in *EJ*, to compare the demands of the teaching of writing to those of the better-funded teaching of science. Whether called *laboratory* or *workshop* practices, the instructional practices that early contributors to *EJ* shared with one another for peer review and community use are ones that other historians tell us developed and evolved in the literary and debating societies and clubs of early American colleges and universities and made their way into composition courses in secondary schools

[handwritten margin note: replaced w/ term "workshop"]

and colleges in the late nineteenth and early twentieth centuries (e.g., Berlin 1984, 1987; Connors 1997; Gere 1987; Schultz 1999).

One of the things I find interesting about the first article published in *EJ* is how Hopkins articulates—in both senses of that word—English and education. As he gives voice to his research and concerns about the teaching of writing, he brings together terms and practices developing in discourses emerging at the time, the discourse of education and the discourse of English studies. In the process, he—and others who wrote for *EJ* in the early years—gave shape to the discourse and discursive practices of English education. Articulation theorists might account for phenomena like the writings of Hopkins and others who contributed to the early numbers of *EJ* and the development of English education by noting how these teacher scholars, most of whom were responsible for teaching English language, literature, and composition all at once, all together, established a scholarly field that was new, generative, and developing coherence, by conjoining teacher-scholars whose intentions, meanings, understandings, values, and practices that were not necessarily in harmony with one another at the outset.

English Education and Composition Studies
in the University of Michigan

bio of Path

My personal history in the intertwined fields of English education and composition studies began some years after the founding of NCTE and Edwin Hopkins' work. In the late 1970s, I joined the faculty in the newly established English Composition Board—the unit created to oversee the equally new writing requirement in the College of Literature, Science, and the Arts (LS&A) in the University of Michigan—and I became a doctoral student in Michigan's Joint Ph.D. Program in English and Education (JPEE). A secondary school teacher of English with experience in urban, suburban, and rural settings, I stepped into a stream of distinguished work forged more than a century earlier when founders of Michigan's educational system made provision in the state's constitution for a dynamic relationship between its common schools and the University of Michigan.

As it happens, the story of composition's roots in English education in the University of Michigan is the story of scholars, themes, and projects that figure significantly in the history of the field of composition studies' roots in the field of English education. English educators in the University of Michigan conceived composition studies even before NCTE was established, even before they knew they were doing so. For this and two other reasons, I share a bit of what I know about the history of their work. First, in this collection of essays written by scholars who have played foundational roles in the development of composition studies, you will read about yet other remarkable individuals whose work launched the field. The story of composition's roots in English education in the University of Michigan contributes to this broader narrative and provides a prologue to it. Second, I tell the story to enliven—to

style note: she gets meta, gives purpose

dramatize with individuals and efforts—one case of the work of English educators, across the twentieth century, that took place in a number of universities in the United States, to realize a community of scholars and a body of knowledge about the teaching of writing.

The Intertwined Roots of English Education and Composition Studies

In the spirit of Michigan's provision for a dynamic relationship between its common schools and the University of Michigan, during his time as acting president of the university (1869–1871), a time when admission to east coast colleges and universities was determined by entrance examinations, Henry S. Frieze put in place "the diploma connection," the first system in the United States for admitting to the university students who graduated from university-accredited high schools (Kitzhaber 1990, 29). This hierarchical system might have become elitist under the stewardship of leaders less egalitarian than James B. Angell, who was recommended by and succeeded Frieze as the third president of the university (1871–1909) and—in the field of English studies—Fred Newton Scott, who attended the university, joined its faculty in English in 1889, and served as head of Michigan's Department of Rhetoric from its formation in 1903 through his retirement in 1927, when the department was refolded into the Department of English Language and Literature.

In his comprehensive history of higher education in the United States, *The American College and University* (1962), Fredrick Rudolph contrasts James B. Angell's conception of the role of higher education at the time of his presidency with that of his contemporary Charles W. Eliot, President of Harvard University, by recalling the following remarks that Eliot made about emerging state universities at an 1873 meeting of the NEA:

> There is a skepticism of the masses in Massachusetts as to the justice of everybody paying for the advanced education of somebody's child. The mechanic, the blacksmith, the weaver says: "Why should I pay for the professional education of the lawyer's son, the minister's son? The community does not provide *my* son his forge or loom." (278–79)

Reflecting on Eliot's remarks, Rudolph observes:

> For Angell higher education was not a luxury but a necessity that should be made available to all. It would not have occurred to him to make the assumption that came so naturally to President Eliot that the blacksmith's son was destined to be a blacksmith. (279)

To have studied in the University of Michigan, served on its faculty, worked in an office in Angell Hall, as I did, was to have known that James B. Angell imagined the state university he worked to establish as a requisite agency of a democratic society. Accordingly, during Angell's presidency, Michigan proved to be a hospitable intellectual environment for faculty who shared his commitment to Jeffersonian democracy, scholars like the philosopher of education John Dewey and the English educator Fred Newton Scott. Dewey, having studied at Johns Hopkins University with George S. Morris—there on leave from his role as chairman of Michigan's philosophy department—accepted an invitation to teach at Michigan in 1884. During his Michigan years, Dewey participated in "the diploma connection." As he traveled in the state, observing and conferring with precollegiate teachers, he became interested in problems of education, and he became a friend of the young Fred Newton Scott,[5] who also participated influentially in precollegiate education within and beyond his work in Michigan's diploma connection.

Fred Newton Scott

Historians tell us that in the establishment and development of the fields of English education and composition studies in the United States, Fred Newton Scott's role is unparalleled (e.g., Berlin 1987; Gere 2010; Kitzhaber 1990; Stewart 1979, 1985; Stewart and Stewart 1997). President of the MLA in 1907, Scott served as the first and second president of NCTE from 1911–1913; president of the North Central Association of Colleges and Secondary Schools in 1913; and president of the American Association of Teachers of Journalism in 1917. He also authored numerous influential textbooks in English education, including *Paragraph Writing: A Rhetoric for Colleges* with Joseph Villiers Denney, that included a program and rationale for the teaching of writing in the secondary school (1893). In the early years of the twentieth century, textbooks like Scott's not only shaped the teaching of English in secondary schools and higher education, but they also served as venues in which scholars in English studies published theories of the teaching and learning of language, literature, and composition. Midcentury textbooks in the emerging field of composition studies functioned similarly (e.g., Corbett 1965; Young, Becker, and Pike 1970). The wisdom of many of Scott's contributions to these textbooks was groundbreaking at the time and speaks instructively to teachers even today. For example, in a textbook written with George R. Carpenter and Franklin T. Baker, published in 1903, at a time when British texts comprised the literature curriculum of subject English, Scott argued that teachers of English should be teachers of American as well as English literature. He also argued that instruction in the English language should value language in use rather than abstract prescriptions for language use.

As historians tell the story of Fred Newton Scott's contributions to American education, those who focus on his work in English education often remind us of his tenacious resistance to college- and university-imposed entrance requirements (Scott 1901). Like Angell, Scott was a nationally known, persuasive spokesperson for education for the common man (sic), for Michigan's pyramidal educational system, for what he called the "organic" conception of education upon which the State of Michigan's education system was founded.

In talks and writing, Scott contrasted this "organic" conception of education with what he dubbed a "feudal" system that based admission to higher education on external entrance examinations rather than completion of precollegiate education. Historians of English education also remind us of the influence on Scott's thinking of other practicing educators in Michigan, particularly of his sister, Harriet M. Scott, principal from 1886 to 1899 of the Normal Training School in Detroit, who advanced Scott's efforts to make paragraph-length compositions—rather than the word or the sentence—the unit of writing instruction in secondary schools; and his student, Edwin L. Miller, principal of Central High School in Detroit, a fellow cofounder of NCTE.

Those historians who focus on Scott's work as teacher and mentor of other influential scholars who went on to accomplish groundbreaking work in various corners of the field of English studies remind us of the work of Sterling Andrus Leonard, Ruth Weeks, and C. C. Fries in language studies and of Gertrude Buck and Clara Stevens (see Emig in this volume) in rhetoric and composition.[6] Reflecting on the revolution of work in composition studies in the 1960s—on the work of scholars like Weaver, Christensen, Rohman and Wlecke, Zoellner, Winterowd—Donald C. Stewart claims: "Looking back to the work of Fred Newton Scott, . . . we discover that we are not the pioneers we thought we were. In many ways we are simply re-discovering and clearing trails first blazed by Scott in the early part of the century" (1979, 542–43). Stewart draws our attention to Scott's 1922 article, "English Composition as a Mode of Behavior," published in *EJ*, to support his claim that Scott's understanding of grammar and usage errors in student writing anticipates "the problem identified later in the CCCC's 1974 resolution 'Students' Right to Their Own Language'" (1979, 545). Attributing errors that composition instructors were finding in the writing of their students to the fact that many students enrolling in the university at the time were children of first-generation Americans, Scott argued that students whose home language differs from school English require time to adjust to new language use. He advised composition instructors to stop concentrating their attention on such errors, to allow students the time to adjust to language use they experienced in school, and to focus their instruction on broader issues of communication (Scott 1922, 463–73).

In another essay in which he posits a conception of writing instruction that anticipates work of the field in the 1960s ("What the West Wants in Preparatory English," 1909), Scott argues once again for a rhetorical as opposed to a "correctness" approach to the teaching of composition.

> It is of course necessary that our young people should spell and punctuate properly, should make the verb agree with its subject, should use words in their dictionary sense and write sentences that can be read aloud without causing unnecessary pain to the mandibles. They should also know the meanings of words in the poetry and prose that they read, and understand the allusions to things ancient and modern. But these matters, after all, are subsidiary

and must be treated as such. They are means to an end. To treat them as an end in and for themselves is to turn education in this subject upside down. The main purpose of training in composition is free speech, direct and sincere communication with our fellows, that swift and untrammeled exchange of opinion, feeling and experience, which is the working instrument of the social instinct and the motive power of civilization. (19)

With Fred Newton Scott's retirement from the University of Michigan in 1927, the work of the Department of Rhetoric—including teacher preparation and collaboration with precollegiate teachers across the state and levels of instruction—was incorporated into the English department. To accomplish parts of this work, in the 1930s, some decades in advance of calls for such degrees,[7] Michigan's English department established a degree program in English education about which I will have more to say later in this essay.

Although it is gratifying to someone who studied and taught courses in English education and composition in the University of Michigan in the 1970s and 1980s to look back on the accomplishments and thinking of Fred Newton Scott, knowing that the legacy of his intellectual work contributed to my education and influenced my work long before I knew it did, it has also been important for me to recall the times and colleagues with whom Scott worked: the time of the emergence of state and land-grant universities; work with colleagues like James B. Angell, John Dewey, Gertrude Buck, Harriett Scott, Edwin L. Miller.

Warner G. Rice

Across the years, the University of Michigan has benefited from more than its share of noteworthy leaders in English education and composition studies. In 1929, two years after Scott's retirement, Warner G. Rice, having just completed his Ph.D. at Harvard, joined Michigan's faculty in English. Like Scott before him, Rice was committed to Michigan's holistically conceived educational system. Across his years in the English department, he visited, observed, and conferred about matters of curriculum and instruction with schoolteachers across the state, and during the years he chaired English (1947–1968), he encouraged a number of faculty in the department to serve on high school accreditation teams.

Historians of composition studies remember Warner Rice most frequently for "A Proposal for the Abolition of Freshman English, as It Is Now Commonly Taught, from the College Curriculum" (1960) that he presented in a session sponsored by the College Section at the 1959 NCTE Annual Convention. Calling for the renewal of Freshman Composition and the development of a "new rhetoric" in "Death—or Transfiguration?" (1960), Albert R. Kitzhaber, then incoming chair of Conference on College Composition and Communication (CCCC) and later—in 1964—president of NCTE, argued the alternative position.[8] Although both Rice and Kitzhaber were persuaded that a body of scholarship and scholar-teachers would need to be developed if Freshman English were to become an academically sound course, Rice did not believe the field was prepared to make the requisite investment of resources. Kitzhaber did. And although both believed that the teaching of writing was the responsibility of all faculty, Kitzhaber was persuaded that faculty with preparation in rhetoric and composition had a special role to play in teaching students to write effectively. Rice was persuaded that faculty across the curriculum avoided their responsibility to teach writing in their disciplines because they were happy to believe that such work could be accomplished in one course, once and for all, in the English department. He had this to say on the subject:

> College faculties will not welcome the abolition of Freshman English, because with it must go the comfortable assumption that the English department is solely responsible for good writing. This assumption is certainly false, but it has been encouraged by the incautious willingness of English departments to sponsor and direct the required course. (1960, 363)

For Rice, with the required course and the revenue and graduate student support it provided the English department, came the false assumption that the English department could teach a course that would prepare all students for all time to write effectively in all contexts. Given his commitment to what Scott called Michigan's "organic" system of education, Rice proposed that the teaching of writing take place in the secondary school and that all university faculty build upon that instruction by asking students to practice writing in their discipline-based courses because—as he put it—"expression is intimately bound up with the argument" (365).

In keeping with his belief that students should come to the university prepared to write in courses where all faculty would require writing in discipline-based courses, Rice argued:

> It is indeed in the education and training of secondary school teachers, rather than through the enlargement of Freshman English programs, that the hope for an improvement in communication skills lies. In discharging this obligation, departments of English must persuade men and women of first-rate ability to undertake the task. They must forge alliances with schools of education, in order to avail themselves of the talents and opportunities which exist there, must participate in the offering of courses in methods, and must aid in the supervision of practice teaching. Members of English departments must go into the high schools, acquaint themselves with the conditions under which teachers are working, and give practical advice toward the solution of real classroom problems. And they must reach agreements, through direct contact with secondary educators and by constant consultation with their colleagues in the schools, as to the standards which college-bound students can reasonably be expected to meet. (364)

Outlining how schools, colleges, and university faculty in English and education might work together to ensure students' proficiency in writing, Rice proposed programs in which that work might take place: in summer institutes like those developed in the 1950s by the College Entrance Examination Board, adopted in the 1960s in National Defense Education Act (NDEA) programs, and adapted in the 1970s by the National Writing Project; in internships for secondary school teachers in freshman English programs; in seminars and workshops offered in the field by university faculty for secondary school teachers; in English departments strengthening English teacher preparation; and in the development of joint degree programs to be offered in English and education.

Kitzhaber's position prevailed in the Rice-Kitzhaber debate. Work to establish a "new rhetoric" and a body of knowledge to guide the practice of the teaching of writing and new programs for the teaching of writing developed and moved forward dramatically in the 1960s, 1970s, and 1980s. An important body of that work took place in the University of Michigan. Some of it was indebted to Rice's insistence that the teaching of writing be conceived as a coherent school–university enterprise and that faculty in all disciplines be involved in writing instruction.

For years, as someone who studied in a setting filled with stories of this man who did not know me, to whom I nodded countless mornings, who tipped his hat to me, as I walked to my office and he to his, I was unaware of Warner Rice's impact, albeit indirect, on my professional preparation. During the 1960s, Rice was responsible for attracting to Michigan a number of scholars who have influenced not only my education but, more importantly, the fields of English educators and composition studies. Among these scholar-teachers are individuals with whom I had the privilege of working at Michigan: Richard W. Bailey, Stephen Dunning, Daniel N. Fader, Jay L. Robinson, Bernard Van't Hul. I have also had the privilege of working in the profession with others, like past president of NCTE, Sheridan Blau. In the late 1970s, when I came to Michigan to work in the English Composition Board and to study in the Joint Program in English and Education (JPEE) Jay Robinson was chair of the English department; Daniel Fader, chair of the English Composition Board; Bernard Van't Hul, director of Introductory Composition, the writing course that replaced Freshman English when the English Composition Board was established; Richard Bailey, graduate chair in English and director of research in the English Composition Board; and Stephen Dunning, director of the JPEE.

The Joint Ph.D. Program in English and Education

Established during the time when Warner Rice was chair of English, the JPEE is the kind of degree program Rice outlined in his 1959 remarks at the NCTE Annual convention. In her article, "Establishing the Field: Recognition,

Interdisciplinarity, and Freedom in English Education Doctoral Studies" (2009), Anne Ruggles Gere, current cochair of the JPEE, tells us that across the thirty years since it was originally established in the 1930s in the English department, doctoral work in English education took various forms in the University of Michigan. When English educator and poet Stephen Dunning joined Michigan's faculty in 1964 and became director of the program, it took its current form. Administered by the university's Rackham Graduate School, the JPEE is an intercollegiate program located in the Department of English Language and Literature in the LS&A and in the School of Education. During the years that Dunning, who served as president of NCTE in 1975, directed the JPEE, it graduated a number of individuals who have been themselves involved in foundation building work in the emerging field of composition studies—to name just a few, Stephen Bernhardt, Barry Kroll, Lee Odell, Irv Hashimoto, and Anne Ruggles Gere.

Gere, whose career is still developing, has already taken her place among Michigan's outstanding leaders in English education and composition studies. In 1989, she returned to Michigan from her first faculty role in the University of Washington to join Jay Robinson as cochair of the JPEE. During her years in Washington, Gere published the first of the ten books, five textbooks, and more than seventy articles that have earned her distinction in English education and composition studies. Since her return to Michigan where she holds two distinguished chairs, Gere has served as cochair of JPEE and chair of the Sweetland Writing Center, the unit that succeeded the English Composition Board. Gere has also led the profession as chair of CCCC in 1992, president of NCTE in 2001, Chair of the MLA Division on Teaching Writing, and member of the Executive Committee of MLA, and currently, as the first director of the James R. Squire Office of Policy Research in NCTE.

The English Composition Board

In 1973 and 1974, the LS&A in the University of Michigan conducted an internal review of its graduate requirements, the first such review since the 1940s. During open hearings, a recurrent theme in the testimony of students and faculty alike was dissatisfaction with the quality of students' literacy both upon entering and leaving college. Responding to this testimony, the dean of LS&A asked English department chair Jay Robinson for guidance on how to begin the effort to develop a new writing requirement for the college.

Robinson, another of Michigan's remarkable leaders in English education and composition studies, began his academic career preparing to be a medievalist in the University of California–Berkeley. In the process of teaching courses in the history of the English language, during his first faculty position in Northwestern University, Robinson became interested and began publishing in linguistics. In university courses and NDEA summer institutes, he also began his work in English education, work he continued when he moved to the University of Michigan. Across the years I studied in Michigan,

Jay Robinson served—in roles that I knew about—as chair of the English department, executive director of the Middle English Dictionary, chair of the English Composition Board, chair of the JPEE, and founding director of the Center for Educational Improvement through Collaboration, a unit established to support collaborative research into issues of mutual concern by teacher-scholars in the university and Michigan schools. *Conversations on the Written Word: Essays on Language and Literacy* (1990), a collection of his most influential essays written during his Michigan years, traces Robinson's ensuing scholarship in sociolinguistics, rhetoric, composition, and the broader field of literacy studies. An extraordinarily generous leader in English education and composition studies, Robinson has mentored more than his share of well-known scholars in these fields, among them Cathy Fleischer and David Schaafsma, who edited a collection of essays written by others of them, honoring the conversations and the work into which Robinson introduced and invited them: *Literacy and Democracy: Teacher Research and Composition Studies in Pursuit of Habitable Spaces: Further Conversations from the Students of Jay Robinson* (1998).

In 1976 when the dean of LS&A asked Robinson who would be the best person to lead the college's development of a new writing requirement, he named yet another remarkable scholar in literacy studies, Daniel Fader. Prepared in British renaissance studies in Stanford University, Fader spent his entire academic career at Michigan. Early in his career, Fader's interest in children suffering the problems of persistent poverty turned his attention from British renaissance writers to American youth. Well known in the United States and beyond for literacy learning practices he developed while working with incarcerated and inner-city youth (*Hooked on Books* [with Morton H. Shaevitz] 1966; *Hooked on Books: Program and Proof* [with E. McNeil] 1968; *The New Hooked on Books* [with James Duggins, Tom Finn, and Elton McNeil] 1976; *The Naked Children* 1971), Fader's reputation for engaging previously unsuccessful students in demonstrable literacy learning made him the logical choice to lead the work of Michigan's college of LS&A to develop a new writing requirement.

Today the innovative teaching practices that Fader developed in the Maxey Boys Training School in Michigan have become commonplace, although, as James Zebroski notes in his essay in this book, few contemporary English educators and compositionists know that in the 1960s Fader was surrounding students with books, magazines, newspapers, asking them to engage in sustained silent reading of self-selected, high-interest materials, to write freely in journals, and to talk about their reading and writing in small peer groups. Although Fader was committed to practices of this kind in his own teaching of writing at Michigan, these were not practices he asked of faculty whom he hired to staff the English Composition Board when he became the first chair of the unit. Like his contemporary James Gray, founding director of the National Writing Project, Fader was a man of his time, working during the beginning of the establishment of the field of composition studies, for him what would come to be considered best teaching practices in the field was an open question. Fader was interested in the practice of successful teachers, convinced—again like Gray (2000)—that teachers' practice was an untapped source of knowledge about the teaching of writing.

Between 1976 and 1978, Fader, worked closely with Robinson and others in the English department who were interested in literacy studies to develop the college's new writing requirement and the English Composition Board, the unit that would oversee and coordinate the requirement. With common commitments to social justice, these faculty had worked together earlier to develop the English department's Doctor of Arts degree, a program designed to serve practitioner scholars who were able to commit limited time to on-campus, in-residence study. Among the foundational scholars in composition studies who are graduates of this program are especially noteworthy leaders in composition studies, including Jacqueline Jones Royster and Barbara Couture.

In January 1978, after failing to approve a proposal that asked students to fulfill the college's writing requirement by completing three courses identified as writing courses offered across the curriculum in the college, LS&A faculty overwhelmingly approved a seven-part program, with six parts within the college and one beyond, the first writing across the curriculum program in a large research university and a program in keeping with the spirit of the Michigan educational system that its founders conceived. Three of the parts of the program within the college were accomplished by an English Composition Board faculty of lecturers: administration of an entrance essay required of all incoming undergraduates; tutorial instruction required of students who demonstrated the need for such assistance in the entrance essay; writing workshop support available to every student.

The fourth—Introductory Composition—was accomplished in the Department of English Language and Literature, initially under the direction of Bernard Van't Hul, who composed and published in-house *English 125* "textbooks" for use during the years he directed the introductory composition course. The *English 125* books, like other groundbreaking textbooks of the era, were theories of writing instruction even as they were methods and activities for translating theory into practice. In the workshops and seminars that he offered in Michigan and beyond and in the *English 125* books, Van't Hul shaped the "new rhetoric" for which Albert Kitzhaber had called and influenced the teaching of writing in Michigan and beyond (Stock 2001).

In the 1970s, Van't Hul introduced his theory of language use to all teaching assistants in the University of Michigan and to countless teachers across the State of Michigan and beyond in a remarkable workshop. Anyone who participated in this workshop remembers the acronym *MAPS*, which Van't Hul introduced to connote what he called "warmed-over Aristotle," Aristotle's theory of rhetoric warmed over by twentieth-century scholarship in sociolinguistics: All messages, spoken and written, are more or less effective, depending on how successfully they meet the rhetorical constraints of the *Medium* or *Mode* in which they are composed; the *Audience* for whom they are composed; the *Purpose* for which they are composed; and the *Situation* in which they are composed. Just as the workshop scholarship of Amherst College's famous teacher of writing Theodore Baird has made its way into the broader circulation that print affords in the work of compositionists like William Coles (1978) and David Bartholomae (Bartholomae and Petrosky 1986), Van't Hul's scholarship in the teaching of writing is circulating in the work of his students.

The fifth part of the program, junior/senior-level writing courses, was offered and required primarily in students' areas of concentration. The director of the English Composition Board reviewed and approved upper-level writing courses proposed by departments in accordance with guidelines developed by the board. The English Composition Board also offered professional development seminars in writing instruction, led in the early years for faculty and teaching assistants who offered and participated in these courses by Barbra Morris, Assistant Director of the English Composition Board. The sixth part of the program, research into its effectiveness, was funded by the Ford Foundation and conducted by the late Professor of English Richard W. Bailey (Bailey and Fosheim 1983). Bailey, who held the Fred Newton Scott Distinguished Chair in the university, is author or editor of more than twenty books and hundreds of articles dealing with his range of research interests: varieties of English around the world, sociolinguistics, composition, lexicography, stylistics, semiotics, historical linguistics, computers in language and literature, and the teaching of English.

The seventh part of the program, supported with a generous grant from the Mellon Foundation, included activities relating the teaching of writing in secondary schools and community colleges to the writing program in the university: writing conferences on the University of Michigan campus, one-day and two-day seminars conducted throughout the state; curriculum and staff-development projects; and publication of *fforum*, a journal designed to place in conversations with one another theorists, researchers, critics, and teachers intent on developing a scholarship of the practice of teaching writing.

fforum, the newsletter of the English Composition Board—later published as one of the conceptual maps of the emerging field of composition studies *(fforum: Essays on Theory and Practice in the Teaching of Writing* [Stock 1983])—moved me from secondary school teaching to the University of Michigan. Following a writing conference I attended on the campus with 125 other K–university teachers, from across the State of Michigan, Bernard Van't Hul, one of the conference leaders, invited those of us in attendance to offer suggestions for how we might productively continue our discussion of the teaching of writing. In my response to Van't Hul's invitation, I proposed a newsletter that became *fforum* and was invited to join the faculty in the English Composition Board to develop the publication in which I imagined scholars and practicing teachers who were developing the field of composition studies discussing the work of the emerging field with one another.

English Education and the Emergence of the Discipline Composition Studies

During the 1970s and 1980s, I studied in the JPEE, edited *fforum*, taught composition and English education courses, worked in the English Composition Board's Outreach program, served as the coordinator of research projects in the Center for Educational Improvement through Collaboration, and began to conduct and publish a body of practitioner research (e.g., Barritt, Clark, and Stock 1986; Robinson and Stock 1990; Stock 1993, 2001, 2005; Stock and Robinson 1989). It was my good fortune to do this work in the midst of the scholars and immersed in scholarship that shaped the field of composition studies. In the process I came to know the authors of this book's collection of essays and people and the work about which they write.

Having thought for some time about the claim I will make now, I make it fully convinced of its accuracy: The discipline—composition studies—would not have come to be and come to be recognized had it not been for the scholars in English education about whom you will read here. Neither would the field have steadfastly focused on student writers and the teaching of writing had it not been for remarkable teacher scholars like the authors who have written the essays in this book, all of whom entered the field in the 1960s, 1970s, and the 1980s, an era about which they write here, a time when work in English education flourished, when the Conference on English Education (1964)—following the model of the CCCC (1949)—was established and developed in NCTE to promote the scholarship of the teachers of teachers of subject English. Each of the authors of the essays in this collection is herself or himself an influential scholar in the field of English education and a foundational scholar in the field of composition studies. Because these essays are, in part, autobiographical, and because their authors are well known, I introduce them only briefly by name and by the subject matter of their essays.

Preceding this introductory essay, in a foreword to the collection, "Remembering Composition," Kathleen Blake Yancey positions this history among others aimed at locating the origins of the field of composition studies. The collection itself opens with three different kinds of articles. James T. Zebroski leads with an overview of intellectual and political events unfolding in the late 1960s, early 1970s, events Zebroski argues led to the formation of the discipline of composition studies. Following the overview, in a poignant memoir, Janet Emig offers a portrait of the journey that led her to become a founder of the discipline that now appears among the National Research Council's recognized fields of study. And although she did not realize it at the time, Emig's essay reveals that she began her purposeful, systematic work to establish the field of composition studies as a secondary school student in the 1950s. Next, Thomas Newkirk reflects on the impact on the field in the 1970s and the 1980s of composition scholars'—like his teacher James Kinneavy's—move from departments of education to English departments.

In the four essays that follow, Anne Ruggles Gere, Sheridan Blau, Bonnie S. Sunstein, and Lil Brannon and Cy Knoblauch tell us about foundational theorists, researchers, and publishers—English educators all—whose work figured significantly in the development of the field of composition studies. As they do so, they draw particular attention to the work of Richard Braddock, James Moffett, Don Graves, Donald Murray, Thomas Newkirk, and Bob Boynton.

The collection concludes with two telling memoirs. Trained in a prestigious university in *belles lettristic* studies—like so many other scholars who entered the fields of English education and composition studies in the 1960s and 1970s—Charles Moran traces his journey from literary to literacy studies and the reasons why he devoted his career to English education and composition studies. A poet and practicing teacher of writing before pursuing doctoral work in English education in New York University in the 1980s, Keith Gilyard tells us how and why he became a compositionist. In the process, Gilyard draws us along the intellectual and ethical paths he traveled en route to the field of composition studies.

Merging Work in English Education and Composition Studies Since the 1990s

After completing my doctoral work in the late 1980s, I began a career that took shape at the corner of the field of English studies where English education and composition studies intersect. Since then, I have worked as a developer and administrator of writing programs, as a teacher educator, as a director of National Writing Project sites, as a journal editor, and in policy-making venues. In other words, my academic career has been very like that of others of us, prepared in the field of English education, who worked in the late twentieth and early twenty-first centuries to establish the field of composition studies. As writing program developers and founders, we have designed programs and curricula, planned and conducted preparation programs for undergraduate peer tutors and consultants, graduate students teaching assistants, and faculty in composition studies and across the curriculum. We have worked with colleagues in K–12 education to improve and articulate literacy teaching across the curriculum and levels of instruction, and—many of us—have published and advocated for the unique value of context-based practitioner research in language and literacy learning and teaching.

But . . . the braided stories of English education's and composition studies' development at the close of the twentieth and the beginning of the twenty-first centuries is another narrative for another time, one that Cathy Fleischer introduces in her afterword to this collection, "A Case for Collaboration: Intertwined Roots, Interwoven Futures."

Notes

1. It is also interesting to note that the authors of these articles were about evenly divided between secondary school and college teachers.

2. In his history *Composition-Rhetoric: Backgrounds, Theory, and Pedagogy* (1997), Robert Connors describes Hopkins' study as the field's first detailed information on teaching loads apart from anecdotal references (192).

3. The article—so far as I know the first report of an empirical study of the working conditions of teachers of composition—is a telling example of how *EJ* figured in its early years as a forum for discussion of the problems of teaching English across levels of instruction. It is also a powerful argument for how English education and composition studies—newly developing enterprises in the field of English studies—were intertwined from the outset.

4. In his important book *Education and the Cult of Efficiency*, Raymond E. Callahan (1962) describes how the model of "scientific management," developed by an engineer, Frederick W. Taylor, to increase the productivity of human labor, spawned an "efficiency model" that shaped the discourse and the discursive practices of education in the early twentieth century. Callaghan traces the origins of the efficiency model to social circumstances and public faith in the power of science to solve social as well as technological problems. After demonstrating in some detail how the principles of scientific management first captured the public imagination, Callahan demonstrates how the discourse of business and industry made its way into the spoken and written language of two influential educators of the time—Frank Spaulding (Superintendent of Schools in Newton, Massachusetts) and Franklin Bobbitt (instructor in educational administration in the University of Chicago). It is interesting to note that in the final report of his committee, Hopkins cites the work of these men whom Callaghan credits with education's adoption of cost-effectiveness as the primary criterion for evaluating what they called the "products" or "results" of the process of education (Callaghan 1962, 70).

5. Among *The Early Works, 1882–1898* is a biographical article that Dewey published locally about Fred Newton Scott (1971, 119–122).

6. A full, rich account of Scott's life and work may be found in Donald C. Stewart and Patricia L. Stewart's *The Life and Legacy of Fred Newton* (1997).

7. Following the Soviet Union's launch of Sputnik in 1957, the federal government passed a National Defense Education Act in 1958. Hoping to gain National Defense Education Act funding in support of the teaching of English, NCTE presented to the U.S. Congress a report entitled *The National Interest and the Teaching of English* (1961). Following release of the report, the U.S. Office of Education allocated funds for Project English. Among the activities funded by Project English was the 1962 Allerton Park Conference at which participants from college and university departments of English acknowledged their responsibility to prepare teachers of English for all levels of education. A study conducted in 1966–67, by Don Cameron Allen, professor of English at Johns Hopkins University, advanced the commitment of departments of English to teacher education for all levels of instruction and recommended the development of doctoral programs in English education in which the research emphasis would be on the teaching of English. In the same year, Erwin Steinberg, then coordinator of Project English and chair of English at Carnegie Mellon University called for development of the Ph.D. in English education.

8. Although it was not published until 1990, Albert R. Kitzhaber wrote his doctoral dissertation on the subject of *Rhetoric in American Colleges, 1850–1900*. In the "Introduction" to the published work, John T. Gage writes:

> More than a necessary work for the student of contemporary composition to know if he or she wishes to understand the history of the discipline as it now exists, *Rhetoric in American Colleges, 1850–1900* is in fact one of the important markers of the beginning of that discipline. It is the first book-length historical study of this subject, by a scholar who helped to initiate the reevaluation of rhetoric in American education that made the so-called "paradigm shift" in composition during the 1960s possible. (1990, vii)

Across his career, Kitzhaber was a groundbreaking researcher and practitioner in the field of composition studies. As Research Professor of English in Dartmouth College, he directed the Dartmouth Study of Writing, funded by the Carnegie Corporation, that he published as *Themes, Theories, and Therapy: The Teaching of Writing in College* (1963). He also directed sizeable writing programs in the University of Kansas and the University of Oregon.

Works Cited

Allen, Don C. 1968. *The Ph.D. in English and American Literature*. New York: MLA.

"Appendix. Proceedings of the Twenty-eighth Annual Meeting of the Modern Language Association of America, 1910." 1910. *PMLA* 25: i–cix.

"Appendix. Proceedings of the Twenty-ninth Annual Meeting of the Modern Language Association of America, Second Union Meeting, 1911." 1911. *PMLA* 26: i–xxxiv.

"Appendix. Proceedings of the Thirtieth Annual Meeting of the Modern Language Association of America, and the Eighteenth Annual Meeting of the Central Division of the Association, 1912." 1912. *PMLA* 27: i–cixviii.

Applebee, Arthur N. 1974. *Tradition and Reform in the Teaching of English: A History*. Urbana, IL: NCTE.

Bailey, Richard W., and Robin Fosheim. 1983. *Literacy for Life: The Demand for Reading and Writing*. New York: MLA.

Barritt, Loren S., Francelia Clark, and Patricia L. Stock. 1986. "Researching Practice: Evaluating Assessment Essays." *College Composition and Communication* (Oct.): 315–27.

Bartholomae, David, and Anthony Petrosky. 1986. *Facts, Artifacts, and Counterfacts: Theory and Method for a Reading and Writing Course*. Portsmouth, NH: Boynton/Cook–Heinemann.

Berlin, James A. 1984. *Writing Instruction in Nineteenth-Century American Colleges*. Carbondale, IL: Southern Illinois University Press.

———. 1987. *Rhetoric and Reality: Writing Instruction in American Colleges, 1900–1985*. Carbondale, IL: Southern Illinois University Press.

———. 1996. *Rhetoric, Poetics, and Cultures: Refiguring College English Studies*. Urbana, IL: NCTE.

Boyer, Ernest. 1990. *Scholarship Reconsidered*. Princeton, NJ: Carnegie Foundation for the Advancement of Teaching.

Braddock, Richard, Richard Lloyd-Jones, and Lowell Schoer. 1963. *Research in Written Composition*. Urbana, IL: NCTE.

Callaghan, Raymond E. 1962. *Education and the Cult of Efficiency*. Chicago: University of Chicago Press.

Carino, Peter. 1995. "Early Writing/Centers: Toward a History." *The Writing Center Journal* 15(2): 101–15.

Carpenter, George R., Franklin T. Baker, and Fred N. Scott. 1903. *The Teaching of English in the Elementary and Secondary School*. New York: Longmans, Green.

Christensen, Frances. 1967. *Notes Toward a New Rhetoric: Six Essays for Teachers*. New York: Harper & Row.

Coles, William E. 1978. *The Plural I: The Teaching of Writing*. New York: Holt, Rinehart and Winston.

College Entrance Examination Board Commission on English. 1965. *Freedom and Discipline in English*. New York: The College Entrance Examination Board.

Connors, Robert J. 1997. *Composition-Rhetoric: Backgrounds, Theory, and Pedagogy*. Pittsburgh, PA: University of Pittsburgh Press.

Corbett, Edward P. J. 1965. *Classical Rhetoric for the Modern Student*. 1st Ed. New York: Oxford University Press.

Crowley, Sharon. 1998. *Composition in the University: Historical and Polemical Essays*. Pittsburgh, PA: University of Pittsburgh Press.

Dewey, John. 1971. "Fred Newton Scott." In *The Early Works, 1882–1898*, edited by Jo Ann Boydston. Carbondale, IL: Southern Illinois University Press.

Fader, Daniel N. 1971. *The Naked Children*. New York: Bantam.

Fader, Daniel N., and E. McNeil. 1968. *Hooked on Books: Program and Proof*. New York: G. P. Putnam's Sons.

Fader, Daniel N., and Morton H. Shaevitz. 1966. *Hooked on Books*. New York: Berkeley Publishing Corp.

Fader, Daniel N., with James Duggins, Tom Finn, and Elton McNeil. 1976. *The New Hooked on Books*. New York: Berkeley.

Fleischer, Cathy A., and David W. Schaafsma. 1998. *Literacy and Democracy: Teacher Research and Composition Studies in Pursuit of Habitable Spaces: Further Conversations from the Students of Jay Robinson*. Urbana, IL: NCTE.

Gage, John T. 1990. "Introduction." In *Rhetoric in American Colleges, 1850–1900*. Dallas, TX: Southern Methodist University Press.

Gere, Anne R. 1987. *Writing Groups: History, Theory, and Implications*. Carbondale, IL: Southern Illinois University Press.

———. 1994. "Kitchen Tables and Rented Rooms: The Extracurriculum of Composition." *College Composition and Communication* 45(1): 75–92.

———. 2009. "Establishing the Field: Recognition, Interdisciplinarity, and Freedom in English Education Doctoral Studies." In *The Doctoral Degree in English Education*, edited by Allen Webb. Kennesaw, GA: Kennesaw University Press.

———. 2010. "The Teaching of Writing, 1912–2010." In *Reading the Past, Writing the Future: A Century of American Literacy Education and the National Council of Teachers of English*, edited by Erika Lindemann. Urbana, IL: NCTE.

Gray, James. 2000. *Teachers at the Center*. Berkeley, CA: National Writing Project.

Harris, Joseph. 1997. *A Teaching Subject: Composition Since 1966*. Upper Saddle River, NJ: Prentice Hall.

Hook, J. N. 1979. *A Long Road Together: A Personal View of NCTE's First Sixty-Seven Years*. Urbana, IL: NCTE.

Hopkins, Edwin M. 1912. "Can Good Composition Teaching Be Done Under Present Conditions?" *English Journal* 1(1): 1–8.

———. 1912. "The Roundtable: Four Problems for the Council." *English Journal* 1(1): 49.

Kitzhaber, Albert R. 1960. "Death—or Transfiguration?" *College English* 21(7): 367–73.

———. 1963. *Themes, Theories, and Therapy: The Teaching of Writing in College*. New York: McGraw-Hill.

———. 1990. *Rhetoric in American Colleges, 1850–1900*. Dallas, TX: Southern Methodist University Press.

Miller, Susan. 1991. *Textual Carnivals: The Politics of Composition*. Carbondale, IL: Southern Illinois University Press.

———. 1998. *Trust in Texts: A Different History of Rhetoric*. Carbondale, IL: Southern Illinois University Press.

Miller, Thomas P. 1997. *The Formation of College English: Rhetoric and Belles Lettres in the British Cultural Provinces*. Pittsburgh, PA: University of Pittsburgh Press.

National Education Association Committee of Ten. 1894. *Report of the Committee of Ten on Secondary Schools, with Reports of the Conferences Arranged by Committees*. New York: American Book Company.

NCTE Commission on the National Interest. 1961. *The National Interest and the Teaching of English*. Champaign, IL: NCTE.

Parker, William R. 1967. "Where Do English Departments Come From?" *College English* 28 (5): 339–51.

Rohman, D. Gordon, and Albert O. Wlecke. 1964. *Pre-Writing: The Construction and Application of Models for Concept Formation in Writing*. East Lansing, MI: Michigan State University Cooperative Reprints.

Rice, Warner G. 1960. "A Proposal for the Abolition of Freshman English, as It Is Now Commonly Taught, from the College Curriculum." *College English* 21(7): 361–67.

Robinson, Jay L. 1990. *Conversations on the Written Word: Essays on Language and Literacy*. Portsmouth, NH: Boynton/Cook–Heinemann.

Robinson, Jay L., and Patricia L. Stock. 1990. "The Politics of Literacy." In *Conversations on the Written Word*, edited by Jay L. Robinson, 271–317. Portsmouth, NH: Boynton/Cook–Heinemann.

Rudolph, Frederick. 1962. *The American College and University: A History*. New York: Vintage Books.

Schell, Eileen E., and Patricia Lambert Stock. 2001. *Moving a Mountain: Transforming the Role of Contingent Faculty in Composition Studies and Higher Education*. Urbana, IL: NCTE.

Schultz, Lucille M. 1999. *The Young Composers: Composition's Beginnings in Nineteen-century Schools*. Carbondale, IL: Southern Illinois University Press.

Scott, Fred Newton. 1901. "College Entrance Requirements in English." *School Review* 9 (June): 365–78.

———. 1909. "What the West Wants in Preparatory English." *School Review* 17 (Jan.): 10–20.

———. 1922. "English Composition as a Mode of Behavior." *English Journal* 11 (Oct.): 463–73.

Scott, Fred Newton, George R. Carpenter, and Franklin T. Baker. 1903. *The Teaching of English in the Elementary and the Secondary School*. New York: Longmans, Green & Co.

Scott, Fred Newton and Joseph Villiers Denney. *Paragraph-Writing: A Rhetoric for Colleges*. New ed. Boston: Allyn and Bacon, 1909.

Stewart, Donald C. 1979. "Rediscovering Fred Newton Scott." *College English* 40(5): 539–47.

———. 1985. "Fred Newton Scott." In *Traditions of Inquiry*, edited by John Brereton, 26–49. New York: Oxford University Press.

Stewart, Donald C., and Patricia L. Stewart. 1997. *The Life and Legacy of Fred Newton Scott*. Pittsburgh, PA: University of Pittsburgh Press.

Stock, Patricia L. 1983. *fforum: Essays on Theory and Practice in the Teaching of Writing*. Portsmouth, NH: Boynton/Cook–Heinemann.

Stock, Patricia Lambert. 1993. "The Function of Anecdote in Teacher Research." *English Education* 24(4): 173–87.

———. 1995. *The Dialogic Curriculum*. Portsmouth, NH: Boynton/Cook–Heinemann.

———. 1997. "Reforming Education in the Land-Grant University: Contributions from a Writing Center." *The Writing Center Journal* 18(1): 7–29.

———. 2001. "Toward a Theory of Genre in Teacher Research: Contributions from a Reflective Practitioner." *English Education* 33(2): 100–14.

———. 2005. "Practicing the Scholarship of Teaching: What We Do with the Knowledge We Make." *College English* 68(1): 107–21.

Stock, Patricia L., and Jay L. Robinson. 1987. "Taking on Testing: Teachers as Tester-Researchers." *English Education* (May): 93–121.

———. 1990. "Literacy as Conversation: Classroom Talk as Text Building." In *Classrooms and Literacy*, edited by David Bloome, 310–88. Norwood, NJ: Ablex, 1989. Reprinted in Jay L. Robinson. 1990. *Conversations on the Written Word*, 163–238.

Van't Hul, Bernard, Ed. 1978–79. *125 Book*. Ann Arbor, MI: Introductory Composition Program, Department of English Language and Literature, The College of Literature, Science, and the Arts, the University of Michigan.

———. 1981–82. *125 Book*. Ann Arbor, MI: Introductory Composition Program, Department of English Language and Literature, The College of Literature, Sciences, and the Arts, the University of Michigan.

Weaver, Richard. 1957. *A Course in Writing and Rhetoric*. New York: Henry Holt.

Winterowd, W. Ross. 1975. *Contemporary Rhetoric: A Conceptual Background with Readings*. New York: Harcourt.

Young, Richard E., Alton L. Becker, and Kenneth L. Pike. 1970. *Rhetoric: Discovery and Change*. New York: Harcourt, Brace, and World.

Zoellner, Robert. 1969. "Talk-Write: A Behavioral Pedagogy for Composition." *College English* 30 (Jan.): 267–320.

1

Hidden from History
English Education and the Multiple Origins of Contemporary Composition Studies, 1960–2000

James Thomas Zebroski

Only that historian will have the gift of fanning the spark of hope in the past who is firmly convinced that *even the dead* will not be safe from the enemy if he wins.

—Walter Benjamin (as quoted in Merlis)

I was having to invent this whole thing, and it was not being invented in a propitious climate. . . . [T]here was nothing but large feet out.

—Janet Emig (on writing *Composing Processes of Twelfth-Graders*, quoted in Ralph Gerald Nelms, *A Case History Approach to Composition Studies: Edward P.J. Corbett and Janet Emig,* unpublished dissertation, The Ohio State University)

Being interested in how children write is not unlike being interested in how cripples skate.

—Peter Noumeyer (dissertation adviser of Janet Emig, quoted by Emig in Ralph Gerald Nelms, *A Case History Approach to Composition Studies: Edward P.J. Corbett and Janet Emig,* unpublished dissertation, The Ohio State University)

At the southern entrance to the Ohio State University campus are two gate posts. On one of these posts is an historical plaque that contains the following text:

Neil Avenue Gate

Construction of these brick columns was authorized by the Board of Trustees of the University on November 6, 1915. The columns later supported iron gates bearing the university seal, which were used to close this south entrance to campus. Matching gates were constructed at the north entrance to campus, on Neil Avenue and what is now Woody Hayes Drive. Of those original north and south gateways, only these two columns survive.

Historical Marker

The only thing stranger than a historical marker on a campus where officials have regarded the institution's past with the zeal of a Los Angeles land developer—as something to be bulldozed and made into a construction site—is a key fact missing in this text. No mention is made of what had, by the fall of 1970 when I first came to OSU as a freshman, become part of the local folklore. The anti–Vietnam War riots of May 1970 that occurred after the Kent State shootings and that closed the campus began at this very gate. Although it is not surprising that an institution would refrain from advertising this part of its history, I would be surprised if this omission were a conscious one. Rather, it is the "common sense" of what is left out of, what is excluded from our discourses that structures this text and most of our histories. It is the repetition of these language practices that omit on a regular and regulated basis that structures our discourse. By consistently calling attention to certain aspects of the world while denying others, the world becomes naturalized, a matter of "facts," rather than of social and discursive constructs.

My major claim in this essay is that in this same time period something similar happened to our histories of composition and rhetoric, whether of a leftist (Berlin, Miller) or a centrist (Connors, Varnum, Harris) variety, which have omitted the crucial contributions of colleges of education, and especially the influence of the discipline of English education on the field. In these histories, composition and rhetoric has increasingly silenced and distanced itself from its multiple origins of only forty years ago. At the very same moment that students were protesting the war in Vietnam at that Neil Avenue Gate to the Ohio State campus, English educators were focusing on public school students and revolutionizing the study of composition.

In 1970, college English departments were not, for the most part, interested in composition as a scholarly area of specialization. We must remember that the first-year writing course was often called *freshman English* rather than *freshman composition* and that one of its key goals was to introduce students to the discourse of literature and criticism. Histories that assume a serious interest in composition in most college English departments in 1970 retroject a current situation onto that historical moment. In contrast, an examination of the archive shows that the primary interest in composition in the early 1970s came from English educators. In fact, colleges of education, as indicated by the extensive research done under their auspices on grammar and writing (Hartwell 1985, 126), had been interested in composition since the twentieth century began.

My second claim is that there are many reasons why these origins of composition in education have been suppressed. These include the passing or retiring of the first generation of compositionists, many of whom received degrees in colleges of education; turf battles; matters of funding; the emergence of poststructuralist theory and cultural studies critique; the decline of social science research—including, for example, sociology and anthropology—in composition and rhetoric; and the location in the 1980s of most of the new doctoral programs in composition and rhetoric within English departments. But certainly one key factor is social class and its stigma, although social class is itself always a highly mediated affair in U.S. education. As in the professions of law enforcement, firefighting, and nursing, it has drawn a larger proportion of students from working-class backgrounds than most academic areas in arts and sciences. Furthermore, the work of educators in the 1960s was especially focused on so-called "disadvantaged children," who themselves were not middle class. Not surprisingly, the materials on writing from the 1960s and 1970s are immersed in social class concerns.

My third claim is that it was largely because of the pressure exerted by students from working-class backgrounds and by teachers who served them in public schools that new ways were found to teach reading and writing. This initiative was supported by the federal government through a variety of funding measures; and these federally sponsored programs, most of which have been long gone since the Reagan budget cuts, had important, if hidden, effects on the formation and the discipline of composition and rhetoric.

Let me put my argument into twelve propositions. These twelve statements are interrelated, because I am trying to capture several events that occurred simultaneously in the period from 1968 to 1973. I am suggesting that behind our official histories are concepts already at work that structure the narratives that follow. For this reason, we need to take care to understand the period from 1968 to 1973 as much as possible on its own terms.

Proposition 1: There was no composition as a social formation before the late 1960s.

This is a difficult but critical place to begin. For many people in the discipline, this goes against the grain of conventional historiography and the archival work that has been done for nearly two decades now. The idea that composition, however defined, does not really go back much before 1960 in the United States will seem very strange indeed. To be sure, the teaching of writing has a long history in U.S. colleges (Berlin, 1987), and also in public schools (Schultz 1999). But I am noting here that the discontinuities that occur from the late 1960s and after are more important for us today, and are more revealing of social class, than the continuities and similarities across the past century. Susan Miller (1991) has the right idea—attending to all those instabilities, shifts, gaps, changes. As I develop my argument, I am going to refer to the early informal, unstable, often antidisciplinary collectives of people interested in composition, especially at the college level, as a social formation. Composition "within" English was antidisciplinary because it was not literary study or New Critical. It often drew on social science research. For the most part, this social formation only occurred in the late 1960s and during the 1970s. Composition as a social formation began to gather in the years 1968–1973.

Proposition 2: There was no composition as a discipline before 1980 or so.

Much of the debate of the early 1980s in composition and rhetoric turned on the question of whether "we" were a discipline or not. Part of the problem is that there has rarely been a sorting through of what precisely we might mean by *discipline*. As I have noted in another essay (1998), a discipline is a relational concept. Composition and rhetoric met the disciplinary criteria I detailed above about 1980 or so (i.e., definitions of and investigations into writing practices, teaching practices, curricular practices, disciplinary practices, professional practices and the theorizing of those practices), as Nystrand, Green, and Wiemelt (1993) have pointed out. Disciplines are late events in part because they presuppose established doctoral programs. Despite the claims of disciplinary histories to a long and illustrious lineage, disciplines are preceded by social formations, loose informal collectives that address needs— in this case, writing and the teaching of writing—not seen worthy of attention by existing social structures—in this case, college English departments.

Proposition 3: A major shift, a break, in social relations in the United States occurred 1968–1973; composition as a social formation emerged from this break.

The periods before 1968 and after 1973 are basically in different worlds. Michel Foucault calls such discontinuities *breaks in epistemes* (1977). To the extent that there are continuities between these two periods, they are continuities of change, resistances to the stabilities of the social relations and social structures. These resistances are part of what I am calling *social formations*. So social formations, changing groups and collectives, bridge this period. College composition by the late 1950s was what Robert Connors (1997) has called a *moribund affair*; composition as a social formation was born from this death.

conn. w/ its
sojo at its
roots

30   Composition's Roots in English Education

Proposition 4: Composition as a social formation was interconnected with the other countercultural events of the 1960s.

Composition was also connected to the new teachers and students who gained access to the schools and to university in this period. One thing that is very important but difficult to communicate to people who came of age after these events is that during the 1960s teaching had perhaps the highest status it was ever to achieve in the United States. It was on par with, and often seen as another form of, the sort of political action taken by Civil Rights workers. It was seen as public service of the highest calling, a sort of everyday domestic Peace Corps or local VISTA (Volunteers in Service to America). Popular culture of the time had many representations of the teacher (and student) as hero. Bel Kaufman's popular 1964 book *Up the Down Staircase* is one. Teachers were often seen in the forefront of social change and social action as in the role that Sidney Poitier, perhaps the most respected black movie star of his generation, played in the 1967 *To Sir With Love*. In a lighter vein, Elliot Gould played a teacher's assistant in an English department and at university during the student riots at the very end of the 1960s in *Getting Straight*. In this moment of a break in social relations, the public school teacher was represented in popular culture as hero and change agent. Out of this appreciation of teachers and teaching came the social formation of composition. The clearest example of this perhaps was the Dartmouth Conference of 1966, which I describe later. This conference and the books that came out of it were central to English education. At the time, teachers in the public schools were more likely to know and care about Dartmouth than college English professors.

Proposition 5: This shift in social relations is associated with the emergence of post-Fordist regimes of capital around 1971 in the United States.

Although postmodern ideas were in circulation long before, the "postmodern" only became economically viable after 1971 or so. There is general agreement now among many social scientists and social critics (Sennett 1998; Harvey 1989; Ohmann 1976/1996; Berlin 1996) that the U.S. economy underwent a dramatic shift from economies of scale to economies of scope in the last third of the twentieth century. This shift was connected with the conservative restoration during the early 1980s that Ira Shor describes and contests in his book *Culture Wars* (1986). The year 1971 becomes a convenient one to examine for several economic and social reasons. Standards of living for American workers, which had steadily risen from the end of the Great Depression, reached a plateau at this point, never to return to the earlier value.

Proposition 6: With shifts in social relations come shifts in what counts as authority and the accompanying shift in concepts of authorship.

This change in our very notion of what counts as authorship had major effects on composition as a social formation as well as on other social formations (e.g., ethnic writers, women writers, gay and lesbian writers, etc.). The fact that authorship is connected to power is widely accepted dogma since Barthes and Foucault. But what is less recognized is the dramatic impact of this shifting conception of authorship in this period in composition and rhetoric. Before 1968, it was rare to find student writing that was published in bona fide forums and treated as bona fide writing. Starting with English educators like Moffett, in his 1968 *A Student-Centered Language Arts Curriculum*, and Janet Emig, in *The Composing Processes of Twelfth Graders* in 1971, and school teachers like John Rouse, who wrote often during the late 1960s in *Media and Methods*, student writing is valued for its own authority. It was also in this time that student writers were published as authors. Only a few years later, scholars in composition and rhetoric, influenced by their colleagues with training and connections in English education, began to look at student writing as authored writing. This changing view of the student writer, occurring as it did in a moment, a liminal moment, on the cusp of the change from Fordism to post-Fordism, provided people working and living in collectives—like groups of teachers of writing—with the exigency to experiment and to imagine new forms and forums, new forms of authorship.

Proposition 7: There is a strong economic connection between federal spending, improvement in working-class conditions, and emergence of composition and rhetoric as social formation.

In the period 1945–1980, programs such as the G.I. Bill, the V.A. home loan program, and even the interstate highway fund improved the lives of working-class Americans. Furthermore, there is a strong economic connection between federal spending during the 1960s and 1970s and the emergence of composition and rhetoric as social formation. There was a variety of federal spending on the arts, humanities, and education during the 1960s and 1970s. Most all of these funds were terminated, or radically cut back, in the economic and budgetary crisis of the early 1980s in the Reagan administration. Following are just a few of the projects that connected to the study and teaching of writing.

- There were the projects related to the establishment of National Endowment for the Arts and National Endowment for the Humanities in 1966. These agencies helped fund the poets in the schools program in the late 1960s, which had a profound effect on college composition. Robert Fox describes some of the effects of the original poets in the schools program in *The World Is Flippied and Damzled About: A 20-Year Retrospective of Writers in School and an Anthology: 1982–1985*. College composition-ists sometimes became aware of this work through the student-authored anthologies put together by the poet-teacher Kenneth Koch, who collected *Wishes, Lies, and Dreams* (1970) and *Rose Where Did You Get That Red?* (1973). Public school teachers were very influenced. According to Elizabeth Kray's essay in Fox's collection, there were teacher in-service projects with poets, as well as work by poets in actual classrooms in New York City (starting in 1966), Detroit, Pittsburgh, Minneapolis, Chicago, Tucson, and Los Angeles (1986, 13). Often matching grants from the states as well as private money from the Rockefeller Foundation, among others, was involved. In these projects, students authored texts and published them with their names attached. Many of these seed projects eventually went on to become part of the National Writing Project.

- Over twenty Project English curriculum study centers were established 1962–1967. Although people in both English (Kitzhaber 1967) and English education (Carlsen and Crow 1967) found fault with the work many of these centers did, there can be little quarrel with the fact that the Project English centers often provided the only extended and intense interaction between college professors, mostly in English education, and public school English and language arts teachers, before or since. A channel was established between the schools and the universities, which often outlasted the project centers. What started as an attempt to have college professors do scientific research on language learning for teach-ers became, by the late 1960s, a site where teachers could critique the ivory tower theory of academe when it came to actual students in actual communities. At least teachers "tested" the materials developed at the curriculum centers. How often are teachers allowed this freedom today? And the university faculty who participated in Project English began to use the word *curriculum* and to think about curriculum, rather than simply their disciplinary specialization.
  - The centers received what even by contemporary standards were large amounts of money—$250,000 for each center. Given twenty-three centers, that is nearly six million dollars for this project alone. Many of the centers according to Shugrue (1966) focused on nonlit-erature areas because these were seen by the public as more useful. The National Endowment for the Humanities and National Endow-ment for the Arts, when they were established four years later, would cover literary projects, one of which was the poets in the schools project. Included among the charges of the various centers was English as Second Language at University of California–Los Ange-les and Teachers College, Columbia University; both writing (Gate-

way English for disadvantaged junior high school students) and the bilingual readiness program at Hunter College of the City University of New York; a secondary curriculum for the deaf at Gallaudet College; a teacher action research project in developing a curriculum for teacher education at the University of Illinois; reading instruction training films at Syracuse University; linguistics for secondary English curricula at Ohio State and New York University; and a focus on adult functional illiteracy in the county around Tuskegee Institute. Almost all of the centers either had some subject matter connection with composition and rhetoric or had a connection with secondary or primary curricula in the public schools. For the English professors involved in such federally supported work, this may have been the only experience they would have with the schools, teachers, and public school students—before or since.

- Daniel Fader makes the case that his literacy work, in both the University of Michigan's centers that did prison outreach and inner-city Washington, DC schools, was a turning point for him. In *Hooked on Books* (1966, 1976), his important accounts of literacy learning, Fader describes how he and his team at Michigan taught reading and writing in a prison environment. They motivated reform school inmates by saturating their environment with large quantities of consumable, attractive print media—paperback books and magazines—that appealed to student interests. They insisted on English (reading and writing) in every class, an unacknowledged forerunner of the writing across the curriculum movement. Asking students to write journals on anything they wanted (including copying in a free form), Fader and his colleagues opened up the sorts of writing the students could do seven years before Peter Elbow pioneered journal use when he wrote about freewriting in his *Writing Without Teachers* (1973). Fader's account of his work with children in the DC public schools, *The Naked Children* (1971), is testament to the profound effect that such work, often supported by the federal government, had on him and perhaps on these working-class children. Daniel Fader is not even mentioned in the official disciplinary histories of composition and rhetoric or on writing across the curriculum. His work, important and heroic, was perhaps too focused on the schools and on basic literacy. There is no better evidence for the narrowness of the disciplinary histories, and the totalizing narratives underlying them, than that Fader's work is kept alive only in English education.

And that point can be made about the Project English centers and federal funding in general. It is simply inaccurate to claim that writing in the Project English programs, with two exceptions, remained largely transparent. Using Shugrue's list (1966), I count eleven centers out of twenty-three that have to do directly with linguistics (English as a second language, transformational generative grammar) and/or writing. The influences these centers had on English and on composition and rhetoric are often made invisible in histories that too narrowly define the field and its origins because they do not conveniently fit into the narratives of what is currently fashionable professionally. For instance, Richard Ohmann's *English in America* (1976/1996) is one of the key critiques of the profession that came out of the 1970s. In that book is a chapter "Rhetoric for the Meritocracy," by Wallace Douglas (1976/1996). Wallace Douglas, according to Shugrue (1966), was involved in the Project English center at Northwestern University, which worked on the art of writing in grades 7 through 12. Helping Douglas prepare documents was Stephen Judy (Tchudi), who became an English education professor in the 1970s at Michigan State University, editor of *English Journal*, and a president of National Council of Teachers of English (NCTE). Tchudi himself went on to coauthor a revision of the James Miller book *Word, Self, Reality*. Miller, at Chicago, had been a participant at Dartmouth. So the federal and foundation money that went to Project English centers and seminars like Dartmouth (funded by the Carnegie Corporation) had long-term effects that remain—for the most part—overlooked; and although the connections of the Project English centers with writing are not always easy to see thirty years after the fact, they are there. For another example, the Center at Ohio State headed by Bateman and Zidonis, although it was written up as a project on transformational generative grammar, was focused on the writing of students in the junior high (see Bateman 1970, 1963). Unquestionably, the Project English centers had significant impact on composition and rhetoric that has been largely erased.

- Other federal funding included research like the Weehauken, New Jersey, Project running from about 1966 to 1974, which worked with students and teachers in a multicultural school and produced *Individualized Language Arts—Diagnosis, Prescription, Evaluation: A Teacher's Resource Manual for the Promotion of Students' Facility in Written Composition K–12*. In this 1974 document, we find some fairly traditional ideas about writing, but also ideas like freewriting, brainstorming, written response to film or music, not to mention the extensive use of talk and small groups, that were all but alien to most college English professors in the 1960s and that were fairly innovative even for many college composition teachers. Other research funded by the federal government included the famous Rohman and Wlecke study of *Prewriting* (1964) at Michigan State, in which students, as well as instructors and outside readers, were asked to assess the success of the project (77–95). Although composition and rhetoric historians do frequently mention this monograph, the role that student feedback and federal funding played take a backseat to the supposed expressivist or cognitivist orientation of the work. I read the work more as a reworking of authorship, which includes student writers. Yet another project, the Wilcox survey of college English departments, was cosponsored by the federal government and the Modern Language Association. The final report, published in 1972, was the largest and most detailed description ever put together of the work of college English departments—everything from the majors and courses offered, to the use of faculty, to the type of textbooks required in freshman English (mostly not expressivist). No history of college English in the 1960s and 1970s can begin without studying closely the results of the Wilcox survey. Yet, in histories of the field of composition studies, it is mentioned in footnotes, if at all.

- Federal funding was not confined to academics doing research. Even more important was the larger amount of capital invested invisibly and directly in the education of working-class students. First, there were Office of Economic Opportunity grants, monies for tuition and books that were provided if parents' income was too low to contribute to college funding. These were grants, not loans. They did not have to be repaid. Second, it was during this same time that work-study programs were established within universities, again federally funded, to pick up for the working-class student what the grants could not pay for. Work-study students worked in university offices or for professors on research projects. For many work-study students this, not the college composition classroom, was the real site where "academic discourse" was observed in its "natural habitat" and was forever demystified. Third, there were specially targeted programs like City College of New York's SEEK (Search for Education, Elevation, Knowledge) and Upward Bound. SEEK was the basis for Open Admissions at Mina Shaughnessy's campus of the CCNY and produced the central work of Marie Jean Lederman. Upward Bound, among other things, published books like *Talkin' Bout Us: Writing by Students in the Upward Bound Program* in 1970. This anthology of student writing and photography was offered as an "alternative" to what was going on in English. It notes: "There is a crisis in English classrooms across this country; teachers need a literature that presents a vision of life that is real to the student" (v). Where better to go than to the students? It would be interesting to find out what happened not simply to the Upward Bound students, but to all of those working-class students who came through and were lucky to have federal and often matching state aid to education. I wonder how many of them ended up in composition and rhetoric. I know of one of them who did.

Proposition 8: The forces that eventuated in composition as a social formation, and later as discipline, came mostly from the bottom and moved up.

The forces that came to be what we call composition came mostly from the public schools and the students, to education colleges and English education, and only then to composition in college English departments. Let me simply list a few of the major names who contributed to composition and rhetoric during the late 1960s and early 1970s: James Moffett, James Britton, Janet Emig, Ken Macrorie, Lee Odell, Charles Cooper, John Rouse, John Dixon, Stephen Tchudi, James Kinneavy, Richard Larson. All of these people either worked directly with teachers or were English education professors who worked with inservice teachers or were trained in English education or wrote for English education publications during this time, for *English Education* and also *Research in the Teaching of English (RTE)*. *RTE* was itself an outgrowth of early conferences among English professors and English teacher preparation people, which were funded by the federal government. *RTE* in the late 1960s and into the 1970s was a different sort of journal than it has since become. Many innovative ideas, especially those in composition, were supported through the research published in the journal. Janet Emig wrote often for *RTE*. And the first scholar I know of who called for ethnographic research on student literacy was Martha King, who was in language arts and elementary education at Ohio State. In the October 1978 issue of *RTE*, she noted a need for writing theory and ethnographic research of writing practices. King and Rentel at that time were just beginning a federally supported research project on the growth of writing in primary school students. These observations lead me to claim: The origin of most of the key ideas in composition and rhetoric from 1968 to 1980 came from those associated with schools of education or with teacher education. Many of the ideas that later scholars in English simply assume came from college English departments instead emerged from people with ties to education schools. The histories in composition and rhetoric so far have been blind to this important contribution.

Proposition 9: The Dartmouth Conference can be interpreted as the first volley in a controversial debate that would last a decade between college professors of English and public school teachers of English and language arts and those allied with them.

Although the Dartmouth Conference can be viewed as a conflict between those who saw English as subject matter and those who saw it as language in use, from a class perspective, Dartmouth can be interpreted as the first volley in a decade-long controversial debate between college professors of English and public school teachers of English and language arts and those allied with them. Although the invited delegates were university faculty, in a very real sense Dartmouth was the scene of a struggle between those who spoke for the middle and privileged classes in university under the rubric of the "discipline" of English and those who served the working classes, who spoke for students.

For years, professors in English did not even know about Dartmouth. The only real in-depth analysis of Dartmouth from that period that exists in the journals that might have been frequented by some English professors was the critique by Ann E. Berthoff in *College English* in 1972.

Funded by big capital in the form of the Carnegie Corporation, the Dartmouth Conference can well be read as part of the ongoing conflict between teachers and scholars for English. Though funded by corporate capital, Dartmouth didn't quite go as planned. Instead it became a site where various related conflicts broke out:

- conflicts over disciplinary discourses, over whether teacher knowledge should prevail or whether psychology, linguistics, literary criticism, social sciences of various sorts should prevail—and be taught as part of "English"

- conflicts over scholars' primary identification as teachers versus their primary identification as researchers

- conflicts between the rising militancy of school teachers versus the control of curriculum by college English professors

- conflicts between a current political shift (i.e., the material demands made by huge baby boomer enrollments and a school teacher shortage) versus outdated institutional structures at university that controlled access to teaching and to English.

These heated disagreements at Dartmouth were class conflicts. Teachers, at the bottom of the disciplinary structure, were often associated with the "new" students who came from the working class. Stephen North (1987) notes that disciplinary structure constructed teachers in research projects like the initial Project English centers as technicians (or even "natives") who would simply learn and apply the newfound discoveries of the more elevated college professors—whether such discoveries were the new grammars of Chomsky, the new rhetorics of Burke, Richards, Hayakawa as delineated in the pioneering work by Daniel Fogarty, *Roots for a New Rhetoric* (1959), or the new criticisms, including that of Northrup Frye, formalized in secondary curricula at Nebraska and Oregon.

At the time of the Dartmouth meeting, teachers who were in the forefront of social change in both Britain and the United States were resisting this subjugated role. Dartmouth was a declaration of independence being voiced by teacher educators because teachers themselves were not invited delegates. Berthoff is absolutely correct in her 1972 critique of the theoretical inadequacies of the language theory behind Dartmouth, though the power struggle that was going on is missing from her analysis. Later in his important book, *A Teaching Subject: Composition Since 1966* (1997), Joseph Harris invokes the conference and the ideas of the teacher advocates as a part of the debate about what college English was, how it was to be defined. Missing from his discussion is the material dimension, that is, social class.

First, most college English professors, aside from some who attended Dartmouth perhaps, *knew* what college English was. Second, they had no interest in composition, let alone in consorting with education people, let alone public school teachers who were reconceiving their roles to define English, very much as the teachers who founded the National Council of Teachers of English, together with like-minded teacher educators, had done a half-century before. Dartmouth was where changes from below ran into changes from above.

John Dixon's account of the background that the British participants brought to Dartmouth is especially enlightening on this point. In 1969, he wrote, "Throughout the early sixties there had been a sudden flourishing of new work in *secondary* departments scattered up and down England . . . without the help of a single curriculum project" (366–67, my emphasis).

> Although one or two American teachers from a similar school tradition were present at the seminar, the U.S. delegation was predominantly drawn from the universities. This reflects the decision of the government funded Project English Centers to involve university scholars in literature, linguistics, and composition in setting up curriculum study centers. . . . [There was a] tendency for the university professor to dominate the work of the schools, and certainly, as regards representation, this was true at Dartmouth. (367)

The British delegation at Dartmouth, often constructed by U.S. scholars as radical, was sharply criticized *back home* by the newly founded National Association of Teachers of English for failure to fully represent the work "(and its Primary school origins) of the delegation sent to Dartmouth" (Dixon 1969, 367). By teachers' lights, the British delegation at Dartmouth was not radical enough. What we see here then is a British delegation, influenced by grassroots social change put forward by teachers working with working-class students in a socialist setting, communicating a watered-down version of that to the U.S. scholars. The movement of change is from the bottom upward, from working-class students to their teachers to their teachers' representatives brought to the United States to bring this message to scholars at Dartmouth by Carnegie Corporation money.

The struggle to define English that ensued at Dartmouth continued over the next decade in the United States. We can see it, for a notable example, in Gerald Graff's 1980 rebuke of John Rouse's critique of Mina Shaughnessy's work. Harris comments on Graff's dismissal of Rouse:

> For what Graff—who was identified by a . . . note on the first page of his response as chair of the English Department at Northwestern University, as well as author of articles in several prestigious literary journals and of a book published by University of Chicago Press—was hinting rather broadly at was that he didn't know who this guy was, that Rouse (schoolteacher rather than professor; article in *College English* rather than *Salmagundi*, book published by trade rather than university press) was not a player in the academic world that he moved about in. (1997, 76)

True enough. But the connection to the teaching counterculture can be traced in what Rouse wrote over the previous decade, not simply where he was positioned in academic and disciplinary hierarchies.

Rouse had, through the late 1960s and into the 1970s, written extensively on alternative schooling and alternative literacies for, among other magazines, *Media and Methods*, the voice of innovation and counterculture for English teachers in the schools. Rouse was part of the very movement of radical school teachers who constructed a social formation where the notion of authorship was refigured to include students, including working-class students, and different media, including film, adolescent literature, popular magazines, paperback books. Rouse was a veteran of a fifteen-year debate between academically privileged college English professors and school teachers representing the "new" students. Ruling class bourgeois meet the working class—in extremely mediated forms, of course. The ruling class won that battle. Although Mina Shaughnessy was fought every step along the way by her own English faculty colleagues at the CCNY, she was taken up widely by English professors, more, no doubt, because she was a trained as a Milton scholar than because her "diving in" to study the errors of open admission students and the expectations of their teachers was a brilliant piece of groundbreaking research.

To be sure, once the discipline composition and rhetoric was established in the 1980s, Dartmouth was reinscribed as an official part of college English disciplinary history.

Proposition 10: Egalitarian change came from the bottom of the social structure, that is, from students reconceived as authors by those in the social formation.

This "birth of the student author" can easily be tracked into composition through a diverse set of materials that originated with the schools and students in the schools and moved into college composition. We can begin to see the birth of the student author in the publication of innovative and extremely popular curricular journals and magazines, especially *Media and Methods*, but also *This Magazine Is About Schools* and later *Learning Magazine*.

The April 1969 student issue of *Media and Methods* was a classic early example of an entire journal given over to student writing. A call went out a few months before in December for a "kid-contributed issue" for what became the "school is a bore" issue. The surprised staff of *Media and Methods* was inundated with submissions. A total of 3,157 students wrote "cubic yards" of a massive response to the call. Much of the material was "sophisticated" and of extraordinarily high quality. The editors reserved an introductory note and an afterword, but the rest of the issue was student-authored. *Media and Methods* had always been sympathetic to students and teachers who centered their curriculum around student activities and interests. For instance, *MM* began a regularly running feature in each issue that focused on Young Film Makers, starting with the September 1968 issue, owing to a great deal of encouragement for and appreciation of student produced films. Each month's issue of *MM* was targeted on hot topics, which the mainstream journals did not get near because they were too controversial. The October 1969 issue was the Peace Issue; May 1970, the Ecology issue; September 1970 dealt with drugs; November 1970, violence; teaching black studies, December 1970; Native American works, April 1971; Women's Liberation, March 1972; Aging, October 1972; and Sex/Ed in November of 1972. Anyone who is interested in the edge of teaching during this period needs to go to *MM*.

Frank McLaughlin, in his "Afterword" to the April 1969 student issue of *MM* tried to account for this response:

> Professional organizations like NCTE and the NCSS serve worthwhile functions as agencies that gather and disseminate research and literature, but they are also committed to their own self-perpetuation and consequently can inhibit the development of needed radical change (e.g. the reintegration of curriculum). (40)

One need only add that histories that focus only on the professional organizations' journals and publications give a skewed view of that period, but also of where the real innovations came from. If the slogan for the Watergate investigative reporters became "Follow the money," the slogan for a history of this period might well be "Follow the student writing": Student writing that without earlier federal and foundation monies and the social class they invited into the mainstream in schools would not have been published, might not even have been composed.

One can continue to track this developing focus on the student as author through the publication of innovative books (e.g., James Moffett's 1968 *A Student-Centered Language Arts Curriculum, K–13*, Ken Macrorie's 1970 *Uptaught*) that published and closely attended to student texts and to the publication of book collections devoted only to student texts (e.g., Kenneth Koch's 1970 *Wishes, Lies, and Dreams*; Stephen Joseph's 1969 *The Me Nobody Knows*; Caroline Mirthes and the children of PS 15's 1971 *Can't You Hear Me Talking to You?*; Upward Bound collections; even a 1971 college textbook from Random House, *Student Voices/One: On Political Action Culture*, and *The University* [Reaske and Wilson 1971]). In 1970, Leonard A. Greenbaum and Rudolf B. Schmerl published *Course X: A Left Field Guide to Freshman English*, which like the college textbook tries to cash in on the increasing importance of the student. Although *Course X* does not have any student writing in it, a revealing omission, it provides a sort of consumer's report that constructs the freshman reader of that time. It also provides some evidence for what the typical freshman composition course is likely to be— not expressivist, but political. The fact that the first-year course is still called

Freshman English in the book's title signifies the absence at the time of a "discipline" of composition and rhetoric.

Finally, one can see student writing emerge in scholarly articles, research monographs, and the professional journals. Marie Jean Lederman in the SEEK program at CCNY published one of the earliest calls for respecting and including student language in the composition course in her 1969 *CCC* essay, "Hip Language and Urban College English." This pioneering article made the case for making the study of student language part of the composition course content. She notes:

> Many educators feel that our hallowed halls of higher education should resound only with the sounds of Standard English. Yet circumstances both inside and outside of college classrooms today make me feel strongly that it is time for urban college teachers to include "hip" language in the bland diet we traditionally serve in our English composition classes. . . . It follows that the English teacher in a composition class might do well to try to set up situations in which students examine their own linguistic behavior. . . . In the freedom and enlightened atmosphere of our college classrooms, where we have already broken down so many barriers, where we can talk freely about war, drugs, sex, and so many other formerly taboo subjects . . . why shouldn't we be willing to talk freely about words? (204, 205, 214)

Student words, it must be added. It shouldn't surprise us that Lederman in a 1973 essay in *College English* mentions that the "best work" that has been done to improve student writing includes Herbert Kohl's *36 Children* and Kenneth Koch's *Wishes, Lies, and Dreams*. These innovations moving into college composition in the mid-1970s grew out of work with children in urban schools, working-class children, and often federally funded projects.

Janet Emig's 1971 monograph, *The Composing Processes of Twelfth Graders*, begins to legitimize the study and publication of students' writing. Journal articles follow. In 1973, *CCC* publishes Lee Odell, whose academic preparation was in English education. Odell argues for making student response a part of the composition course. Continuing down this path, we can track the development of the profession's interest in student authorship into *College English* under Richard Ohmann's editorship ("The Student Speaks" section and later an entire student issue); into *English Journal* under Stephen Tchudi's editorship, 1973 to 1980 (the annual spring poetry issue); and *Language Arts* (1972), which begins to regularly feature student writing during this time. And theorists add their voices. David Bleich in 1974 publishes *Readings and Feelings*, calling for subjective criticism, in an argument for putting student experience and student response at the center of literature courses.

These are, in fact, but a few examples of how student authorship grew from the grass roots, well watered by federal and foundation monies, on up the social hierarchy, from working-class children in the schools and teachers like James Herndon (1966, 1971, 1985), who taught them and wrote about that experience, to basic writers in new introductory courses in college composition, to the journals and publications of English education, and only then, *much later* to college composition. The stone that the builders rejected had become the cornerstone, as Vygotsky was fond of reciting (1962/1986).

Proposition 11: Student writing leads scholarship.

Student writing with attached author lines, its publication, and its acceptance as a bona fide effect of authoring and an increasingly legitimate object of study and appreciation, shaped so-called process theory, which shaped the subsequent discipline of composition, which, ironically, as time goes by, has begun to exclude the publication of student writing and then to turn away from student writing that does not rigidly adhere to the conventions of so-called academic discourse. By the 1990s, the student becomes more of a drag on goals of the discipline whether those goals are political or scholarly. Student experience, interests, and writing become less important as the discipline professionalizes and becomes increasingly constructed by and serving corporate interests and legislated mandates (Zebroski 2002).

Proposition 12: The discipline of composition and rhetoric begins to coalesce in the late 1970s; the Ottawa Conference of 1979 is one site where the discipline is born.

There had been an increasing interest by the mid-1970s in viewing composition and rhetoric as a disciplinary formation. Frank D'Angelo (1999) traces this disciplinary beginning to small groups of like-minded people who met during this time—what I have called a *social formation.* Yet I would argue that the discipline's emergence from this social formation can be charted by its primary internal conflict. As the social formation of composition begins to set itself apart from English and other established disciplines by including student writing and new forms of authorship as subjects of study, the emerging discipline begets academic schools of research and pedagogy that bring together different traditions of knowledge making, which are often in conflict from the start. These schools of composition and rhetoric are arrayed on a spectrum between the most humanities-oriented approaches, often associated with rhetoric, to the most social science-oriented approaches, often associated with English education. Much of the struggle for composition and rhetoric has been enacted in the space created by these competing traditions, which have in some cases proved to be a productive, creative tension, in others a counterproductive binary.

In 1975, *The Writing Processes of Students* came out of SUNY Buffalo reporting on the annual conference on the language arts held there in 1974. SUNY Buffalo was at this time an important center of English education and of the emerging interest in university in composition. Many later researchers in the discipline got their training or taught at SUNY Buffalo. It is fascinating to look at the contents of this report because it shows both the promise and the potential conflicts as composition shifts from a social formation to a discipline. Included in the collection are articles by James Squire, Janet Emig, Donald Graves, Charles Cooper, and Lee Odell—all people associated more with English education than college English. James Squire points out the conflicts between rhetoricians from English departments and education people.

> During the past decade or so, the revival in rhetoric and rhetorical studies is offering us many new insights about the nature of discourse. We have a generative rhetoric of the English paragraph, transformational sentence combining, tagmemic study of the contexts of writing, a restatement of Aristotelian logic, and ever so many other new insights. Well and good, of course, in extending the teacher's insight into his [sic] own writing for these new rhetorical approaches are based almost entirely on the study of adult models, of specimens of the most mature and sophisticated stylists and craftsman who have written in the English tongue. (1975,6)

Squire is setting up his argument against the rhetoricians by first listing some of the accomplishments and noting that they are not student centered, but teacher centered. The argument is very much the same argument that James Britton launches at the start of his *The Development of Writing Abilities (11–18)* (Britton et al., 1975), which will come out a year after Squire's remarks. But we can also read these remarks as an indication of a bigger turn from a social formation to discipline, from a period of social antistructure to a period of slow, but sure, increasing social structure. Squire continues:

> Indeed, rhetoricians themselves by the very nature of the discipline devote virtually their entire efforts to analyzing mature prose passages selected from printed texts. Almost all of the analysis deals with the final product, not with the process itself. Almost all deals with writing of adults. (1975,6)

So the rhetoricians not only are oriented toward adult rather than student writing, but they are also product rather than process people. What had been circulating as conventional wisdom for well over a decade, the distinction between product and process is here used as a slogan to call into question—but also in a sense to construct—the opposition. Squire, however, still sees value in compromise and accommodation.

> Reject the rhetoricians then? I say not. But let us use their insights more to suggest ways for the teacher to study the writing of children than as subject matter to be taught in a program designed to teach people how to write. . . . On what then can our programs of composition be based if not the rhetorical analysis of standard prose? Much more, I think on the reading of writing by children—on the rhetorical analysis of their own writing. Until we learn to listen to the modes of our children's discourse, we are not likely to discover the problems they encounter in communicating. Until we have a generative

rhetoric of their paragraphs, we are not likely to know how best to help them through such an approach. (1975,6)

Remarkable words nearly thirty years later in a time when genre theory touts adult forms that college students must master and rhetoric pushes argument on social issues of interest to adults. The strangeness of the words shows clearly how far we are from this social formation and protodiscipline.

What had been a tension at the SUNY Buffalo conference in 1974 became a conflict at the Ottawa Conference in 1979. Aviva Freedman and Ian Pringle (1980) provide some contextualization of the conference in *Reinventing the Rhetorical Tradition*, the published papers of the conference. Janet Emig also provides some commentary about her presentation there in the dialogues with the editors of her essays *The Web of Meaning* (1983), as well as in other interviews she has since done. She tells Gerald Nelms, for example, that she was bored and angry with the emphasis on classical rhetoric and linguistics as sources of information about writing or instruction in writing (Ralph Gerald Nelms, *A Case History Approach to Composition Studies: Edward P.J. Corbett and Janet Emig*, unpublished dissertation, The Ohio State University). She notes that "differences in the kinds of research done separated the two fields" of English and English education (165). Her presentation was one attempt to articulate those differences. But the "tacit tradition" that Emig describes at the conference in an essay of that title is *her* tradition, *the English education tradition*, not the tradition of the rhetoricians, nor twenty years later, the tradition of any remaining sizeable school of the discipline of composition and rhetoric. Emig was moving the struggle for students—and implicitly for working-class students and teachers—from the social formation to the discipline. As it became clear that teachers were beginning to lose whatever say they briefly had between Dartmouth and Graff, Emig moved the struggle to the discipline.

Freedman and Pringle are among the very first to call composition and rhetoric a discipline.

> Of course, those presenting papers at the conference were not representative of the *discipline* as a whole. As leading researchers and composition theorists in the English-speaking world, they are at the vanguard; they do not so much represent the attitudes and beliefs of the practitioners in the field as indicate the direction in which the field is moving. (1980, 176, my emphasis)

In their epilogue. Freedman and Pringle use the word *discipline* six times in the first section alone. They describe the buoyant mood of excitement, the conference being a culmination of all that had been achieved in the "recent resurgence of interest in the discipline" (173). Throughout the book, however, lies a gaping fault line between rhetoric and English education, between humanities scholarship and social science research (and by social science research conducted in the human science tradition), and between a teacher-centered and a student-centered approach to writing. Freedman and Pringle and the participants were clear about much of this.

> Clearly, in identifying these forebears of our tradition, Emig made explicit many of the underlying assumptions of the discipline. At the same time, as John Dixon commented publicly after the presentation, she has been unconventional and somewhat outrageous in suggesting that our true heritage is not the classical or Aristotelian rhetorical tradition, but rather the contemporary intellectual matrix. (1980, 178)

Of note is the participation of John Dixon at the conference and his characterization of Emig's remarks. Note too the use of the phrase the *discipline*. Note too the title of the collected papers of the conference, *Reinventing the Rhetorical Tradition*. The use of the word and the resort to rhetoric are clarified by Freedman and Pringle.

> Until now, the discipline as a whole has consistently appeared to define its home within the classical tradition of antiquity. Early on, Corbett (1965) placed the teaching of composition within this tradition which despite having fallen on bad days, clearly had vital roots. Since then, it has been a commonplace to point to this heritage *not least for rhetorical purposes, to give the discipline legitimacy by invoking names almost canonized.* Yet there is no great difficulty in reconciling the conventional view that we hark back to Aristotle with Emig's claims for that tacit tradition of twentieth century thought. That two separate traditions can be traced does not imply a polarization within the discipline. The reinvented rhetoric has multiple roots. (1980, 178–79, my emphasis)

This is one of the most remarkable passages written in composition and rhetoric in the last twenty-five years. But I think the writers doth protest too much. The polarization was already there, already existent, and in fact, was the very foundation of the "discipline" so frequently invoked and constructed here.

The need for unity and harmony that runs through this whole book and, I assume, that conference, can only be understood as a reaction to the prior reality of conflict between the college English professors and English educators with their advocacy for public school teachers and students.

There is so much clarity in this passage—a correct evaluation of the narrative that rhetoric projects, which was only really taken up by Susan Miller a decade later in her *Textual Carnivals* (1991). There is an accurate description of how rhetoric is invoked for disciplinary legitimacy, how an idea and a tradition function as cultural rhetoric. There is a clarity about different and multiple roots for "the discipline." Yet the final hopes that polarization might be avoided were not fulfilled as indicated by the final title of the book. The final conflict was simply postponed, differed, until full-fledged schools of composition, almost all located in English departments and not in colleges of education, had produced several generations of recruits armed and ready for disciplinary battle. I dislike the war metaphors, but I think they capture the sense of the years from 1985 to 2000 in composition and rhetoric. And there is little evidence at the time of this writing of an impending cessation in hostilities.

Works Cited

Barthes, Roland. 1989. "The Death of the Author." In *The Rustle of Language*, translated by Richard Howard, 49–55. Berkeley, CA: University of California Press.

Bateman, Donald. 1959. *Speculations Concerning Symbolism, the Communication Core, and Language*. Columbus, OH: Center for School Experimentation.

———. 1963. "The Psychology of Composition: (I) Suitable Conditions for Composing." In *Center for School Experimentation Bulletin 1*, 1–15. Columbus, OH: Center for School Experimentation.

Batman, Donald, and F. Zidonis. 1970. A Grammatico-Semantic Exploration of the Problems of Sentence Formation and Interpretation in the Classroom. Volumes I and II. Columbus, OH: Ohio State University Research Foundation. Final Report.

———. 1964. *The Effect of a Knowledge of Generative Grammar upon the Growth of Language Complexity*. Columbus, OH: The Ohio State University, Cooperative Research Program, Office of Education, U.S. Department of Health, Education, and Welfare.

———. 1966. *The Effect of a Study of Transformational Grammar on the Writing of Ninth and Tenth Graders*. N.C.T.E. Research Report No. 6. Urbana, IL: NCTE.

Berlin, James. 1987. *Rhetoric and Reality: Writing Instruction in American Colleges, 1900–1985*. Carbondale, IL: Southern Illinois University Press.

———. 1996. *Rhetorics, Poetics, and Cultures: Refiguring College English Studies*. Urbana, IL: NCTE.

Berthoff, Ann. 1972. "From Problem Solving to a Theory of Imagination." *College English* 33(6): 636–49.

Bleich, David. 1974. *Readings and Feelings*. Urbana, IL: NCTE.

Britton, James, T. Burgess, N. Martin, A. McLeod, and H. Rosen. 1975. *The Development of Writing Abilities (11–18)*. London: Macmillan Education Ltd.

Carlsen, G. Robert, and J. Crow. 1967. "Project English Curriculum Centers." *English Journal* 56(7): 986–93.

Connors, Robert. 1997. *Composition-Rhetoric*. Pittsburgh: University of Pittsburgh Press.

D'Angelo, Frank. 1999. "Professing Rhetoric and Composition: A Personal Odyssey." In *History, Reflection and Narrative: The Professionalization of Composition 1963–1983*, edited by Mary Rosner, B. Boehm, and D. Journet, 269–82. Stamford, CT: Ablex Publishing.

Dixon, John. 1967/1975. *Growth Through English: Set in the Perspective of the Seventies*. Edgarton, Huddlesfield, Yorkshire, England: National Association of Teachers of English and Oxford University Press.

———. 1969. "Conference Report: The Dartmouth Seminar." *Harvard Educational Review* 39(2): 366–72.

———. 1991. *A Schooling in "English": Critical Episodes in the Struggle to Shape Literary and Cultural Studies*. Philadelphia: Open University Press.

Douglas, Wallace. 1976/1996. "Rhetoric for the Meritocracy." In *English in America. A Radical View of the Profession*, edited by Richard Ohmann, 97–132. Hanover, NH: Wesleyan University Press.

Emig, Janet. 1967. "On Teaching Composition: Some Hypotheses as Definitions." *Research in the Teaching of English* 1(2): 127–35.

———. 1971. *The Composing Processes of Twelfth Graders*. Urbana, IL: NCTE.

———. 1972. "Children and Metaphor." *Research in the Teaching of English* 6(2): 163–75.

———. 1983. "The Tacit Tradition: The Inevitability of a Multi-Disciplinary Approach to Writing Research." In *The Web of Meaning: Essays on Writing Teaching, Learning and Thinking*, 145–56. Portsmouth, NH: Boynton/Cook–Heinemann.

Elbow, Peter. 1973. *Writing Without Teachers*. New York: Oxford University Press.

Fader, Daniel. 1971. *The Naked Children*. New York: Bantam.

———. 1976. *The New Hooked on Books*. New York: Berkeley.

Fader, Daniel, and E. McNeil. 1966. *Hooked on Books: Program and Proof.* New York: G. P. Putnam's Sons.

Finn, Patrick, and Walter Petty, eds. 1975. *The Writing Process of Students: Report of the Annual Conference on Language Arts*. Buffalo, NY: SUNY at Buffalo, Department of Elementary and Remedial Education.

Fogarty, Daniel. 1959. *Roots for a New Rhetoric*. New York: Russell and Russell.

Foucault, Michel. 1972. *The Archaeology of Knowledge*. New York: Pantheon Books.

———. 1977. "What Is an Author?" In *Language, Counter-memory, Practice: Selected Essays and Interviews*, edited and translated by Donald Bouchard, 113–38. Ithaca, NY: Cornell University Press.

Fox, Robert, ed. 1986. *The World Is Flippied and Damzled About: A 20 Year Retrospective of Writers in the Schools and an Anthology: 1982–1985*. Columbus, OH: Ohio Arts Council.

Freedman, Aviva, and I. Pringle, eds. 1980. *Reinventing the Rhetorical Tradition*. Conway, AK: L & S Books.

Greenbaum, Leonard, and R. Schmerl. 1970. *Course X: A Left Field Guide: A Left Field Guide to Freshman English*. New York: J. B. Lippincott Co.

Harris, Joseph. 1997. *A Teaching Subject: Composition Since 1966*. Upper Saddle River, NJ: Prentice Hall.

Hartwell, Patrick. 1985. "Grammar, Grammars, and the Teaching of Grammar." *College English* 47(2): 105–27.

Harvey, David. 1989. *The Condition of Postmodernity*. Cambridge, MA: Blackwell.

Herndon, James. 1968. *The Way it Spozed To Be*. New York: Simon and Schuster.

———. 1971. *How To Survive in Your Native Land*. New York: Simon and Schuster.

———. 1985. *Notes from a School-Teacher*. New York: Simon and Schuster.

Joseph, Stephen, ed. 1969. *The Me Nobody Knows: Children's Voices from the Ghetto*. New York: Avon.

Judy (later Tchudi), Stephen. 1981. *Explorations in the Teaching of Secondary English: A Sourcebook for Experimental Teaching*. New York: Dodd, Mead and Co.

————. 1981. "A Note on the Second Edition." In *Explorations in the Teaching of Secondary English: A Sourcebook for Experimental Teaching*, 2d ed. New York: Harper and Row.

King, Martha. 1978. "Research in Composition: A Need for Theory." *Research in the Teaching of English* 12(3): 193–202.

King, Martha, and V. Rentel. 1983. "Conveying Meaning in Written Texts." *Language Arts* 56(6): 721–28.

Kitzhaber, Albert. 1967. "A Retrospective View of the Government and English Teaching." *College Composition and Communication* 56(7): 135–41.

Koch, Kenneth. 1973. *Rose Where Did You Get That Red? Teaching Great Poetry to Children*. New York: Vintage Books.

Koch, Kenneth, and the Students of PS 61 in New York City. 1970. *Wishes, Lies, and Dreams: Teaching Children to Write Poetry*. New York: Vintage Books.

Kohl, Herbert. *36 Children*. New York: New American Library, 1967.

Larsen, Richard. 1970. " 'Discipline' and 'Freedom' for Teachers of Composition." *English Education* 1(3): 153–58.

————, ed. 1975. *Children and Writing in the Elementary School*. New York: Oxford University Press.

Lederman, Marie Jean. 1969. "Hip Language and Urban College English." *CCC* 20(3): 204–14.

————. 1973a. "A Comparison of Student Projections: Magic and the Teaching of Writing." *College English* 34(5): 674–87.

————. 1973b. "Taught." *CCC* 24(3): 251–55.

Macrorie, Ken. 1970/1996. *Uptaught*. Portsmouth, NH: Boynton/Cook–Heinemann.

McLaughlin, Frank. 1969. "Afterword to School Is a Bore Issue." *Media and Methods* April: 62.

Merlis, Mark. 1996. *American Studies*. New York: Penguin.

Miller Jr., James. 1972. *Word, Self, Reality: The Rhetoric of the Imagination*. New York: Dodd, Mead and Co.

Miller, Susan. 1991. *Textual Carnivals: The Politics of Composition*. Carbondale, IL: Southern Illinois University Press.

Miller, Thomas.1997. *The Formation of College English*. Pittsburgh: University of Pittsburgh Press.

Mirthes, Caroline, and the Children of PS 15. 1971. *Can't You Hear Me Talking to You?* New York: Bantam.

Moffett, James. 1968. *A Student-Centered Language Arts Curriculum, K–13: A Handbook for Teachers*. Boston: Houghton Mifflin.

North, Stephen. 1987. *The Making of Knowledge in Composition: Portrait of an Emerging Field*. Upper Montclair, NJ: Boynton Cook.

Nystrand, Martin, S. Green, and J. Wiemelt. 1993. "Where Did Composition Studies Come From? An Intellectual History." *Written Communication* 10(3): 267–333.

Odell, Lee. 1973. "Piaget, Problem-solving, and Freshman Composition." *CCC* 24: 36–42.

Ohmann, Richard. 1976/1996. "Introduction to the 1995 Edition." In *English in America. A Radical View of the Profession*, xii–lii. Hanover, NH: Wesleyan University Press.

Reaske, Christopher, and R. Willson. 1971. *Student Voices/One: On Political Action, Culture, and the University*. New York: Random House.

Rohman, D. Gorden, and A. Wlecke. 1964. *Prewriting: The Construction and Application of Models of Concept Formation in Writing*. Cooperative Research Program of Office of Education, U.S. Department of Health, Education, and Welfare. CRP No. 2174. East Lansing, MI: Michigan State University.

Sennett, Richard. 1998. *The Corrosion of Character*. New York: Norton.

Schultz, Lucille. 1999. *The Young Composers: Composition's Beginnings in Nineteenth-Century Schools*. Carbondale, IL: Southern Illinois University Press.

Shor, Ira. 1986. *Culture Wars: School and Society in the Conservative Restoration 1969–1984*. London: Routledge and Kegan Paul.

Shugrue, Michael F. 1966. "New Materials for the Teaching of English: The English Program of the USOE." *PMLA* 31(4): 3–38.

———. 1968. *English in a Decade of Change*. New York: Pegasus.

———. 1970. "Educational Accountability and the College English Department." *CCC* 21(3): 250–255.

———. 1970. "Educational Accountability and the College English Department." *CCC* 21(3).

Small, Robert. 1972. "Student Authority." *English Education* 3:3 (Spring 1972): 151–61.

Squire, James. 1975. "Composing—A New Emphasis for the Schools." In *The Writing Process of Students: Report of the Annual Conference on Language Arts*, edited by Patrick Finn and Walter Petty, 1–10. Buffalo, NY: SUNY at Buffalo, Department of Elementary and Remedial Education.

Upward Bound Students. 1970. *Talkin' Bout Us*. New York: Random.

Varnum, Robin. 1996. *Fencing with Words: A History of Writing Instruction at Amherst College During the Era of Theodore Baird, 1938–1966*. Urbana, IL: NCTE.

Vygotsky, Lev. 1962/1986. *Thought and Language*. Cambridge, MA: M.I.T. Press.

Weehauken Board of Education. 1974. *Individualized Language Arts—Diagnosis, Prescription, Evaluation: A Teacher's Resource Manual for the Promotion of Students' Facility in Written Composition K–12*. Weehawken, NJ: Board of Education with State of New Jersey Department of Education, validated by U.S. Office of Education.

Wilcox, Thomas. 1967. "Non Serviam." *CCC* October.

———. 1972. "The Varieties of Freshman English." *College English* 33(6): 686–701.

———. 1973. *The Anatomy of College English*. San Francisco: Jossey Bass.

Zebroski, James T. 1998. "Toward a Theory of Theory for Composition Studies." *Under Construction: Working at the Intersections of Composition Theory, Research, and Practice*, edited by Christine Farris and Chris Anson, 30–48. Logan, UT: Utah State University Press.

————. 1999a. "The Expressivist Menace." In *History, Reflection and Narrative: The Professionalization of Composition 1963–1983*, edited by Mary Rosner, B. Boehm, and D. Journet, 99–113. Stamford, CT: Ablex Publishing Corp.

————. 1999b. "Textbook Advertisements in the Formation of Composition: 1969–1990." In *(Re)Visioning Composition Textbooks: Conflicts of Culture, Ideology and Pedagogy*, edited by Xin Liu Gale and Frederic Gale, 231–248. Albany, NY: SUNY University Press.

————. 2002. "Composition and Rhetoric, Inc.: Life After the English Department at Syracuse University." In *Beyond English Inc.: Curricular Reform in a Global Economy*, edited by David Downing, M. Hurlbert, and P. Matheiu, 164–80. Portsmouth, NH: Boynton/Cook–Heinemann.

2

Under the Influence
A Prequel

Janet Emig

This essay was difficult to write. I do not say this to elicit sympathy, much less empathy. It was difficult to write chiefly because of my stance toward the past. Some claim the older we grow, the more the past tightens its grasp while at the same time flashing and dimpling its charms. Not for me. The only two tenses I find of interest are the present and the future. Joan Didion, one of my seven favorite writers, once said, "Every day is all there is." Yes.

Yet we all know that the past inevitably shapes, even as it informs the present. And this project that Patti Stock initiated is not only worthy but also seriously needed in an era when too many texts misrepresent themselves as histories of our field. History implies accuracy; doesn't it?—rather than at times as dismissive and self-serving category systems. I mean: Would YOU want to be called an expressivist (such a graceful term!) or a cognitive rhetorician, for that matter?

Just what were the contributions made by those of us who elected to work early in this curious field? Were we actually responsible for all this? All that? While at the same time clearly having so much more fun than our colleagues down the hall?

We took writing seriously again, after an unhappy hiatus, rescuing it from being regarded simply as a skill and a domestic drudgery. Instead, we honored it as a central symbolic process worthy of being a subject and an object of inquiry, possibly constituting a unique field, perhaps even a discipline. We took children and adolescents seriously as learners. We took schools, especially public schools, seriously, noting how they both form and deform learning.

We connected writing with its indigenous, by which I mean, American philosophical roots pragmatism and neopragmatism. We foregrounded the complex interplay of learner with researcher, including teacher-researcher, dealing necessarily, if at times only implicitly, with issues of gender, race, and culture. We did this through naturalistic inquiry—notably, case study and ethnography—at a time when the very few studies of written composition were being conducted as experimental studies only.

From the outset we were, as our signifier indicates, cross-disciplinary by predilection, background, or both. We acknowledged a role for the social sciences and even, rarely, the contributions the hard sciences could make. Consequently, we conducted studies that possibly possess biological as well as cultural accuracy about how writers actually write, learners actually learn, rather than metaphysical pronouncements and prescriptions about how students should be required to write. If we had a mantra, it might be the one Stephen Marcus phrased simply, "We are, more than anything else, born to learn."

And if we succeeded, it was because we elected to form a community—a noncompetitive community—not difficult because we genuinely liked one another and chose to play first what one of us happily called "the believing game."

So, cheered by scanning these not inconsiderable accomplishments, I pulled up my socks and almost immediately made discoveries that turned duty into joy. I read the not-yet-but-I've-always-been-meaning-to read. I reread the not-read-for-decades, including my own writings, recalling that I once upset Alan Purvis at some reception or other when asked some detail about *The Composing Processes,* by saying I really couldn't remember.

More vitally, I reconnected with colleagues long out of sight, if not mind. And I want to thank them up-front. Perhaps I'm wrong in these attributions, but I think one of the side effects of the feminist movement and of the writing projects is that so many authors are so much more open and effusive in their acknowledgments. Very little writing has ever occurred in a vacuum, but now we are more honest about our debts.

Deciding how to organize this essay represented a vexed rhetorical question. History pristine and unadorned by the personal? Herstory informed by history? A possibly uneasy interplay? Perhaps I could give the shuttling cache if I called it *contrapuntal.*

Roots, origins, genealogies. That tangle. Those intertwinings. I don't find it curious that at the very time I am seeking out my roots in English education—my intellectual genealogy—I also find myself in the genealogy library of the Latter Day Saints Center in Tacoma, Washington, trying to learn something about my maternal grandmother, Anna Everson, who died at twenty-eight of tuberculosis. (Yes, just as I thought, and hoped: I am a corner Irish.)

Identity. What those of us who still know and believe in evolution call *hereditability*: literally, the measure of the percentage of variation in a trait that can be attributed to genes allowing a role for human uniqueness. There is, I believe, a cultural analogue: that percentage of variation in an artist or writer that stays outside a cultural and a linguistic explanation. Again, uniqueness. (Some in our field just fainted away at this heresy.) Others of you might just be saying irritably, "Just quote T. S. Eliot, who put it elegantly, simply, as 'tradition and the individual talent.' "

What was striking upon introspection was how for a complex of reasons, some probably unconscious (I am not a Scientologist), I found myself in three academic settings with deep and often ambivalent connections with composition and rhetoric: Mount Holyoke College, the University of Michigan, and Harvard University.

To stay on theme means, of course, I cannot honor all those who sponsored and shaped my literate life starting with my mother and father, my grandmother, and my great-aunt Nora. For that accounting, you will have to wait, and I am certain you can, for my full-length memoir *The Satisfactory Dusk* (or me-moir, as Louise Rosenblatt so charmingly pronounced it).

I happened to attend both an elementary school—Williams Avenue in Norwood, Ohio—and a high school—Walnut Hills in Cincinnati—where we wrote regularly. Indeed, at Williams Avenue we pursued all the arts with vigor and élan under the curious *rubric of auditorium*, a term Yetta Goodman also remembers from her school in Detroit. Only many years later, when first reading Dewey in Israel Scheffler's Philosophy of Education class, did I realize that the Norwood schools were clearly Deweyan in curriculum and approach. Lucky for all of us there at that time.

Walnut Hills was pure anti-Dewey, a classical high school where although Greek stopped being required the year before I entered, we were required to take the equivalent of five years of Latin. Ninety-eight percent of us went on to four-year colleges, many, Ivy League and Seven Sister schools. Looking back on our English department, I realize that it was one of the last outposts of the British Empire. I can remember reading only three American writers: Langston Hughes (one poem), Susan Glaspell (you remember her, don't you?), one one-act play, and Vachel Lindsay ("The Congo," what else?). All tests in English were essay tests. My crowd was almost ludicrously literate. When we were reading *The Return of the Native*, for example, we wrote sonnets about Egdon Heath—for fun! To give some notion of the quality of *The Gleam*, our literary magazine, Kenneth Koch was an editor and John Ziegler drew the cartoons, as he still does for *The New Yorker*. My greatest literary thrill came my sophomore year when I won *The Gleam*'s $2 poetry prize for my poem "The Great Lover," an open imitation of Rupert Brooke—my Sinatra.

Mount Holyoke College

Although I went to Mount Holyoke College for its science—I wanted to be a doctor—I loved my English classes from the very first day. Helen Griffith, chair of the department, taught my section of Freshman Composition. Very early on, we were assigned to write a poem. My first conference with her—I think it lasted at least half an hour—was taken up with her scrupulous analysis of why spelling the title *Grey* with an *e* was far superior to spelling it with an *a*. Lesson from my first writing conference ever: Writers, even seventeen-year-old writers, were to be taken seriously, as was their writing itself.

By checking with that infallible source, my freshman roommate, I realized that where reading was concerned, freshman comp our year must have represented some kind of experiment by a faculty member or committee imprinted by dealings with Franz Boas and his group at Columbia who so influenced Louise Rosenblatt. Although we later turned to Cleanth Brooks and Robert Penn Warren, like good little New Critical neophytes, our initial texts were *Patterns of Culture* by Ruth Benedict, *Coming of Age in Samoa* by Margaret Mead, and *Philosophy in a New Key* by Susanne Langer.

Only as I was writing this chapter did it occur to me that reading under the rubric of English what otherwise might have been required in anthropology or sociology perhaps was the origin of my belief that insights from the humanities and the social sciences might actually inform one another.

As a sophomore, I took the next course open in the English composition sequence, entitled simply (starkly?) *Description*. (Yes, Virginia, at Holyoke at that time one could take a major in English composition.) At the time all aspects of my academic world were unquestioned givens, but as I was reading for this essay, some historical strands intertwined. Thanks to Joann Campbell and others, I learned that at the turn of the last century Holyoke's curriculum in writing and rhetoric was undergoing a revision comparable to Gertrude Buck's at Vassar. It turned out that Clara Stevens, the chair at Holyoke, like Buck, studied with Fred Newton Scott and Dewey at Michigan, earning a Master of Philosophy degree in 1894. Buck graduated from Michigan in 1899 and received Scott's first Ph.D. in rhetoric four years later.

The next is pure speculation, but I believe that it was likely Stevens and Buck knew each other and that there was cross-pollination between the programs at Vassar and at Holyoke, where Stevens started the rhetoric department in 1897 and served as its chair until 1921. I base this on two suppositions: The first, how many women could there possibly have been in rhetoric at Michigan at the turn of the last century? The second, the course title, *Description*. Vassar, it seems, offered such a course with the same title, a course that survived at Holyoke for forty years.

In addition, we took advanced description (!) and versification, and we had the opportunity both junior and senior years for honors work, either critical or imaginative. Junior year I wrote about Elizabeth Bowen, whose novel *Death of the Heart* had blown me away. Senior year, with no sense of hubris I wrote a novel (serious when the title is the best part of the project, and the words are Hart Crane's anyway). My tutor was Joyce Horner, the British novelist and Oxford graduate St. Hilda's, whose own novel *Greyhound on the Leash* had received quiet critical acclaim.

In addition, we wrote critical essays in every class. I mean, every class. At Holyoke no such entity as a non–intensive writing course existed. In the late 1940s, we were all paper-writing factories, churning out lengthy dispositions on the MicMac Indians of Nova Scotia and living our eighteen-year-old conclusions to such minor questions as "Does God exist?" while back in English, by now good little New Critics that we were, we snuffled out new strands of imagery like truffles (serpents in Antony ah!). Our opinions were both sought and honored, although our professors felt free to tell us off if they found us aesthetically wanting: Alan McGee, chair of the department, wrote on my dis-appreciation of "The Lotus Eaters," "Miss Emig, you are too damn moral to read Tennyson!" Bracing.

For most of the time, however, our teachers were gentle and encourag-ing, particularly about imaginative writing such as stories and poems and pre-tentious and plotless novels. Peter Viereck, Pulitzer Prize–winning poet and our history professor, was especially kind. But then so were Sydney Maclean, another established novelist on the faculty, and May Sarton, when she served as a judge for our Glascock Poetry Contest (Sylvia Plath won the year before I read and lost). Unlike any professor I met later in graduate school, my Holyoke professors did not take themselves over seriously. After we spent, it seemed, a half semester or more on Eliot's *The Cocktail Party* (verse dramas were very big in that era), I wrote a satire called *The Beer Picnic* in which our three senior Lit Crit professors were featured, which they found hilarious.

At Holyoke living writers were actually welcomed. There seemed to be, to use Robert Coles' devastating phrase about professor/critics, "no envy of the storyteller." Thomas Mann spoke; and I was present for the famous eve-ning when Dylan Thomas made his entrance onto the American academic stage, as described by John Malcolm Brinnin in *Poet in America*. I missed Auden by a year, alas.

Today at Holyoke there is no composition major, and there are many non–intensive writing classes. Instead, there is a Center for Writing and Critical Thinking: important, I think, to siphon off both those processes from the actual curriculum!

The University of Michigan

When I went to Michigan in 1950, I knew nothing of our, or its, tradition. I noted above how I learned about Dewey, through enactment and then reading at Harvard. I never heard of Fred Newton Scott or of Gertrude Buck or, indeed, of Clara Stevens. No, I went to Michigan to pursue another tradition: Among English comp majors at Holyoke, we went to Ann Arbor to try to win a Hop-wood Prize in writing (in 1952 Hetsy Howell Slote finally redeemed our honor).

We were required, of course, to take regular lit courses along with our twelve-credit seminar in writing. My first course was with the chair, Warner Rice, in American lit. The first assignment: to write three hundred words about a quatrain from an Emily Dickinson poem. When I looked at my grade the fol-lowing Monday, it was a *D* with the comment, "You have written 308 words." I went up to Professor Rice almost laughing and said, "Professor Rice, this is a joke, isn't it?" He replied, "Young woman, I never joke."

My second course in pre-Shakespearean drama was with the famous Shakespeare scholar G. B. Harrison. Our first assignment was to compare and contrast two early plays, say, by Marston and Jonson. My grade here was a

B− with the comment, "Dear Miss Emig, Throughout this paper you persist in giving me your opinion. Clearly, you went to one of those fashionable Eastern girls' schools interested in your opinions. I am not. Simply compare two plays." Perhaps you can imagine my shock.

Experiences like these had their effect. I never could take Michigan as seriously as it undoubtedly deserved, except as a negative instance. Harvard was to provide another. In the writing seminar under Roy Cowden, weekly we analyzed revisions from very tired and indigo-blurred versions of Hardy and Arnold and critiqued—quite gently, actually—one another's writings. My Holyoke novel stayed plotless, and I stayed clueless that it was. The only memorable moment came when my classmate Frank O'Hara—Frank O'Hara!— expressed relief that I had also entered the poetry Hopwood because he had admired a poem of mine in *Generation*, the Michigan literary magazine.

At Michigan, I was divested of my innocence about the chances for women in academe, particularly in the era of veterans returning under the G.I. Bill. None of the women in the master's program was admitted to the Ph.D. program, although many of us had higher grade point averages. After not being accepted at Michigan, I tried the University of Cincinnati, interviewing with William S. Clarke, a longtime social acquaintance, thanks to my closest friend Elizabeth Bettman, doyenne of Cincinnati's small literary salon. His exact comments are, for some reason, still incised somewhere on my frontal lobe: "Well, Janet, I could admit you; but since no one would ever hire you, why should either of us bother?" (Later, a childhood friend did bother, and she was psychologically destroyed by the experience.)

I know, I then thought: I'll try England: I'll read for a B.Litt. at Oxford, the university, as I noted earlier, of my senior honors tutor. I decided that I wanted to study George Eliot. The word came back through Roberta Teale Schwartz, the Holyoke alum who sponsored me: "Sorry: the author contemplated is too modern." As a recent TV commercial put it, "You can't make this stuff up!"

Happily, during this dire decade, I met John Berryman. He was poet in residence at the University of Cincinnati the spring semester of 1952. I am not the first to write of John as a teacher. In a marvelous essay a number of years ago in the *New York Times Book Review*, Philip Levine described John when he served as faculty member at the Iowa Writers' Workshop.

I first experienced John during a phone call during a week I was home from teaching with one of those faded-flannel-pajamas-and-Vaporub kinds of flu. "It's a man," my father called to me. "I don't recognize the voice."

"Black and hanged," the voice was high and faintly querulous. I thought 1 might be speaking with Lord Peter Wimsey. (Yes, I was a Dorothy Sayers aficionado.) I understood the allusion because it was a line from "The Fool," one of the poems I submitted for consideration to his workshop.

"'Ack,' 'anged,' great assonance. I called to tell you that for that line alone I'm admitting you to my workshop. Would you like to go out for a drink?"

I explained about the flu, glad of a cover for being both awed and unnerved, although we did go drinking (that is, John drank; I drove) many times during the semester. His wife of the time, Eileen Simpson, who later wrote the touching *Poets in Their Youth*, seemed happy to wave us on our way. She was probably less happy with John's affairs in Cincinnati.

The workshop was extraordinary. John taught by admiration. His view of critiquing our work was to admire whatever he believed we had done well. You can imagine our shock when, in subsequent years, Stephen Spender ignored most of the men and all the women; and Randall Jarrell savaged us all.

And since John believed that reading fed writing, we read. I remember *The Tempest*, which John saw as a treatise on work; *Daniel Deronda*, which he liked for the double narrative; and Styron's *Lie Down in Darkness*, just because. Were we asked to read *Don Quixote*? I may have balked because I feel about Quixote as I do about Alice: Who can possibly care?

And although John was in open and obvious competition with such contemporaries as Robert (Cal) Lowell and Elizabeth Bishop, he admired them ferociously as well. And like Lowell, he did not believe that being a scholar was antithetical to being a poet. I am very happy that with the astounding Henry poems he forms the trifecta of that memorable generation. The cost of being John was very high, however. I once met a purported biographer of John who told me that as a child John had witnessed his mother kill his father. That would do it. And I will not describe my last anguishing encounter with John when we happened to take the same plane after he'd spent a disastrous week at the University of Connecticut. When he jumped from that bridge onto the frozen Mississippi a short time later, one bystander said he waved good-bye. I was grief-stricken but, like many others, unsurprised. I learned from John the habit of admiration, a characteristic, I believe, of English educators and of English education—at least most of the time. But, for better or for worse, I also internalized from knowing John—and later, May Swenson—that the cost of being a poet was very high, possibly fatal. And perhaps because I possess a very un-American trait—I am hopelessly moderate—I have elected for the most part to stand at the edge of the forest looking in, while inordinately admiring those who elect to enter like Adrienne Rich and James Merrill. Am I alone in this? I doubt it.

Harvard University

I first met Priscilla Tyler, and learned of that relatively new entity English education, at the 1960 Conference on College Composition and Communication (CCCC) Convention in Cincinnati. Elizabeth Williams, the chair of my English department at Wyoming (OH) High School, suggested that I attend and covered my teaching responsibilities with several days of substitutes.

John Berryman and Priscilla Tyler: Could two personalities seem more disparate? The poet who, for one year, wrote a sonnet a day "just for practice" and the thwarted writer who found putting words on paper such an agony that she could not write enough of them to stay at Harvard. But there were likenesses. Both were ferociously scholarly; both were extraordinary teachers of vast generosity. Both played upon my sensibility and formed so much more than, until recently, I comprehended, my career and any contribution I may have made to English education and to the teaching of writing.

Priscilla graduated from Radcliffe, taught public school in Cleveland, her home city, and received her Ph.D. from Case Western Reserve, where she also taught. In 1960 she codirected the English education program at Harvard with Edwin Sauer, formerly a teacher at Walnut Hills. She did not speak of composition at that workshop. Rather, at the time, caught up in one of her many enthusiasms, she was immersed in structural linguistics: Names like Fries and Marckwardt and Joos floated by. But she also described the coming summer session, alluding somehow to a connection with writing.

I signed up shortly thereafter. My memory of those six weeks is dominated by a single concept: revision. Murray-ites before Murray, we were converted to the notion that writing means rewriting and rewriting. I wrote a kind of prose poem to Eden Park, my favorite setting in Cincinnati. In retrospect, it seemed I rewrote it daily after responses from all my classmates and Priscilla (no small groups as I remember it). Again, only fairly recently did I understand that by not choosing to write, and revise, another piece, writing obsessively about Eden Park was one of the tortuous routes I followed to separate myself from Cincinnati, and from the then tight and probably unhealthy ties that bound me to my recently widowed mother.

I entered the formal, if amoeba-like Ed.D. Program in English education that fall. The course requirements were few; the range, wide. I took any course that beckoned, from Anglo-Saxon with William Alfred to the Psychology of Language with Eric Lenneberg. Priscilla herself taught a course about early American readers, spellers, and textbooks. The subject of her own dissertation (1953) was *Grammars of the English Language to 1850*. The next summer, as her research assistant, I visited the historical societies of many of the thirteen colonies, as well as the Folger and limitless New England barns. I think I was the first to find a copy of a Fox speller at the Free Library in Philadelphia. If you have ever had such a find, you know that unique joy of unearthing a primary source not acknowledged for centuries.

But Priscilla's interests were as catholic as they were fervent: lexicography, with visits from such noted editors as Henry Gleason and Raven McDavid; lectures on structural linguistics; fascination with transformational grammar as well (we were urged to cross-register with MIT); and we, of course, studied Englishes of the world. We read Chinua Achebe and Derek Walcott (actually, Priscilla was the first to bring Walcott to the United States). She learned Inuit legends through visits to Alaska and the northern reaches of Canada, pursuing some connection she perceived with the Arthurian myth. Always she held a persistent, abiding interest in the processes of composing.

Let's see: pursuits historical, linguistic, anthropological, aesthetic, literary, writing as process. At the beginning of the 1960s, Priscilla was developing many of the major clusters of concerns and interests that help identify uniquely English education as a field today. Priscilla also believed in developing community. She was responsible for the no-nonsense entry of all of her students into the profession. In 1963, she served as chair of the CCCC convention in San Francisco, one that possessed even more verve and energy for me than subsequent ones, undoubtedly in part because it was my first as a participant. I remember the seminar when Priscilla announced that we were all going (think imperative); more, we were already assigned to chair sessions. Chair? I drew the panel on eighteenth- and nineteenth-century grammar with Marckwardt, Fries, and immersion with an *I*; terror with a *T*. Of course, we coped; we had no choice.

We also met informally outside Cambridge. Priscilla owned a cabin on Lake Nubanusit in New Hampshire, to which we were invited with steady generosity. I even spent a summer there ostensibly working on my dissertation. Across the lake were Jim (former Executive Director of National Council of Teachers of English) and Barbara Squire (the Squires retired there after Jim left Ginn) and my classmate Henry Olds. Weekends were spent barbecuing and arguing amiably. On Saturday nights, we square-danced at the church where the males competed to see who could stomp the loudest.

As for Harvard itself, its contributions to the teaching of rhetoric and then, briefly, to the teaching of composition have been well rehearsed and well documented by many of our own scholars, Berlin, Brereton, Crowley, Miller, and Connors, to name a few. We all remember its firsts: the first to require an admission essay on an assigned prompt; the first to require daily themes; indeed, the first to require a version of freshman composition. But by the time I arrived at Harvard, the status of composition was so problematic that I could not find, even with Priscilla Tyler's help, a faculty member in English to serve as one of the readers on my qualifying paper on writing. We were particularly struck by the refusal of her acquaintance, the writer Theodore Morrison, with whom Robert Frost was living at the time. A flat, nonexplanatory "no."

Perhaps a greater reason for my difficulty was that Harvard in the early 1960s was owned by Noam Chomsky and his followers. At the time, if the hype was to be believed, "transformational" grammar was to transform the entire intellectual universe as we had known it. One way some in English education decided to get in on the action was through studies in sentence-combining. Those pursuing such studies did find a far quicker route out of Harvard than I, although as we now know, the long-term value of those studies has proved anomalous. I suppose the major reason that I stayed with composition is that Chomsky himself told me that he saw no contribution transformational grammar could make to the study of composition. For some reason, I found his statement compelling.

My experiences with the ten advisers on my dissertation is part of the field's lore so I won't revisit those years, with two exceptions. At one point,

Peter Neumeyer wrote at the top of one version: "Being interested in how children write is like being interested in how cripples skate." As with other comments I have noted, I am fairly certain that at the time he regarded his sentence as the essence of cuteness. Just remember, please, he was a faculty member in the Graduate School of Education with profound interest in children. And two, I want to thank a linguist, Wayne O'Neil of MIT, who returned to chair my committee and sign off on my dissertation after no one at Harvard would.

I do not call up these experiences out of self-pity. It's all too long ago. I do so because some historians in the field proceed as if those of us at the beginning had the same network of support as they found later. Rather, think Sisyphus.

Conclusion

What, if anything, do those of us who call ourselves English educators have in common? We seem to be mavericks, with very few of us entering the field through the front door. Rather, it could be claimed, we entered by breaking and entering, *B and E* as it is called in too many police procedurals.

Temperamentally, we seem a self-assured lot, possessing a keen and cheerful sense of irony, dismissing even as we were being dismissed. From this distance, our commitment to teaching and children often seem greater than what we see around us. We believe in the transformative power of the imagination. And I still think a characterization by Renata Adler years ago obtains: "They kept their language, their energy, and their heads."

> And we have kept our beliefs as well. We believe in the transformative power
> of writing to examine ourselves and others; to deepen and to expand learning;
> and perhaps above all, to enhance, if not free, the imagination.

3

Lunch at the Night Hawk
Or Kinneavy Moves His Office

Thomas Newkirk

> Literacy in the English department? Maybe. It could be, but I doubt it.
> —Jay Robinson, "Literacy in the English Department"

The Night Hawk II Restaurant looked a little like a bird about ready to take off, with angled roofs rising like wings from the entrance way. Or maybe it was designed by someone who really wanted to design car fins because if you squinted your eyes, you could imagine it as the rear end of a vintage Cadillac. Before anyone had heard of cholesterol, the Night Hawk chain was known throughout Austin for its top chopped steaks, and for the fact that Janis Joplin had sung there before she made it big. Located on the Drag that bounded the west side of the University of Texas, it was a favorite hangout for students, and it was there that James Kinneavy made his announcement in the spring of 1975.

As I recall, we were sitting in a big booth, Kinneavy surrounded by a group of teaching assistants in the English Education Program, and he casually mentioned that he had been offered the Directorship of the Freshman English Program in the English department, and asked us what we thought about his taking it. Apparently there was great contention in that department about the directorship, and Kinneavy with his impeccable record as a rhetorical scholar, his *Theory of Discourse* (1971) having been published just a few years before, had the stature (and temperament) to appease all factions in a notoriously difficult department. Someone asked if that meant he would be leaving the College of Education and the English Education Center for good. He hesitated and said that the appointment was for only three years, that he would still be able to work with education students, but in all likelihood it would be a permanent shift.

Geographically it was not a big move—from the basement of Sutton Hall to the first floor of Parlin, maybe fifty yards as the crow flies. And he was good to his word, working with us on our dissertations, all of which at some point reproduced the rhetorical triangle that became foundational in composition theory with its corresponding aims—referential, persuasive, expressive, and literary. As major events in educational history go, Kinneavy's move will probably not rank among the most dramatic, but even then it seemed to symbolize a shift—the movement of composition from departments of education to departments of English. Within a few years, Steve Witte would join the composition program, followed by Lester Faigley, and later by Davida Charney and Linda Brodkey. Texas had long been a leader in textbook publishing with rhetorics written by Maxine Hairston, Susan Wittig, and John Trimble's exquisite *Writing with Style* (1975); but with Kinneavy's move, it soon became one of the first major universities to establish a Ph.D. program in composition and rhetoric. Many of us who experienced this shift there would inhabit two worlds: spending a morning in an East Austin high school supervising student teachers, and an afternoon in a Kinneavy seminar (the only graduate course in rhetoric) struggling to see how Merleau-Ponty provided the rationale for Kinneavy's view of expressive discourse. It was the beginning of a fragmentation that I feel to this day, as I suspect is the case for many who went from English education programs to careers in literature-oriented English departments. We would be strangers in a strange land, regularly at odds with norms and customs of our new home. Or at least that is my story, my particular sense of alienation, which may or may not generalize.

Although Kinneavy and his encyclopedic knowledge of the rhetorical tradition were welcomed by the English department, the low status of writing instruction became apparent in the fall of 1975 when two senior faculty members, James Sledd and Neill Megaw, proposed that all tenure-track faculty be required to teach one section of Freshman English every three semesters. The proposal gained some support, but it met with vigorous opposition from some literature faculty who made clear their low opinion of introductory writing courses and their limited sense of what such a course could be. The internal memos of the debate were collected by George Nash, a teaching assistant in the English department, and excerpted in a *College English* essay, "Who's Minding Freshman English at U.T. Austin?" (1976). I will quote one at length because it lays out the nightmarishly myopic vision of "English" that continues to haunt those of us committed to composition teaching and scholarship:

> There is one absolutely central reason why freshman rhetoric is avoided by the regular faculty whenever possible—it involves an overwhelming amount of dull, tedious, drudgery. Let me be more precise. While classroom contact with freshmen may be challenging and watching them develop intellectually during a semester may be extremely rewarding, marking the hundreds of pages of essays they write in a semester is a time-consuming, boring, uninspiring chore, primarily because so much of one's effort is spent correcting merely mechanical errors. . . .

(margin note: like Staunton's text!)

> Does it make good sense to use our resources more wisely and to have
> T.A.s teach composition while reserving literature courses at every level for
> the more highly trained regular faculty? . . . What I would like to see our
> department do is to respond to this motion—and to pressures by deans and
> presidents and regents—by reaffirming that its basic activities are scholarly
> research and the teaching of literature, and that while it teaches composition
> as a service to the university, such service is by no means it's *raison d'etre*.
> (quoted in Nash 1976, 127)

What a cluster of assumptions—that teaching writing consisted almost wholly
in marking mechanical errors; that this marking helped students and provided
a "service" to the university; that teaching literature of any kind required
advanced training, but the teaching of composition can (and should) be assigned
to graduate teaching assistants; that the pressures to shift professorial resources
to introductory literacy instruction should be resisted (as one faculty member
remarked, this basic instruction is more properly the function of junior colleges). Teaching introductory writing courses was the price graduate students
would pay until a select few of them could move on to faculty positions where
they would be freed this tedium. As one literature teacher put it over a hundred years ago, "I thank God I have been delivered from the bondage of theme
work into the glorious liberty of literature" (Carpenter et al. 1903, 329). In other
words, I may have made it out of the basement of Sutton Hall, but in a more
significant way, as a composition specialist, I was still in the basement.

In the spring of 1977, I met this prejudice again when I interviewed for
a newly created tenure-track composition position at the University of New
Hampshire. After my presentation to the department, a distinguished looking
faculty member (later to be department chair!) took me aside and said, "To be
honest with you, I don't think this position should exist. I'm not convinced this
is really a field of study."

I stuttered something about the rhetorical heritage of composition that
went back at least as far as literary scholarship, then asked, "So who do you
think should be overseeing the teaching of composition?"

"Oh, someone with a literature specialty who happened to take an *interest* in composition." Just as at Texas, I was blindsided and puzzled by the
presumption of English departments to claim possession of composition
while denying it any conceptual or scholarly foundation. "Literature" came to
resemble some of the absentee landlords from my Boston days—they owned
the property, but they didn't want to take care of it.

From a longer historical perspective, this resistance was nothing new.
Classicists resisted the entry of British literature in the late nineteenth century,
and fifty years later American literature had to fight its way into the mainstream, and more recently advocates of Women's Studies, American Studies,
Queer Studies, and Critical Theory had to confront the skepticism of established specialties. What made composition different—and less swallowable—

was the fact that its full integration required more than the addition of a new group of faculty specialists. It sticks in the throat. As Nash pointed out in his exposé, most university English departments, like other empires, are built on an exploited underclass, in this case one that teaches introductory writing courses. These courses help the bottom line in English departments, and they furnish graduate students for advanced literary study, a fraction of whom can realistically expect to gain tenure-track appointments. Hiring a few composition faculty may help in the management of this underclass but cannot eliminate the cruel hierarchy and exploitation. In some ways, it allows literature faculty to distance themselves even more from the system they sit on top of.

After thirty years in an English department, I am still mystified by the capacity of bright, enlightened, progressive, humane, socially conscious faculty members to tolerate (and benefit from) a system so clearly at odds with their political values. Most, in my department at least, would protest the outsourcing of U.S. jobs, when in fact we have been outsourcing the teaching of composition for years. They teach students the new vocabulary of critical theory, with terms like *hegemony*, while failing to see the hegemonic domination of composition and its teachers.

Let me cite just one example. At a department meeting several years ago, a few of us raised the issue of adjunct pay, which had been set at $3,000/section in the late 1980s and had not changed *for thirteen years*. We pointed out that even with the low inflation of the 1990s, the purchasing power of this pay rate had declined by almost a third, and unless we did something it would continue to decline. There was general head nodding and agreement until one faculty member—whose specialty, is, ironically, the construction of "race"—argued that if we increased the pay for adjuncts it would be harder for "regular" faculty to buy out course releases. I was literally speechless, unable to respond to such a nakedly self-interested argument. As the Director of Freshman English, I was the one who hired the adjuncts, and knew the quiet desperation of the gypsy scholars who would float between the University of New Hampshire, Hesser College, and the Sylvan Learning Center, hoping their car held up in the New England winter, and that they avoided any health problems because none of these jobs gave them any benefits. I thought of one particular adjunct, a Ph.D. in British literature, who had just adopted a Korean child and was trying to meet the new expenses of child rearing.

The only way I have been able to make sense of this attitude, this indifference, is to make analogies to racial prejudice. This is not to suggest that anything I have experienced approaches the severity of racial oppression, or even that I can begin to imagine what that must feel like. Yet books like Charles Mills' *The Racial Contract* (1997) make clear the dynamics of prejudice, specifically the capacity of the oppressor to operate in a situation of privilege while maintaining a sense of moral integrity. According to Mills, whites are able to do this by subscribing to a "contract," a tacit collective agreement not to see certain things or recognize certain social realities. This "contract" is not visible to the dominant race (which does not even imagine itself as a "race") and claims to adhere to "universal" principles, which in fact they apply only to their own race. Significantly, Ralph Ellison's central character is an "invisible" man. Within English departments, the "contract" involves imagining the "faculty" as tenure-track faculty and failing to notice part-timers: not knowing their names, their working conditions, their pay rates—and certainly not the life a marginal teacher must live. It does not manifest itself as "overt" discrimination because an active prejudice would at least recognize the object of prejudice. Instead, it is an agreement to remain ignorant. How else to explain the callous resistance (or indifference) to adjunct pay? If these adjuncts assumed human proportions, if they become three-dimensional, the "contract" would be harder to sustain. As any pedestrian in Manhattan knows, it is sometimes best to avoid eye contact with the street people.

I realize that my own alienation within an English department may be partly a product of my own temperament or perhaps all that reading in existentialism in my formative years. And to be fair, I was personally well supported after some rocky early years. And to be even fairer, I have come to see that even faculty in established areas of literary study (even Shakespeareans!) can feel beleaguered and marginalized. Nevertheless, my thesis finally is this: that key to the disciplinary formation of composition in the mid and late 1970s was a rejection of certain principles that seemed to undergird literary study as it was practiced then. This was the case clearly for Ken Macrorie, Peter Elbow, Mike Rose, and Janet Emig. It was the case for the British reformers like James Britton and John Dixon at the Dartmouth Conference who argued for a "growth model" of English. Jay Robinson, a highly respected former chair of the Department of English Language and Literature of the University of Michigan, felt that English departments would never take "literacy" seriously (1985/1990). It was the case for Donald Murray who argued that writing teachers should turn to practicing writers who might describe their processes and habits—rather than to literary scholars. It was even true for a new group of reader response critics (Bleich, Holland, Purvis, Squire Tompkins) who were rediscovering Louise Rosenblatt and her 1938 masterpiece, *Literature as Exploration*. Her later delineation of a transactional model of reading seemed a good fit with the new emphasis on the writing process.

This collective estrangement from literary study played a key role in the early formation of composition studies as a discipline. In fact, it is impossible to understand the disciplinary roots of composition without reference to the dominant literary culture of English departments as we perceived it. It is not too much of an exaggeration to claim that composition studies *inverted* the values of literary studies; that it defined itself in opposition to the prevailing set of values we saw in operation. This inversion was powerfully illustrated in Mina Shaughnessy's *Errors and Expectations* (1977), which I read just as I was finishing graduate school. Working with the same student errors that some U.T. English department found so degrading, such a misuse of faculty time, she painstaking laid out the patterns and "logic" of the deviations from grammatical academic writing. It was for me the first and most powerful demonstration of what it means to penetrate the *systematic* thought processes that lead to work that fails to meet institutional expectations (an insight I would come back to twenty years later in *The Performance of Self in Student Writing*). But maybe even more significantly, it established "access" as a central preoccupation of composition studies. If literacy scholars were being acculturated to see real fulfillment in the teaching of skilled and advanced students, where they might work within their scholarly specialties, Shaughnessy was encouraging us, teaching us, to "dive in" to the messy democratic work of helping the underprepared.

Another way in which this inversion operated had to do with the focus on "processes" or in Rosenblatt's term, *transactions*. Donald Murray in one of his early articles urged writing teachers to "teach the process, not the product," a slogan that was not without its problems. It could easily be taken to mean that writing teachers should not care about the quality of writing produced, something Murray never intended. And by suggesting such a split between processes of writing and written products, Murray may have obscured the way a knowledge of products (genres, styles, conventions) *affects* the processes of writers. But Murray's intent was at least partly political—to distinguish composition teaching (and scholarship) from what he perceived as the text-centered focus of literary studies, which in his view regularly failed to probe the activity of the writer in producing the text. Examining writing processes had the promise of demystifying a process that often appeared as inspiration or the manifestation of "talent." It could create a workmanlike and teachable set of practices and options—insights that literary study, in his view, had little interest in producing. For someone coming out of an education department, this focus on "process" seemed entirely congenial as it drew on some of the qualitative research techniques like protocol analysis that we were learning.

One great advantage of this research focus on process was the way it complemented the teaching we were doing. Universities regularly claim that scholarship enhances teaching, something that any faculty member knows is not always true. More often it seems that teaching, particularly teaching in introductory courses, gets in the way of scholarship. Yet this early composition research—Mike Rose (1985) on writer's block, Sondra Perl (1980) on "felt sense," Linda Flower (1987) on "task representation"—seemed to arise out of our teaching and speak directly to it. By contrast, it often seemed that literary scholars had to get into more advanced and specialized courses (and certainly escape from composition responsibilities) to really teach their specialties, thus creating a "higher is better" scale of valuation. There would be no rewards for them in studying the processes of struggling, inexperienced readers—even though the bulk of literature teaching involves teaching a reading process.

To contemporary graduate students in composition studies, this "process" focus can seem narrow, dated, overly individualistic, not sensitive to differences in race, class, and gender, and ultimately prosaic. As Gary Olson (2002) and others have argued, it may limit the discipline by tying it too closely to introductory writing courses and not moving out to the use of writing in various disciplines and in cultural contexts outside the university. Still I would argue that by inverting the perceived disciplinary biases of literary studies, composition studies has responsibly established itself as a field committed to access, as a field intellectually interested in the difficulties and promise of marginalized students. Because the majority of U.S. colleges are essentially open admission, a field focused on the processes of literacy learning may be a better fit in many cases than one focused on specialized literary study.

There were other ways in which those of us with English education backgrounds worked against the "higher is better" ethos of the departments we were joining. Because many of us had taught high school or supervised teachers, we naturally sought alliances and collaborative projects with public schools, as did the scholars who helped form the discipline. James Britton and Nancy Martin were regulars at the Bread Loaf program for teachers in northern Vermont, and Mina Shaughnessy was set to join them at the time of her tragic final illness. Jim Moffett was influential in the establishment of the Bay Area Writing Project, later expanded into the National Writing Project, which attracted regional leaders like Bill Strong of Utah State who had a strong background in English education. Janet Emig was closely associated with both the New Jersey Writing Project and the summer program for teachers sponsored by the University of Vermont (where Don Murray also taught). I was able set up a modification of the Bay Area model in New Hampshire with a grant from the National Endowment for the Humanities, a program still active today. Anne Gere's work similarly straddled high school and college composition, making significant contributions to both.

Because there was no established academic audience for composition, many of the key books in these formative years were written for practitioners. Early publishers like Boynton/Cook promoted authors who could reach both college and high school teachers (typically distrustful of university faculty). Elbow's *Writing Without Teachers* (1973); Murray's *A Writer Teaches Writing* (1968); Kirby and Liner's *Inside Out* (1981); Macrorie's *Telling Writing* (1976); and later Mike Rose's *Lives on the Boundary* (1990)—all found a readership among both high school and college writing teachers. Boynton/Cook's publication of Nancie Atwell's *In the Middle* (1987) signaled a major shift, however, with practicing secondary school teachers, not affiliated with universities, creating the major resources for K–12 literacy educators. She would be followed at Heinemann (which purchased Boynton/Cook largely to acquire Atwell's title) by Linda Rief, Regie Routman, Kylene Beers, Jim Burke, Ellin Keene, and Susan Zimmermann, none of whom worked out of universities. At the same time, new academic presses (or new lines within established presses) at the University of Pittsburgh, the State University of New York, Southern Illinois University, and Utah State were becoming the major outlets for composition scholarship.

In effect, the "literacy" audience interested in writing had split in two. Public school teachers were attracted to the practicality and credibility of authors like Atwell, and compositionists in English departments were drawn to a level of theorizing and complexity (and difficulty) that seemed irrelevant—even "precious"—to K–12 teachers oppressed by heavy teaching loads and state mandates. But by the mid 1990s, when Maxine Hairston (1992) and Peter Elbow (1991) criticized what they saw as the abstraction and jargon that was making its way into composition journals, they were often written off as reactionaries by younger members in the field, educated in English departments, and attracted by the conceptual power of theorists like Foucault, Bourdieu, Derrida, and Bakhtin. Increasingly, these new scholars lacked experience or interest in public schools and identified themselves with the same modes of scholarship and the same critical frames as their literary counterparts. Even the basic vocabulary was different—high school teachers taught "writing," college faculty taught "composition." And some of us were still trying to straddle the two.

A few years ago, I watched an interview with an old Irish Republican Army terrorist who fought the British in the 1920s, a frail old man who seemed to weigh no more than one hundred pounds. For all the world, he looked like a gentle harmless nursing home patient—except when he talked about the British, when his hatred seemed to animate his entire body, as if it were the very source of life for him. Without that cause, that reason for being, I could imagine him shriveling up into nothing. When asked about attempts at reconciliation between Catholics and Protestants, he denied that as a possibility, as if it would undermine his very identity.

On a much reduced scale, I could imagine myself as someone whose professional identity has been shaped by opposition, or as I have argued by inversion, by distancing myself from a value system that I saw operating in English departments. And despite the generous treatment I have personally received at the University of New Hampshire, and the changes in English studies over the last quarter century, this alienation is part of who I am as a professional. I still see myself as a stranger in a strange land. But as composition studies attains disciplinary status and becomes acculturated in English departments, losing any trace of its roots in English education, I see newly minted Ph.D.s who feel nothing of this alienation, and in my more reasonable moments, I think that my fights do not necessarily have to be their fights, and that this acceptance, after all, was something that we worked hard to achieve. But at some cost.

As composition studies becomes acculturated in English departments, there is the danger that researchers might try to align themselves with the prevailing value systems to be accepted as equals. They might, for example, come to adopt the "higher is better" bias and avoid introductory writing courses as assiduously, as adeptly, as their colleagues in literature. Based on two recent national searches that I directed, I was stunned by how few young researchers were actually studying students in any systematic way. In part, this reflects a healthy turn that does not restrict composition studies to a focus on introductory writing courses, that looks at writing in the wider culture. But even so, there seemed to me an attempt to fit in to English department culture—and avoid dissertations that might mark the researcher as someone with an interest in learning or in processes of reading and writing (that is, someone who might have spent time in an education department, or worse, a psychology department). There seemed a retreat from the kind of systematic qualitative data gathering that we had worked hard (fighting the positivists in education departments) to create a space for. As I complained about this situation, I did my best not to sound like that aging terrorist, endlessly refighting old battles, but I did feel that many of these new Ph.D.s seemed way too comfortable in English departments. When Kinneavy, himself, responded to the U.T. proposal for faculty to teach freshman English, he was characteristically generous and expansive:

> The intent of the Sledd-Megaw proposal, as I see it, is to maintain the English Department as the stronghold of the liberal arts tradition, a stronghold where rhetoric, poetic, (and logic also) are respected and maintained in a fruitful balance, fruitful for the faculty and especially for the student. He can see the intellectual life as a healthy organic whole, not as a discrete set of suspicious fragments. (Nash 1976, 127)

This was his utopian vision of a robust and comprehensive English department in which its components not only respected each other—but formed an organic unity. I suppose I want to close by saying a good word for suspiciousness, for resisting a unifying ethos that I believe has drawn composition studies away from its originating concerns for public education, literacy, and access. Writing almost thirty years ago, Mina Shaughnessy eloquently reminded us all of this mission:

> The work is waiting for us. And so irrevocable now is the tide that brings the new students into the nation's classrooms that it is no longer within our power, as perhaps it once was, to refuse to accept them into the community of the educable. They are here. DIVING IN is simply deciding that teaching them to write well is not only suitable but challenging work for those who would be teachers and scholars in a democracy. (1976/1988, 68)

The work is still out there.

Works Cited

Atwell, Nancie. 1987. *In the Middle: Writing, Reading, and Learning with Adolescents.* Portsmouth: Boynton/Cook–Heinemann.

Bleich, David. 1975. *Readings and Feelings: An Introduction to Subjective Criticism.* Urbana, IL: National Council of Teachers of English.

Carpenter, George, et al. 1903. *The Teaching of English in Elementary and Secondary Schools.* New York: Longmans.

Elbow, Peter. 1973. *Writing Without Teachers.* New York: Oxford.

———. 1991. "Reflections on Academic Discourse: How It Relates to Freshmen and Colleagues." *College English* 53: 135–55.

Flower, Linda. 1987. *The Role of Task Representation in Reading-to-Write.* Berkeley, CA: University of California/Office of Educational Research and Improvement.

Hairston, Maxine. 1992. "Diversity, Ideology, and Teaching Writing." *College Composition and Communication* 43(2) (May): 179–95.

Holland, Norman. 1975. *5 Readers Reading.* New Haven, CT: Yale University Press; 1975.

Kinneavy, James. 1971. *A Theory of Discourse.* Englewood Cliffs, NJ: Prentice Hall.

Kirby, Dan, and Tom Liner. 1981. *Inside Out: Developmental Strategies for Teaching Writing.* Montclair, NJ: Boynton/Cook.

Macrorie, Ken. 1976. *Telling Writing.* New Rochelle, NJ: Hayden.

Mills, Charles. 1997. *The Racial Contract.* Ithaca, NY: Cornell University Press.

Murray, Donald. 1968. *A Writer Teaches Writing: A Practical Method of Teaching Composition.* Boston: Houghton Mifflin.

———. 1972/1982. "Teach Writing as a Process Not a Product." In *Learning by Teaching: Selected Articles on Writing and Teaching.* Montclair, NJ: Boynton/Cook.

Nash, George. 1976. "Who's Minding Freshman English at U.T. Austin?" *College English* 38(2) (October): 125–31.

Newkirk, Thomas. 1997. *The Performance of Self in Student Writing.* Portsmouth, NH: Heinemann.

Olson, Gary, ed. 2002. *Rhetoric and Composition as Intellectual Work.* Carbondale, IL: Southern Illinois University Press.

Perl, Sondra. 1980. "Understanding Composing." *College Composition and Communication* 31: 363–69.

Purves, Alan with Victoria Rippere. 1968. *Elements of Writing About a Literary Work: A Study of Response to Literature.* Champaign, IL: National Council of Teachers of English.

Robinson, Jay. 1985. "Literacy in the English Department," *College English* 47(5) (1985): 482–98. Reprinted in Robinson, Jay. L. 1990. "Literacy in the English Department." In *Conversations on the Written Word.* Portsmouth, NH: Boynton/Cook–Heinemann.

Rose, Mike, ed. 1985. *When a Writer Can't Write: Studies in Writer's Block and Other Composing Problems.* New York: Guilford Press.

Rose, Mike. 1990. *Lives on the Boundary.* New York: Penguin.

Rosenblatt, Louise. 1938/1983. *Literature as Exploration.* New York: Modern Language Association.

Shaughnessy, Mina. 1976/1988. "Diving In: An Introduction to Basic Writing." In *The Writing Teachers Sourcebook*, edited by Gary Tate and Edward P.J. Corbett. New York: Oxford University Press.

———. 1977. *Errors and Expectations: A Guide for Teachers of Writing*. New York: Oxford.

Squire, James R. 1964. *The Response of Adolescents While Reading Four Short Stories*. Urbana, IL: National Council of Teachers of English.

Tompkins, Jane P., ed. 1980. *Reader Response Criticism: From Formalism to Post-Structuralism*. Baltimore: Johns Hopkins.

Trimble, John. 1975. *Writing with Style: Conversations on the Arts of Writing*. Englewood Cliff, NJ: Prentice Hall.

4

What's in a Name?

Anne Ruggles Gere

Tecumseh, Michigan is a small town about thirty minutes outside Ann Arbor on the River Raisin. With picturesque nineteenth-century houses, a refurbished old mill in a park next to the river, and tree-lined streets, it is the second largest city in Lenawee County. The Tecumseh website explains that its first white settlers were three Quakers. Actually, it doesn't say that. The exact language is "Tecumseh was first settled in 1824 by three Quakers, Joseph W. Brown, Musgrove Evans, and Austin E. Wing." There is no suggestion that Tecumseh had been inhabited by anyone before Brown, Evans, and Wing arrived. Yet the city is named for Chief Tecumseh, a Shawnee leader famous for his skills in organization and military strategy. Tecumseh insisted that Indian land could not be sold, "No tribe has the right to sell, even to each other, much less to strangers. Sell a country! Why not sell the air, the great sea, as well as the earth? Didn't the Great Spirit unite in claiming a common and equal right in the land, as it was first, and should be now, for it was never divided." Tecumseh organized a pan-tribal confederation of American Indians to preserve their way of life, and he died in the War of 1812, fighting on the side of the British, a dozen years before Tecumseh, Michigan was named.

In conducting what my son Sam calls "a small survey" of people in the area, I found few who knew much about Chief Tecumseh except that he was an American Indian. Details about Chief Tecumseh's life and accomplishments have faded much as the history, traditions, and life experiences of nineteenth-century Osage, Wyandotte, or Ottawa peoples have largely faded from the popular imagination, leaving only the shard of memory embodied in the name. Seeing the lives of prominent individuals and whole groups of people reduced to a place name has, sadly, been the experience of many American Indians. But the reduction of individuals and whole populations to place names is not limited to that group. Richard Braddock, the designation attached to one of the most prestigious awards given by *College Composition and Communication* (CCC), is fast becoming a place name in our field.

I'd wager that many of the people who cheer winners of the Braddock Award—and perhaps even the winners themselves—could not tell you much about the accomplishments, intellectual orientation, and significance of Richard Braddock's work. Here is the description of the award:

> The Richard Braddock Award is presented to the author of the outstanding article on writing or the teaching of writing in the CCCC journal, *College Composition and Communication*, during the year ending December 31 before the annual CCCC spring convention. The award was created to honor the memory of Richard Braddock, University of Iowa. Richard Braddock was an extraordinary person and teacher who touched the lives of many people in ways that this special award established in his name can only suggest. (CCCC)

Lovely as this statement is, it doesn't tell us what Richard Braddock actually *did* for the field of composition studies. As our field matures and those who remember the contributions of Richard Braddock fade from view, we lose a portion of our history. And it is not just the history of an individual; it is a portion of our collective identity that is at risk of disappearing from our concept of the field and its work.

Richard Braddock was the lead author of what might be described as the urtext of composition studies, the 1963 monograph, *Research in Written Composition*, but before he undertook that project he had been a high school English teacher, he had taken an M.A. in American literature at Columbia, and an Ed.D. in the teaching of college English from Teachers College, Columbia. He had, in other words, moved between English and education, combining an interest in literature with a deep commitment to pedagogy. As he moved into university teaching, first at Iowa State Teachers College (now the University of Northern Iowa) and then at the University of Iowa, he continued this oscillation between English and education. As a professor of English and rhetoric at the University of Iowa, he taught a variety of writing courses, courses on adolescent literature, and summer courses for teachers. From his background in education, Braddock drew upon a statistically based model of research and emphasized pedagogy, but at the same time he frequently articulated values that emphasized his connection to the humanities, to English departments. A very early article "An Introductory Course in Mass Communication" (1956) demonstrates Braddock's dual approach. In explaining why undergraduates should take a course in mass communication, Braddock appeals to a liberal education and argues that such a course instills responsible citizenship, cultivates taste for "quality magazine stories and artistic radio, television and film dramas," and develops communication skills (1956, 56). This emphasis on liberal arts education gives way to pedagogical concerns as Braddock deals with several pedagogical issues, including the lack of an appropriate textbook, organization of the course, and specific assignments. With this combination of emphasis on a liberal arts perspective and careful attention to strategies of teaching, Braddock shows how his background in English *and* education both contribute to his scholarship.

When Braddock served as Director of Iowa's Communication Skills program, he emphasized taking a rhetorical approach to writing. In "Crucial Issues," an article he published in 1965, Braddock begins, "Ideally, what distinguishes a rhetorical approach from the usual approach to composition is a deliberate concern not only with the composition itself but with the writer and the readers as well—especially the readers" (165). He goes on to urge the importance of asking students to write an argument, which he defines as an "intellectual and ethical attempt to convince an audience through reasoning and evidence" (165) rather than simply seeking consent. In addition, he urges that students consider *crucial issues*, those that occur between the writer and specific readers. Braddock argues that students who address these crucial issues become ethical both because they inform themselves more fully and because they consider the views of those with whom they disagree. He concludes:

> The process of understanding others and modifying oneself is fundamental to liberal education. We cannot neglect it because it is difficult. On the contrary, we who teach rhetoric have a unique responsibility here, for it is we who are granted a portion of the college curriculum to help students become conscious of what is involved in thinking deliberatively and, as they reveal their thinking in their writing, to help them shape their ideas into clearer and more responsible communication. Thus the crucial issues approach is indeed crucial, not merely to rhetoric but to education itself in the most liberal sense. (1965, 169)

Here Braddock articulates his commitment to a liberal arts education, one that puts rhetorical values of ethos and logos at the center.

At approximately the same time that he was writing this article, Braddock was working on the research that would become *Research in Written Composition* (Braddock, Lloyd-Jones, and Schoer 1963). In 1961, Braddock had been named chair of the NCTE Committee on the State of Knowledge About Composition, a committee charged with reviewing, as the introduction to the book explains, "what is known and what is not known about the teaching and learning of composition and the conditions under which it is taught, for the purpose of preparing for publication a special scientifically based report on what is known in this area" (1). In other words, Braddock's committee was supposed to do the first meta-analysis of research on composition. The impetus for this project grew from Basic Issues, a 1958 conference where the National Council of Teachers of English (NCTE), the Modern Language Association, and the College English Association reconsidered the goals of English teachers. At this conference, it became evident that little was known about writing instruction, and Braddock took the lead in persuading representatives of federal agencies that it was essential to consolidate information on this topic. Braddock received a grant from the U.S. Department of Health,

Education, and Welfare to support the work of his committee and spent the next two years reading and analyzing over 485 studies, selected five studies for detailed examination, and compiled the findings into the report titled *Research in Written Composition.*

Braddock was joined in this project by two colleagues at the University of Iowa, Richard Lloyd-Jones, a member of the English Department, and Lowell Schoer, a professor of educational psychology. The composition of this group underscores Braddock's dual perspective. On the one hand, he embraced the perspective of Lloyd-Jones, a rhetorician, and on the other he called upon the statistical skills of Schoer, who drew his expertise from the field of education. Looking back on the process, Richard Lloyd-Jones describes Braddock's approach: "Braddock's predilection toward exact observation and fairness in comparisons made us very fussy about each step in comparatives studies. The rules for inclusion of research in our report at all favored those studies with comparisons between experimental and control groups. Braddock was a thorough empiricist" (1985, 163).

Braddock was not, however, interested in empiricism for its own sake; he held studies to a high standard to be able to say something definitive about composition instruction. Accordingly, he and his colleagues agreed to focus on studies that involved actual writing, a decision that eliminated many empirical studies from their book. This insistence on actual writing, as opposed to indirect measures such as multiple-choice tests and surveys of teaching practices manifested Braddock's liberal arts and/or rhetorical values. Similarly, he was interested in the substance or significance that lay behind quantitative measures. For example, as Lloyd-Jones recounts, Braddock was particularly concerned about the lack of consensus among researchers on what constituted an error (or nonstandard form) in writing. As Lloyd-Jones puts it, "Braddock also objected to lists of errors that concealed the importance of differences between items on the count. How many errors of what kind were significant according to what principle of significance?" (1985, 163). Given Braddock's abiding interest in pedagogy, it makes sense that he would insist upon categories that could be translated into instructional terms.

Research in Written Composition, now forty years old, adheres to the principles laid out by Braddock's committee. It emphasizes the importance of research methods; it advocates using appropriate statistical procedures, controlling variables, and attending to reliability. Stepping back from their close reading of individual studies in the field, Braddock and his coauthors observe:

> Today's research in composition taken as a whole, may be compared to chemical research as it emerged from the period of alchemy: some terms are being defined usefully, a number of procedures are being refined, but the field as a whole is laced with dreams, prejudices, and makeshift operations. Not enough investigators are really informing themselves about the procedures and results of previous research before embarking on their own. Too few of them conduct pilot experiments and validate their measuring instruments

before undertaking an investigation. Too many seem to be bent more on ob-
taining an advanced degree or another publication than on making a genuine
contribution to knowledge, and a fair measure of the blame goes to the faculty
adviser or journal editor who permits or publishes such irresponsible work.
And far too few of those who have conducted an initial piece of research
follow it with further exploration or replicate the investigations of others.
(1963, 5)

The standard by which Braddock and his colleagues judged research in
composition is evident here. Their language about using statistics, doing pilot
studies, controlling variables, validating instruments, and replicating findings
makes it clear that they adopted the value structures of empiricism as it was
practiced in educational research at the time. Although today's research in
education is more varied and includes qualitative as well as quantitatively
based work, in 1963, the dominant model for research depended on validity,
reliability, and controlled variables, making it easy to understand why Braddock would have insisted on this standard. The very organization of the book
is designed to emphasize this research methodology. The opening section
considers suggested methods of research, including rating compositions while
keeping in mind the various factors—writers, assessment method, rater, and
colleagues—that shape such evaluations; frequency counts, with admonitions
about the need for care in defining features, attending to sampling strategies,
and the need to focus on features that are reasonably significant. The next section considers the state of knowledge in composition, pointing to what can be
claimed about such issues as the primacy of the writer's background and experience, the ineffectiveness of formal grammar instruction, and the relationship
of oral and written language. This section also includes the category of "unex-
plored territory," which includes a list of questions focused on topics such as
motivation toward writing, the development of writers, and the relationship of
reading to writing. The most extensive section of the book consists of a close
examination of five studies judged "most soundly based" in terms of five criteria: examination of actual writing; a generous sampling, defined as seventy
to eighty students; clear description of features considered; appropriate use of
statistics; and objectivity of researcher.

Taken as a whole, this book can be seen as a comprehensive introduction
to a field—research in composition—that had not yet been called into being.
Through a combination of careful attention to the work of others and the application of rigorous standards for evaluating this work, Braddock and his colleagues offered ways to assign value to work in composition. As Lloyd-Jones
later observes, "Probably the most significant use of the book has been as a
guide to research method—or perhaps to presenting the results of research"
(1985, 162), and looking at subsequent meta-analyses of research in composition like those of George Hillocks and Peter Smagorinsky, one can trace a
palimpsest of Braddock's work.

"Frequency and Placement of the Topic Sentence in Expository Prose," Braddock's most famous article (1974), was cut from the same methodological cloth as *Research in Written Composition* in that it adhered to the standards set out in the book. Here Braddock used frequency counts to investigate the extent to which professional writers adhere to textbook guidelines about use and placement of topic sentences. Braddock selected twenty-five essays published in journals like *The New Yorker*, *The Atlantic*, and *The Saturday Evening Review* and through analysis that included dividing prose into T-units and looking at discourse blocks, he determined that only 13 percent of the essays began with a topic sentence, and only 55 percent contained an explicit topic sentence anywhere in the opening paragraph. By following his own advice about identifying an observable feature in writing—topic sentences in this case—and counting how often it appears, Braddock was able to demonstrate the inaccuracy of generalizations about the proper use of topic sentences, and on the basis of this, he could advise teachers against a uniform insistence on topic sentences in student writing. This article was published in the journal *Research in the Teaching of English* in the winter of 1974, shortly after Braddock's death, and it received the first ever Braddock award.

Braddock's untimely demise cut short a career that could have had an even larger effect on the field of composition studies. During his relatively brief life, he spent considerable energy on issues surrounding the evaluation of writing. Topics he investigated included a comparison of the reliability of the Educational Testing Service (ETS) general impression method with the University of Iowa's analytical method; the effects of considering two papers rather than just one in looking at the quality of student writing; the role of a first-year writing course (versus being excused from the course) on the quality of student writing; various procedures for granting first-year college students advanced standing in writing; and the compensation and training of graduate student assistants who teach first-year writing. Many of these topics attract interest from today's researchers, and it is tempting to think about how different the field might look if Braddock had lived long enough to build upon his early work.

Braddock clearly saw himself as a contributor to composition studies. He taught a wide variety of writing courses, he was chair of CCC in 1967, and he argued that students needed to develop a clear sense of audience to become effective writers. At the same time, Braddock's interests extended into other areas. A longtime member of NCTE, he was the founding editor of *Research in the Teaching of English*, a member of NCTE's standing committee on research, a trustee of NCTE's research foundation, a founding member of the Iowa Council of Teachers of English and later its president, an active participant in Iowa programs that brought together university and high school teachers of writing, and architect of an alternative to the Advanced Placement test that gave college credit in Iowa to specially designed high school writing courses.

Braddock was, in other words, an English educator. He was a teacher of teachers. Like many of us whose route to composition studies comes via English education, Braddock had a deep interest in writing instruction, and, as the title *Research in the Teaching of English* suggests, he saw a clear connection between research and instruction. Even though he contributed to the methodology of the field, he did not position himself as a methodologist. His was a career devoted to improving teaching.

I rehearse Braddock's career to remind us of the accomplishments and intellectual affiliations of the person whose name is affixed to one of our most highly prized awards. Braddock's work makes it clear that he envisioned composition as an interdisciplinary field and, in particular, that he believed it could benefit from, even be guided by, the field of education. Indeed, one could argue that Braddock *needed* education—its language, its access to funding, and its methods—to make composition visible. Like Tecumseh and the many other American Indians who contended with European Americans in the nineteenth century, Braddock had to speak a language and follow procedures that could be "seen" and understood by established populations. Tecumseh spoke English, became literate, and studied European American governance to be able to meet whites on their own terms. Similarly, Braddock, working before composition had begun to reclaim its rhetorical roots or establish itself as a field, schooled himself in existing research traditions within the academy and used them to help create a place for composition.

Like Tecumseh, Braddock's career, his commitments and his accomplishments are connected to larger populations, groups that have faded into relative obscurity, leaving only traces of their history and traditions. Within composition studies, it is the English educators whose history and traditions seem to be fading. In addition to Braddock, I can recite dozens of other names—Bazerman, Bernhardt, Brannon, Bridwell-Bowles, Burns, Emig, Gere, Gilyard, Harris, Hashimoto, Kroll, Malinowitz, Mutnick, Newkirk, Nystrand, Odell, Perl, Qualley, Selfe, Smitherman, Stock, Zebroski—of individuals whose background and training mark them as English educators. Some came from English education programs in schools of education and others from joint programs like the one I direct at Michigan, but the common feature is a focus on teaching. It was Lee Odell, a graduate of Michigan's joint Ph.D. in English and education, who said that composition is a pedagogical field, and those who share a background in English education have done a great deal to sustain that claim.

Within the recent past, there have been an increasing number of concerns raised about current directions within composition studies. In particular, many observers point to a growing division between practice and theory, between those who focus on teaching and those who favor the development of theory. In a 2003 article in the *Chronicle of Higher Education*, for example, Howard Tinberg, as reported by Scott McLemee, claims, "It may very well be composition's dirty little secret that many of us who teach writing would rather talk about cultural studies or critical theory and not trouble ourselves with the writing that our students do." Not surprisingly, those in the field of composition who focus on teaching often have roots in English education. Significantly, however, in discussions of the interdisciplinary nature of composition studies, education is often omitted. For instance, when the *Chronicle* article portrays composition studies in interdisciplinary terms, it does not include education as one of the fields from which compositionists have borrowed. It mentions linguistics, developmental psychology, sociology, anthropology, and rhetoric, but not education. And this is typical of most accounts of our field. When we tell our history, we do not include the education part, and as a result people like Braddock become place names in our field, fading, like Chief Tecumseh, into a few honorific sentences.

To be sure, there have been attempts to highlight the role of English education in composition. The Composition Studies/English Education Connections SIG, a part of the annual CCC conference meeting since 2001, was created to highlight the connection between the two fields. Robert Tremmel (2001) traces a history that highlights the relationship of English education and first-year composition. Janet Alsup (2001) describes the "contact zone" between English education and composition as a space where the two can come together. And Doug Baker and his colleagues (2007) write about how composition theory can be used in teacher education and what successful writing/methods faculty might attempt to do. It is worth noting, however, that all of these initiatives have come from English educators; there has been no corresponding initiative from composition studies.

Writing about American culture, Philip Deloria (1999) claims American identity has been shaped by an inability to deal with American Indians, and I think we can make a related point about composition studies. Our conflicted identities as compositionists result, in part, from our inability to deal with the educationists among us. It's time to claim the part of our history and tradition that comes from education and make figures like Richard Braddock more than place names. It's time to recognize that education is not just part of our history but a key component of composition studies today.

Works Cited

Alsup, Janet. 2001. "Seeking Connection: An English Educator Speaks Across a Disciplinary 'Contact Zone.'" *English Education* 34(1): 31–49.

Baker, W. Douglas, Elizabeth Brockman, Jonathan Bush, and Kia Jane Richmond. 2007. "Teaching and Mentoring New Composition Teachers." *The Writing Instructor.* Retrieved from www.writinginstructor.com/cseeconnections. Accessed February 5, 2011.

Braddock, Richard. 1956. "An Introductory Course in Mass Communication." *Journal of Communication* 6: 56–62.

———— 1965. "Crucial Issues." *College Composition and Communication* 16(3): 165–69.

————. 1974. "Frequency and Placement of the Topic Sentence in Expository Prose." *Research in the Teaching of English* 8: 287–302.

Braddock, Richard, Richard Lloyd-Jones, and Lowell Schoer. 1963. *Research in Written Composition*. Urbana, IL: National Council of Teachers of English.

CCCC. "Richard Braddock Award." Retrieved from www.ncte.org/cccc/awards/braddock. Accessed February 5, 2011.

Deloria, Philip. 1999. *Playing Indian.* New Haven, CT: Yale University Press.

Hillocks, George. 1986. *Research on Written Composition: New Directions for Teaching.* Urbana, IL: NCTE.

Lloyd-Jones, Richard. 1985. "Richard Braddock." In *Traditions of Inquiry*, edited by John Brereton. New York: Oxford University Press.

McLemee, Scott. 2003. "Deconstructing Composition." *The Chronicle of Higher Education.* Retrieved from http://chronicle.com/article/Deconstructing-Compositon/6127/. Accessed August 21, 2011.

Smagorinsky, Peter. 2005. *Research on Composition: Multiple Perspectives on Two Decades of Change.* New York: Teachers College Press.

Tecumseh (Chief). Address to William Henry Harrison. Vincenes, Indian Territory, 1810. http://www.americanrhetoric.com/speeches/nativeamericans/chieftecumseh.htm. Accessed August 21, 2011.

Tremmel, Robert. 2001. "Seeking a Balanced Discipline: Writing Teacher Education in First-Year Composition and English Education." *English Education* 34(1): 6.

5

Theory for Practice
James Moffett's Seminal Contribution to Composition
Sheridan Blau

The Genesis of a Foundational Disciplinary Figure

Like many of us who represent the previous generations of academic special-ists in English education and composition, James Moffett never had a graduate course in either composition or English education and came to both fields by stumbling into a secondary school teaching job. He went to Harvard on a full scholarship in 1947 and graduated as an English major in 1952 (a year late, because he took his junior year off to study French at the Sorbonne), and then abandoned English temporarily to earn a Harvard M.A. in French in 1953, after which he was immediately drafted into the Army for two years (rising to the lowly rank of corporal). In the fall of 1955, fresh out of the Army, married, with a baby on the way, he took a job—with housing—as a French teacher at the prestigious Phillips Exeter Academy in New Hampshire (a prep school for boys, but now co-ed), where he taught French for three years, before he switched to English for the next seven. Nothing in Moffett's earlier history and no document yet discovered in the Moffett archive of letters, biographi-cal notes, manuscripts, and other literary remains suggests that he had ever thought about teaching in a secondary school or had any special interest in education before he took the needed Exeter job.[1]

Yet by the early 1960s, Moffett was deeply engaged in the teaching of English, conducting experiments in semantics, literature, and writing in his English classes at Exeter, and discovering that he could draw upon what he had learned from his research for his prize-winning undergraduate senior hon-ors thesis at Harvard[2] to solve problems he was encountering in his teaching at Exeter. For that thesis (conducted under the supervision of his mentor, Albert

Guerard Jr.), Moffett studied the relations between inner speech or interior dialogue and more externalized narrative voices in Virginia Woolf's novels. Applying what he learned from that study to his new interest as a teacher of literature in the problem of various narrative voices and the narrative perspectives they represent, he began to work out for himself and his students "a spectrum of fictional techniques scaled according to the point of view of the character" starting with inner speech and moving toward an anonymous third-person perspective (1981b, 133). This schema for thinking about narrative point of view became the rationale and organizing principle of an anthology of short stories that Moffett and his Exeter colleague, Kenneth McElheney, published in 1966 under the title *Points of View*.

Then, Moffett retrospectively reports, "matters got out of hand" as he "began to see such a scale not only in narration but in all discourse." The first product of his focus on the full range of discourse types was a sequence of writing assignments that he designed for his classes and shared with his colleagues as a way of leading students from more personal and less abstract writing, up a scale of discourse types to expository and persuasive essays requiring increasingly abstract thought about a range of increasingly academic topics. (This sequence of assignments of which pirated copies were circulating widely by the late 1970s was eventually published in a revised and expanded form in 1981 under the title of *Active Voice: A Writing Program Across the Curriculum*).[3] Still obsessed by a schema that seemed to be growing in its explanatory power, he claims (1981b, 133–34) that he tried to write himself out of it (modestly minimizing the monumental theoretical task he had undertaken) by composing essays that he published individually and eventually incorporated as chapters in his 1968 book, *Teaching the Universe of Discourse*, which secured his place as a seminal theoretician for English education and composition studies.

Let us note that there is also a developmental progression in the way Moffett's obsession plays itself out: from an intellectual interest in an author's narrative style and perspective, to an interest in a range of literary strategies employed by different writers (still material for lectures or essays), to an interest in what students might do with the scales he was developing of intellectual complexity and abstraction. It is an intellectually and professionally crucial movement for a teacher to make: moving from telling about literature and writing to helping students develop as writers themselves.

In his tenth year at Exeter, at age thirty-six, married and the father of two daughters, Moffett received a Carnegie grant to begin work in the following academic year on the development of a comprehensive curriculum and curriculum theory in the English language arts that eventually yielded the two books establishing his reputation as one of the leading spokespersons in America for the field of English education. These were the "methods" text, *A Student-Centered Language Arts Curriculum, Grades K–13: A Handbook for Teachers* (1968), and in the same year the book he referred to as "a companion volume" designed to provide a "pedagogical theory of discourse" for the curriculum and teaching practices presented in the methods text. I am referring, of course, to the now classic book, *Teaching the Universe of Discourse* (1968), which, despite Moffett's ostensibly modest ambition, presented a theory for the teaching of English that would be revolutionary and uniquely generative for an entire profession in the sense that it could help English language arts teachers across the grades determine what they ought to teach, and in what sequence, and through what procedures. It was a theory that would also be authoritative to the extent that it was founded on a set of nonarbitrary principles for instruction—principles that could be said to inhere in the nature of the subject of English as well as in the nature of learners and the nature of learning.

Moffett's Carnegie grant funded him for two years of study and writing, which he stretched into three and spent in residence at the Graduate School of Education at Harvard, where he held an appointment as a Research Associate from 1965 to 1968 when both of his books were published (a remarkable accomplishment, but one that will appear less miraculous when it is recognized that most of the chapters of his book on theory—or substantial portions of them—were published in earlier versions starting in 1964). During this same period, in the summer of 1966, he was also one of the fifty participants in the historic Anglo-American Seminar on the Teaching and Learning of English held for a month at Dartmouth College and known thereafter as the Dartmouth Seminar.

After 1968, Moffett never again held any long-term academic appointment, but made his living mostly as a lecturer and writer, sometimes teaching in the summer at the Breadloaf School of English, often visiting and occasionally codirecting summer institutes at sites of the National Writing Project, and from time to time accepting short-term visiting professorships at such places as the University of California, Berkeley and San Diego State University. Up until just before he died at age sixty-seven in December of 1996, he relished travel and almost all opportunities to work with classroom teachers, and he regularly attended National Council of Teachers of English (NCTE) conferences, but turned down well-paying and tenured university appointments that were—despite his lack of a doctoral degree—offered to him.

Moffett's Theory in Its Historical Context

Moffett was not, of course, the first theorist to attempt to discover some rational ground for organizing the unruly body of knowledge and constellation of practices—reading, writing, speaking listening, language, literature, composition—that were the province of subject English. As Arthur Applebee shows us in his authoritative history of the teaching of English (1974), whenever the field of English as taught in the schools sought to find some basis for shaping its curriculum outside of the demands of college entrance exams or lists of canonical texts dictated by college English departments, theorists and theories emerged to provide what appeared to be a rational basis for identifying and sequencing what should be taught in English classes. And what emerged was almost invariably an expression of whatever broader trends in public education and in the intellectual community seem to have captured the imagination of policy makers and educational leaders. These trends included the application of science—which was translated as the principle of efficiency—to curriculum and instruction in English, and more thoughtful and promising theories deriving from the progressive movement, from reformist political agendas, from conceptions of mental health and social adjustment, from behaviorist psychology, from humanistic psychology, and the emergence of modern scientific linguistics. Not that all of these frameworks and cultural influences were intellectually impoverished (though the cult of efficiency clearly was), but they all represented a momentary fashion, a swing in the educational pendulum, that yielded a framework for the English curriculum that would necessarily pass as the pendulum oscillated in the opposite direction. What makes Moffett's theory different—among its other differentiating virtues—is that is has lasted.

Like every other modern theorist of English education, Moffett begins his discourse on theory with the observation that English is an "untidy" and "amorphous subject," whose ill-defined and undertheorized character undoubtedly explains why it is "the caboose on the train of educational renovation" (1968, 3). He then begins to articulate the foundational principles for his theory by lamenting the widespread confusion in the field between the problem of covering content and the need to develop authentic performative capacities, which amounts to confusion about the difference between learning about something and learning how to do something. Because—as he says in his unpretentious homespun conversational style—it is easier to tell somebody about something than it is to teach somebody to do something, English is treated in schools as a subject parallel to history or geography, as if it were a body of information about literary texts and the names of language features and parts of an essay. Hence the subject of English in schools, he says, has generally been "misconstrued" and "mistaught" (1968, 3).

What English teachers have to recognize as the first step in curricular and instructional reform, according to Moffett, is that English as a subject of study is fundamentally a symbol system, like mathematics or foreign languages, and as such it is not a discipline of information about its own content, but an instrument for working with any content. To learn a symbol system, says Moffett, is not to learn information about it, but to learn "how to operate it" (1968, 6). Hence Moffett calls for teaching practices which place students in "realistic communication 'dramas'" (1968, 12), where they participate as writers and readers, speakers and auditors of language in real or simulated situational contexts, "with better motivation and in a way more resembling how [they] will have to read, write, speak, and listen in the 'afterlife' [Moffett's playful term for the world beyond school]" (1968, 12). To teach writing, Moffett calls for a set of practices that anticipate the next two generations of sociocultural research and theory about rhetorical exigencies (Bitzer 1968; Miller 1984), situated learning (Lave and Wenger 1991), activity systems (Russell 1997), and classrooms as cultures (Green and Dixon 1993), recommending that students be "trained to write for the class group, which is the nearest thing to a contemporary world-at-large," getting them accustomed to having their papers "read and discussed workshop fashion" and having them write about their own experience and discoveries. "It is amazing," Moffett concludes (1968, 12), "how much so called writing problems clear up when the student really cares, when he is realistically put into the drama of somebody with something to say to somebody else."

Moffett and the Dartmouth Seminar

Nor was Moffett the only educator of his generation to be calling for a more thoughtfully theorized and intellectually coherent English curriculum. The decade of the 1960s, was, in fact, a period of considerable foment for the field of English, and reform efforts abounded, including federally sponsored summer institutes for teachers, the curriculum study centers funded by Project English, and the Dartmouth Seminar of the summer of 1966, where, as I have mentioned, Moffett was himself an invited delegate and participant (one of only three K–12 teachers among the twenty-four American delegates). That seminar—generally regarded as a watershed moment in the history of English education—was also famously contentious for the polarized theories of English education that came to be identified (somewhat inaccurately) as a debate between the British and American positions at that historical moment not only on the aims, methods, and ends of education in the English language arts across the grades, but on how to conceive of the problem in need of solution (see Dixon 1967/1969/1975; Muller 1967; Bryan 1974; Applebee 1974; Harris 1997). The British, represented most notably by delegates from the British Schools Council and University of London, where questions of child language and development framed an agenda for research and reform, advocated a child-centered, experiential, inquiry-oriented "growth" model of learning the arts of language, and the Americans, many of whom had been involved in the federally funded curriculum study centers of Project English, were inclined to focus on the content of the curriculum itself or the scope and sequence of the body of knowledge thought to define the subject of English that teachers were responsible for teaching.

Surprisingly, given his age and his relatively junior status, Moffett appears to have been more influential for than influenced by the mostly senior scholars who were his coparticipants at Dartmouth. James Britton (a generation older than Moffett and already a respected senior scholar by the time of Dartmouth) made explicit use of Moffett's discourse schema for the project he later undertook with his colleagues at the University of London Institute of Education to classify a vast corpus of student writing samples collected from British classrooms at every level of schooling for their now classic study, *Development of Writing Abilities in Children (11–18)* (Britton et al. 1975). Moffett, however, makes little mention in his published writing of the Dartmouth Seminar or of his delight in meeting such like-minded colleagues as he had to have found his British colleagues to be and whose ideas about teaching he would certainly have understood in a way that many of the American delegates apparently did not (see Muller 1967).[4] But the only mention Moffett makes in *Teaching the Universe of Discourse* (1968) of the 1966 conference is in the head note to his chapter on "Drama: What Is Happening," where, among those he thanks for helpful criticism of his manuscript (a manuscript for the version of the chapter that appeared as an NCTE publication in 1967, the year after the conference), he mentions his "fellow members of the Study Group in Drama of the Anglo-American Seminar in the Teaching of English . . . Douglas Barnes of the University of Leeds, Anthony Adams of the Crutchfield Comprehensive School, West Bromwich England, and Benjamin DeMott of Amherst." In the same note he also thanks Arthur Eastman of the University of Michigan and Alfred Grommon of Stanford, both of whom were also Dartmouth participants, but he thanks them not in their role as colleagues in the Anglo-American Seminar, but in their separate capacity as readers for the NCTE committee on publications.

Many years later, in *Coming on Center*, in the introduction to the title essay of the book, Moffett (1981b, 1–2) again recalls the Dartmouth Seminar and the status of English education in Great Britain and the United States at that time, noting that he attended the monthlong Dartmouth Seminar in the summer of 1966, right in the middle of the two years afforded him by a Carnegie grant to be in residence at Harvard, "writing up" his "two books of theory and practice." What he found, among many of the British delegates at Dartmouth, he says, was "a gratifying corroboration" of his own approach to teaching, "which included much drama and other peer interaction." On the other hand, "many of the American participants were involved either in government-sponsored curriculum centers that were more often than not perpetuating wrong-headed tradition or in efforts to found a new English on recent linguistic triumphs."

That Moffett emerged as a major influence on the profession of English just after the widely celebrated and intensely documented Dartmouth Seminar has occasioned what seems to be a significantly distorted view of the history of English education in the post-Dartmouth years. As Joseph Harris (1997, 1–17) points out in his trenchant revisionist history of the Dartmouth Seminar, the summer of 1966 has come to represent for much of the profession of English a defining moment in the history of English education, marking a kind of Copernican shift in how the discipline of English defined itself as a teaching field. Harris attributes this "heroic" view of Dartmouth to the "highly skewed" report on the conference written by John Dixon, one of the leaders of the British delegation. The report was initially published in 1967 under the title *Growth Through English*, and has been reprinted several times and published in two subsequent editions, with the 1975 edition extending the title to read "Set in the Perspective of the Seventies." Peering behind the veil of the commonly accepted history, Harris points out (2) that the Dartmouth Seminar accomplished much less than Dixon seems to have imagined; that the delegates could hardly agree on anything; that the recommendations they adopted were either so vague or innocuous that nobody could object to them; and that the few that were substantive (about tracking and testing, for example) were almost entirely ignored by the profession. More importantly, he says, the conference seems to have had little or no impact on what actually transpired in American classrooms.

Harris notes, however, that the "growth model" for English education did find an advocate after Dartmouth whose writing actually influenced the field, and that advocate was James Moffett (1997, 11). In other words, if the teaching of English in American schools underwent a transformation after the Dartmouth Seminar, the transforming event was not the Dartmouth Seminar nor the subsequent publications about the seminar, but the intellectual work that, as we have seen, began before the Seminar and eventuated immediately after Dartmouth (largely uninfluenced by that Seminar itself) in the publication of James Moffett's now classic book, *Teaching the Universe of Discourse* (1968).

Which is not to say that Moffett's theory or book was produced without any intellectual influence from the most significant currents of thought about teaching, learning, and the English language arts in his own period. On the contrary, he references and makes explicit use of the most salient developments in the early and mid 1960s in linguistics (including Mellon's experiments in transformational sentence-combining), semantics, literary theory, sociolinguistics, and sociocultural learning theory, including Vygotsky, who was just being rediscovered and made available by Jerome Bruner, who wrote the preface to Moffett's book. Bruner was in the psychology department at Harvard, while Moffett was a research associate in the School of Education, and Moffett apparently crossed departmental and college borders either to study with Bruner or otherwise get to know him. Where Moffett was indifferent or hostile to contemporary currents of thought was in the arena of what was intellectually fashionable or currently celebrated as the latest approach to reform in the curriculum, in assessment, in academic rigor.

It is Moffett's intellectual integrity and scrupulously rigorous thinking rather than his insularity that has accounted for his consistent stands against the meretricious reforms and theories of teaching and learning that took over professional discourse in English in recurring waves in the decades following his influential book. If he were alive today, he would speak as clearly against "the race to the top" and the culture of common standards and assessment as he did in his anti-assessment book of a generation ago, *Detecting Growth in Language*, and as he did most famously in his 1970 speech on "Misbehavioral Subjectivities" (reprinted in *Coming on Center* [1981b, 10–17]) with which he resigned from a prestigious national commission appointed to identify behavioral objectives (an earlier incarnation of standards) for English instruction.

But as Moffett's writing and workshops also demonstrated over the nearly thirty years of his life that he was a dominant figure in English education, he was never resistant to the genuine insights offered by new and intellectually rigorous research and theory, including the virtual paradigm shifts in literary theory, literacy studies, and rhetoric and composition that he witnessed in his professional lifetime and that his own theory—with an almost mystical prescience—either engendered or seemed to encompass and anticipate. Nor am I aware of any theorized account of the subject of English as a subject for study in the schools that is as independently grounded, as Moffett's is, not on intellectual fashion or the claims of tradition or unexamined ideological principles or even on an already elaborated system of thought (like rhetoric), but on a compelling newly synthesized theory of the structure and development and operation of the mind and of the role of language in shaping and reflecting mental development.

Because English as a subject to be taught and learned is essentially and ineluctably a discipline for the exercise of language and mind in ways that are increasingly mature and intellectually demanding, a theory of learning the discipline of English that is essentially a theory of linguistic and mental development has a kind of self-evident and compelling authority, linking as it does every stage in a student's learning to the mental and linguistic faculties that must of necessity also be under development in the student to account for growth in knowledge or skill in the discipline. Moffett's theory explicitly makes these links and in doing so also presents us with a model of mental and discourse development (or cognitive maturity or sophistication or complexity) that is elegant in its simplicity and easily translatable into a taxonomy of discourse types and writing assignments.

Moffett and the Emergence of Composition as a Discipline

And this, of course, is what accounts for its early and commanding importance to the field of composition as that field was just beginning to claim for itself the status of a legitimate field for scholarship and inquiry as well as a specialized area of teaching. In the early 1970s, as composition was just emerging as a discrete discipline, those who wanted to identify themselves professionally as part of a disciplinary community (mostly nonenfranchised English instructors in year-by-year appointments and wayward teaching assistants) and who were in need of a theorist to cite whose work might legitimate their practice and authorize their claim that they were in possession of some body of specialized knowledge to distinguish them from the mass of English professors and teaching assistants (who tended to think of composition as an untheorized intellectual slum presided over by professional outcasts) could and did name Moffett as the principal theorist for the field. James Gray, the founding director of the Bay Area Writing Project and the National Writing Project, frequently asserted that the writing project, as a matter of principle, must be atheoretical, deriving its collective wisdom, as it does, not from any theory but insistently from the best practices of the teacher-participants whose own successful classroom experience gives authority to what they teach and learn from each other. Yet Gray (1997) also liked to tell of the time (it must have been in the late 1970s) when he gave a talk about the writing project to a group of visiting teacher educators from the Soviet Union and Soviet Block nations, and at the end one of them asked him "Who is your theoretician?" Though it was a question he wasn't prepared for, his response was immediate and came to him, he says, without thinking: "Jim Moffett," he blurted out. For most college teachers of composition, Moffett would have been a more premeditated choice, yet perhaps also the only choice they would have known to make.

I remember a time in about 1980 when I read an evaluation report written by an English department colleague of mine, reporting on the teaching performance of one of our department's temporary composition instructors, where the evaluator noted that in a conversation following up on a classroom observation, the instructor justified most of what he did with reference "to somebody called Moffett." I also remember interviewing applicants for non–tenure-track appointments in our campus composition program during the mid 1980s, when most candidates spoke of being guided by a teaching philosophy based largely on Moffett's theory of discourse (though many also mentioned Peter Elbow or Don Murray, while former UCLA teaching assistants cited Richard Lanham and former University of Chicago teaching assistants were invariably disciples of Joe Williams).

Of course, other modern theorists (putting aside classical rhetoricians) were available to have been cited by then. Kinneavy's *A Theory of Discourse* (1971) and Frank D'Angelo's *A Conceptual Theory of Rhetoric* (1975) were being read in the few serious graduate programs that were already operating by 1980, like the distinguished doctoral program in linguistics, literature, and composition, run by Ross Winterowd at the University of South Carolina (who also had and deserved a large group of disciples); but neither Kinneavy nor D'Angelo offered a theory of discourse that was as translatable to practice or—dare I say—as accessible as Moffett's to thoughtful practitioners, nor as readily available for summary, paraphrase, and visual representation to writing teachers in professional development contexts. In other words, the elegant simplicity of Moffett's theoretical framework made his theory the one that emerging specialists in the teaching of writing could most easily and readily appropriate for their own use in teaching and in theoretically justifying their teaching practice.

Such a description of Moffett's theory does not suggest that his theory is simplistic as well as elegantly presented or that it is insufficiently well informed by scholarship or intellectually reductive and therefore less intellectually sophisticated or demanding than some others or that it compromises complexity and depth for the sake of accessibility; but it would appear that Moffett's work is not immune to such charges. I am not aware of any dismissive critique of Moffett's theory by any scholar in the field of rhetoric or composition or English education, but it has to trouble Moffett's disciples and all exponents of his theoretical perspective that two of the major theoretical works immediately subsequent to his—Kinneavy's monumental study of 1971 and D'Angelo's (1975) deeply learned theory of rhetoric that accounts for the relationship between thought and discourse—both ignore Moffett's earlier contributions as if their authors never heard of Moffett or, more likely, regard his work as unworthy of citation in a serious scholarly study of discourse types and discursive and rhetorical operations. It is perhaps not surprising that E. D. Hirsch's eccentric *Philosophy of Composition* (1977) also makes no reference to Moffett, but it is hard to explain why Victor Villanueva's (2003) more recent and widely used collection of classic documents in modern composition theory (*Cross-Talk in Comp Theory: A Reader*) excludes any selection or excerpt from Moffett among the forty-three selections of seminal and influential theoretical documents (D'Angelo and Kinneavy among them) that he does include.

Many of Moffett's disciples might be inclined to attribute his marginalization in some precincts of the scholarly community to his acknowledgment of nonstandard intellectual and spiritual sources (most notably the European philosopher, social critic, and esoteric Rudolph Steiner)—sources that, as Moffett himself asserted, make conventional academics uncomfortable and lack the intellectual authority that is granted to university theorists in "white lab jackets" (1981b, 62). But Moffett's spirituality was generally hidden from the academic community until 1981 and would not have been known to conventional scholars like Kinneavy or D'Angelo when they were writing their widely referenced volumes of theory. A more likely explanation of Moffett's marginalization, at least by some scholars, might be the orientation of his theory to the practical needs of classroom teachers and his evocation of an audience that specifically included elementary and secondary language arts teachers. Moffett is explicit in his forward to *Teaching the Universe of Discourse* (whose title alone surely declares its pedagogical orientation) about his audience and his purpose, where he calls the collection of essays that make up his classic book "one teacher's efforts to theorize about discourse expressly for teaching purposes" (1968, xi). Many academics in the field of English education or in composition whose work has been reviewed by university personnel committees in tenure and promotion cases will find the problem of Moffett's status in the research community a familiar one. For among traditional researchers in most fields at most major research universities, no work of scholarship can count unequivocally as research, unless it is addressed to problems that are largely theoretical and to an audience of other researchers and theorists. A book addressed to classroom teachers and that theorizes strictly in the interest of the practice of teaching in most prestigious academic communities—including leading departments of English and, ironically, even in departments of education—will be subject to challenge and discussion as a problematic case (if not preemptively deniable), if it should ever be put forward as an instance of a substantial and creditable contribution to knowledge.[5]

What may be surprising about the reception of Moffett's work in the academic community, then, is not the degree to which it has sometimes been discounted or ignored, but the degree to which—despite its pedagogical orientation and acknowledgment of an audience that would include many K–12 practitioners—it has taken a prominent place among the seminal texts in the field of composition, a field dominated by expatriates from traditional university English departments whose leading figures have been engaged in a self-conscious struggle to achieve academic respectability as members of a new and legitimate field for research and theory. For, although one can cite notable instances where Moffett's theoretical work seems to have been deliberately neglected by leading scholars in the field, *Teaching the Universe of Discourse* (or key essays within that volume) has nevertheless become a canonical text for composition researchers and practitioners alike, most especially, perhaps, for those who are not ashamed of its roots in a K–12 teaching practice or in its popularity among well-informed K–12 teachers. Moffett is, for example (pulling instances from my nearby bookshelf), among the most cited sources (along with Linda Flower and James Britton) in McClelland and Donavan's 1985 Modern Language Association (MLA)-published collection of essays by major composition researchers, *Perspectives on Research and Scholarship in Composition*. Moffett's discourse typology is cited as one of the three most important postmodern classification schemas by Robert O'Connors in his widely consulted and frequently taught account of the field, *Composition-Rhetoric: Backgrounds, Theory, and Pedagogy* (1997). And in Stephen North's groundbreaking study, *The Making of Knowledge in Composition: Portrait of an Emerging Field* (1987), Moffett is given more attention than any other theorist in a chapter on "The Philosophers," where North insists that philosophical inquiry produces knowledge that is not instrumental and does not lead to action, and where he claims that Moffett's contribution is a philosophical one, despite Moffett's own insistence on his status as a teacher speaking to other teachers about an inquiry into theory conducted strictly for its value to practice.

Yet Moffett's theory, contrary to what North claims about philosophical inquiry, has remained important to the profession of composition, it seems to me, precisely because it has remained of instrumental value to practitioners, including teacher-researchers and researchers on teaching who have conducted systematic inquiries into classroom practice, including their own practice. And what has been of most value instrumentally is the central trope of his discourse theory, the idea that every act of discourse can be described in terms of its location on two axes or lines of longitude and latitude, measuring degrees of "distance" that are also measures of cognitive demand or complexity (also related to intellectual development or maturity). In fact, Moffett's schema is now so familiar to practicing teachers and has been so widely employed by textbooks, by assessment systems, by curriculum guides, and by course outlines that it may not be recognized as Moffett's distinctive contribution by many of the very teachers of writing who depend on it in their practice.

Moffett's Discourse Schema

Moffett's schema, in case any need reminding, posits two axes of "distance," the first of which is the longitudinal axis of distance between a speaker (or writer) and an auditor that Moffett calls the "I–you" relation, the distance between first and second person being measured by how much the auditor already knows what is in the mind of the writer and conversely how much awareness the speaker or writer needs to achieve through an act of empathy or projective identification to know what cues or information to provide to compensate for the auditor's missing knowledge. The most intimately knowledgeable auditor of one's discourse would be oneself engaged in a process of inner speech or what Moffett calls "reflection" and defines as "intrapersonal communication between two parts of one nervous system." The other distance categories Moffett identifies along the I–you continuum, beyond reflection, are "conversation" ("two people in vocal range"), "correspondence" ("interpersonal communication between remote individuals"), and "publication" ("impersonal communication to a large anonymous group, extended over space or time") (33). It takes almost no effort of imagination to translate all these forms of communication to acts of writing (with virtually no change in labels). If some readers were anticipating that I would be laying out a more finely calibrated scale of discourse distances running from self to intimate others to various kinds of more distant others, that's because we have grown accustomed to such elaborated categories, introduced not by Moffett himself, but by the adaptation of Moffett's discourse schema by Britton and his London colleagues for their now classic 1975 study of school-sponsored writing in *The Development of Writing Abilities in Children (11–18).*

The second, and possibly more important, axis of distance posited by Moffett's schema is the latitudinal axis measuring the distance in what Moffett calls the "I–it" relation between the speaker/writer and his subject as measured by a scale of "abstractive amplitude," moving from discourse about what is here and now experienced in the moment through one's own senses, to discourses that represent experiences, events, or ideas at a further remove in time, space, or abstractive category. On this scale, discourse about one's experience in the moment, what is happening to me as I sit at my computer writing this draft of this essay, how my body feels, how I am hungry or tired or frustrated, and so on represents the least remove up the ladder of abstraction and requires the engagement of no faculties except those of sense perception and the skills required to record perceived data. But if I begin to tell about what happened to me earlier this morning or yesterday, to look back and narrate or report rather than to record, I must use my faculty of memory and organize my discourse by the logic of time or chronology, a kind of logic that requires more abstract thinking than the check on one's senses required for recording experience in the present moment. Merely having to reframe experience or events in a chronological scheme for oneself requires an act of mind that entails more abstract thinking than is required for the mere recording of what is happening as it transpires.

At the next level of abstraction, Moffett identifies a kind of thinking more demanding than remembering and one that must organize data by a more sophisticated principle of reasoning or logic than chronology. This kind of thought—which Moffett calls *analogic* or *analogical thinking*—addresses not the question of *what is happening* or *what happened*, but *what happens*, which is to say, what generally happens or what generalizations or statements can be proposed as true over time to account for how items in a data set are classified together to yield a generalization that applies to all of them. Moffett identifies this kind of thinking with the discourse of exposition, which characteristically employs the intellectual processes of generalization and classification and calls upon the faculty of mind that Moffett identifies as analogical reasoning.

At the next and "highest" level in Moffett's schema is the discourse that Moffett labels in his "happening" sequence as *what should or might happen*. This kind of discourse requires thinking at a level of abstraction that subsumes the generalizations and classifications of exposition and uses them as evidence in the interest of larger arguments or as the data undergirding some larger theory. When I note my experience of this morning as immediate data, I am recording it. If I later remember that experience and organize it as a narrative, I am reporting it. If I ask my colleagues about how they spent their mornings and then classify our activities and report on what sorts of things people like us do in a typical morning, I am writing exposition. If I then use those generalizations as evidence for an argument about how hard we academics work, I am writing argumentation or persuasive discourse. But if I move from those same generalizations to a claim (that looks much like an argument) about how intellectuals are people who love to play with ideas all the time so that their free time and their work time are indistinguishable, then I am writing theory. In both argument and theory I am engaged in a mental process that Moffett calls the *tautologic of transformation*, by which he refers to the way that theory and argument both operate by taking a body of information or ideas and transforming that material into either an argument or a theory, thereby reframing but not changing the underlying data. What is *tautological* (an unfortunate word choice) about that operation is that it doesn't change the underlying data at all. The data remain intact, potentially to justify an opposing theory or argument. The term *tautologic* is unfortunate, I think, because it lends itself to more confusion than clarity, because a tautology to logicians is both an infelicitous (because redundant) way of reasoning (therefore sometimes classified as a logical error) and an indisputable but useless logical claim by virtue of defining something by it own definition, as in *arguments that are tautological are those that employ tautology*. Moffett's important point, in any event, is that both argument and theory are operations of mind that transform material lower down on the abstraction scale, but that are themselves already products of abstraction built on evidence and data that have been organized by a prior act of mind (chronological thinking), which itself operates on the concrete data of perceived experience. There is, in other words, a ladder of thought based on level of abstraction and this ladder defines different kinds of discourse as they are ordinarily practiced in writing and speech and apprehended by auditors in reading or listening.

The power and utility of this schema for teaching and research in composition over the past thirty-five years are incalculable. First of all, it generates a huge array of writing assignments, allows for the development of logically and sequentially related sequences of assignments, and provides a sound basis for classifying almost any piece of written discourse. For teachers of writing who want to think about a range of assignments, for example, the scale of abstraction alone (without considering the I–you axis) can yield a chart (Blau 1983, 301) like the one in Figure 5.1.

Moffett's Discourse Theory in Practice

Classroom teachers who learn Moffett's schema quickly recognize it as a guide to evaluating the difficulty or maturity level required for any writing assignment and also see how it can guide them in strategically constructing assignments so that they control at what point on the I–you axis (measuring cognitive load or difficulty in terms of audience) they would have an assignment intersect with the I–it axis (measuring the cognitive load or difficulty in terms of abstractive amplitude). They can see readily, for example, how and why it might be wise to ask students to explain the motives of characters in a novel to themselves in their journals, before they explain them to a classmate or teacher, while at the same time they ask students to do a brief retelling of a story for a classmate. It has served as a framework for curriculum planning in schools and as the rationale for the sequences of writing assignments included in widely used language arts textbooks for grades 6–12 in schools (e.g., *The Writer's Craft* [Blau et al., 1993]). It also serves as the framework for many of the most widely used college textbooks in writing (e.g., Axelrod and Cooper 1990/2010).

For researchers and evaluation specialists, Moffett's schema has provided a measure of difficulty and a range of types for experiments designed to examine writing competence and processes and to measure skills. It served as the theoretical foundation for the state assessment program in writing for elementary and secondary schools in the state of California in the 1980s and for a number of state assessment programs that subsequently adopted the

Figure 5.1   Scale of Intellectual Ascent for Discourse

Perspective	Discourse Acts	Informing Faculties	Examples
What is happening	Describing, recording	Discourse organized by the senses	Field notes, love notes, diary notes
What happened (or will happen)	Reporting, narrating (or planning)	Discourse organized by memory (chronological thinking)	Memoirs, news reports, summaries of field notes, plans
What happens	Generalizing (using examples), explaining, analyzing, classifying, advising from experience	Discourse organized by analogical reasoning— the capacity to recognize a basis for excluding and including instances into classes and categories (i.e., generalizations)	History, scientific inquiry and explanation, literary analysis, prudential wisdom
What might happen, what should happen	Arguing (using reasoning), advising (from theory), speculating, theorizing, disputing	Discourse organized by the formal logic of argument or by the "tautologic" that generates new theoretical frameworks, yielding new perspectives and arguments	Professional advice and speculation, literary theory, philosophical and scientific theories and proofs, legal argumentation

California model. It guided numerous evaluation studies conducted by sites
of the National Writing Project, where Moffett is widely read and where his
theory and the instructional models that he endorsed and developed in connection with his theory are typically demonstrated and employed in summer
institutes for teachers and in other professional development programs. Moffett's accounts in his 1968 methods text (*A Student-Centered Language Arts
Curriculum, Grades K–13*) and in his writing across the curriculum book of
1981 (*Active Voice: A Writing Program Across the Curriculum*) of the writing
workshops that will ideally be employed to support the research and thinking
that are demanded for different types of writing have been widely adopted by
college and secondary school teachers and were part of the teaching repertoire
of those who have been influenced by Moffett for over a decade before Nancie
Atwell introduced her writing workshops to middle school teachers and the
rest of the profession.

Under the influence of Moffett's perspective in *Teaching the Universe of
Discourse* (1968) on the importance of talk and conversation as the ground
from which writing and all the advanced modes of thinking and discourse
develop, composition classes in colleges and universities all over the country
became organized as intellectual communities where students discuss their
reading in small groups, share ideas for papers, conduct research collabora-
tively, and read each other's writing in drafts as essays develop. If these practices have been promoted by other scholars and influential practitioners in
recent years—by Peter Elbow, for example, or by the model learning communities constructed in summer institutes at sites of the National Writing Project,
and by a growing body of theory about communities of practice (Lave and
Wenger 1991) and more recently by genre theorists of the North American
School (Miller 1984; Bazerman 1994; Freedman and Medway 1994)—Moffett nevertheless anticipated and directly or indirectly influenced the writers
and theorists and practices that began to be reflected in professional discourse
and classroom practice in composition well before they made their appearance
in other precincts of the academic community.

Moffett and the National Writing Project

The relationship between Moffett and the National Writing Project presents an
especially telling story about the influence of Moffett's theory on practice in
the field of composition and the dissemination of both theory and practice. The
Bay Area Writing Project, from which the National Writing Project emerged,
was founded at the University of California, Berkeley in 1974 by James Gray,
who was then a supervisor of teacher education in English in the Graduate
School of Education. While Gray's own vision of a professional development
project built on the principle of teachers teaching teachers was the foundational principle for the project, his vision was shared by a small group of colleagues from the beginning, and the design and implementation of the project

was very much a collaborative effort of a group under Gray's leadership that included other teacher educators and several highly influential teacher-leaders from Bay Area high schools and junior highs.[6] These included Albert "Cap" Lavin, Miles Myers, Mary K. Healy, Keith Caldwell, Mary Ann Smith, and Jo Fyfe, among others. All of these leaders including Gray himself were among the earliest readers and exponents of Moffett's work as that work is represented in his methods text as well as in his book on theory and (by 1973) his *Interaction* language arts and reading program (from Houghton Mifflin) for K–12 classrooms. Lavin was probably the first of that group to know Moffett personally, because he had spent a month with Moffett at Dartmouth in the summer of 1966 as the only currently working classroom teacher invited to the historic Anglo-American Seminar (the mere token representation of K–12 classroom teachers at the Dartmouth conference is today shocking evidence of the top-down structure of the profession of English in the decades before the National Writing Project overturned that pattern for the entire profession). Miles Myers (1997–1998) reports that at the urging of Tom Gage (who was later to become one of Moffett's closest friends and most knowledgeable interpreters), he read Moffett's NCTE monograph (eventually incorporated into *Teaching the Universe of Discourse*) on *Drama: What Is Happening* (1967), and as a result changed the way he taught composition, even before he read the rest of Moffett's work, which he did as soon as it was published in the two early volumes of 1968. Myers then came to know Moffett personally when in the course of working on the *Interaction* program Moffett came to Oakland High School to watch Miles teach. Miles was subsequently one of the first teachers invited to use the *Interaction* program in his English classes, as were Mary Ann Smith and Jo Fyfe. Moffett, in one of his own autobiographical notes in *Coming on Center* (1981b, 81), mentions that beginning in the mid 1960s, even before he moved to California, he maintained a working relationship with a group of "devoted veteran educators" who were later instrumental in founding the Bay Area Writing Project, mentioning by name Jim Gray, Cap Lavin, Miles Myers, Mary K. Healy, and Keith Caldwell.

My point in recounting these incidental connections, is that they all took place before the founding of the Bay Area Writing Project, and that added together they demonstrate that most of the key figures in the founding of the Writing Project actually knew Moffett himself, and virtually all of them were familiar with his theoretical and methodological writing by the time they were involved (along with some twenty other outstanding secondary and college teachers) in the process of dialogue and experimentation that constructed the historic first writing project summer institute, where Moffett was not present in person, but was surely present in the ideas and spirit of open inquiry and critical discussion and experimentation in writing that marked that institute and shaped the prototype for all subsequent writing project summer institutes. Nor was Moffett present merely in the spirit of that first institute. His theory and the practices informed by that theory were explicitly invoked and demonstrated in at least one presentation conducted by a team of innovative teachers who were later to become two of the most respected and influential teacher-leaders of the National Writing Project. As Jim Gray (2000) tells the story in his memoir of that memorable first summer:

> Mary Ann Smith and Joe Fyfe, who were team teaching at Loma Vista Inter-mediate Junior High School . . . had been using the James Moffett *Interaction* series, which drew on booklets and activity cards, readings and prompts, and which introduced students to many forms of creative and real-world writing. . . . Mary Ann and Jo were committed to Moffett's key pedagogical idea: students need to experiment with genres, finding topics that interest them and working at their own pace. They explained Moffett's ideas and showed us examples of student work and a video of their own classroom in action. (54–55)

All of this, of course, helps to explain how it happened that most of the characteristic features of the writing project summer institute, as it initially took shape in Berkeley and eventually took on the status of the model for all National Writing Project sites to adopt, are entirely consistent with Moffett's own model of how writing should be taught and learned in schools in the context of a community of writers. Some of the notable features of the Berkeley model include writing response groups where writers share work in progress; frequent opportunities for writing with only selected pieces taken further in the process than an early draft; rich opportunities for discussion to discover, share, and reshape ideas; and a good deal of experimentation with writing from various points of view, to different audiences and in different genres. Moffett himself often spoke of the Writing Project as an ideal learning community and spent a good portion of every summer for twenty years giving presentations at National Writing Project sites around the country, sometimes remaining in residence for days or weeks at a time, and for several years serving as the codirector of summer institutes in Berkeley, Chicago, and Long Island. Through the writing groups of writing project summer institutes, he said, he found the only success he ever had in convincing teachers of the power of small groups as sites for important learning (Moffett 1981b, 82). Significantly, even at writing project sites where Moffett made no personal appearance, site leaders have almost always taken it as an intellectual and professional duty to introduce teachers in the summer institute through assigned readings and discussions to Moffett's discourse schema along with some of his published reflections on authorship, essaying, or assessment.

Moffett's Continuing Influence on Composition in the New Century

Given the degree to which Moffett's theory and models for instruction are inscribed in the discourse of the National Writing Project and in its signature practices, it is very likely that Moffett's influence on the teaching of writing will remain visible in K–12 and college writing classes, wherever the teachers of those classes have themselves been influenced by the summer institutes and extended professional development programs of sites of the National Writing Project. And the National Writing Project now sponsors roughly 200 sites (almost all of them located on college or university campuses) with at least one project site in every state in the nation and at least one site within a fifty-mile radius of virtually every public school in the continental United States and surely every college.

Beyond the National Writing Project, Moffett's work and theory and pedagogical aims are most emphatically perpetuated and celebrated in NCTE's Assembly for Expanded Perspectives on Learning (AEPL), an assembly that emerged as a subgroup within the Conference on College Composition and Communication and that continues to maintain much of its initial emphasis on the teaching of writing. Moffett served during the last years of his life as the presiding guru and spiritual mentor for the founders of that assembly, and remains (along, more recently, with Peter Elbow) its most frequently cited and most revered authority. In fact, in the years immediately following Moffett's death, a number of members of the NCTE AEPL (including me) argued that the assembly should change its name to the "James Moffett Society," but the idea was rejected on the grounds that such a name would suggest a narrower focus and mission than the assembly wanted to advertise, though there was no disagreement about the significant degree to which the society recognized itself as an organization committed to carrying on a vision of learning and of education that was articulated by Moffett in his writing and workshops for teachers.

Within the past year, however, the idea of a Moffett Society reemerged in a more modern incarnation (under the technologically sophisticated leadership of my former student, Damian Koshnick), with the establishment of an online association of senior and junior Moffett disciples known as the "James Moffett Consortium," which defines itself as "a diverse consortium of teachers and researchers dedicated to dialogue on the value of James Moffett's theories and practices in English and education and our own uses of his ideas within K–16 classrooms." Interested teachers and scholars can join the consortium at its multifunctional ning: jamesmoffettstudies.ning.com. Within the past decade, moreover, subgroups of AEPL and other NCTE-affiliated teachers and scholars have organized two national conferences to share research and classroom practices inspired by or related to Moffett and his contributions to theory and pedagogy, and I anticipate that the steady growth of the Moffett consortium will lead to additional virtual and actual Moffett conferences in the future.

In the field of composition studies, I can think of only one other figure whose writing and intellectual influence has spawned a society named after him and meetings organized to celebrate, explicate, and build on his work. And that is Kenneth Burke. Moffett, it must be acknowledged, does not rank

with Kenneth Burke among the leading American intellectuals of the twentieth century, revered and quoted extensively across the globe by rhetoricians,
literary critics, philosophers, and other scholars in the arts and humanities. But
it must also be acknowledged that Burke (himself, ironically, a college drop-
out) exclusively addressed an audience of university academics and highly
sophisticated intellectuals, including literary critics and theorists, rhetoricians,
language philosophers, and other humanists and social scientists who read the
most sophisticated and prestigious intellectual and scholarly journals. Moffett,
on the other hand, primarily and deliberately addressed K–12 classroom teachers of the English language arts, teacher educators, and composition instructors at every level of education—some of the least prestigious subgroups in
the academic and intellectual communities. Within those subgroups and even
beyond them, as we have seen, he remains, like Burke, a uniquely revered
mentor and guide for two generations of his intellectual heirs and disciples
who will undoubtedly carry his practices and theory and pedagogical wisdom
forward to the generations that succeed them. Unlike Burke, however, Moffett
is revered not only among university researchers and theorists, but by practitioners at every level of education where theory shapes curriculum, assessment, textbooks, and the experience of students. Hence Moffett's influence on
the field of composition is ubiquitous, unavoidable, and probably perpetually
relevant in a way that can be claimed by almost no other figure in the modern
history of research and theory in composition and rhetoric.[7]

Notes

1. The biographical information I present here is drawn from my own conversations with Moffett over the course of our sixteen-year friendship, as well as from
personal revelations scattered among the essays and head notes to essays he published
in *Coming on Center* (1981b), along with information generously shared with me by
Moffett's younger daughter, Judy, some of it based on biographical notes and other
documents on Moffett collected and composed by Janet Moffett, the late Mrs. James
Moffett. See also John Warnock's (2000) informative critical appreciation of Moffett,
"James Moffett" in *Twentieth Century Rhetorics and Rhetoricians: Critical Studies
and Sources*, which benefited from correspondence with Moffett himself and some
subsequent correspondence with Janet Moffett.

Researchers seeking additional biographical and bibliographical data on Moffett
will want to know that in 2006, almost a decade after the death of James Moffett in
1996 and Janet Moffett in 1997, the literary remains of James Moffett (amounting to
roughly a dozen cartons containing books, published and unpublished manuscripts,
audiotapes, videotapes, correspondence, teaching materials, lecture notes, biographical
and autobiographical notes, and other archival materials) were donated by the Moffett
family, through the good services of Judy Moffett, to the library of the University of
California, Santa Barbara (UCSB), where Moffett visited every summer without fail
(always accompanied by his wife Janet, who celebrated her birthday almost every year
in Santa Barbara) from 1980 through the summer of 1996 (when he arrived using a
walker) as a guest presenter of the South Coast Writing Project of which I was the

director from 1979 until my retirement from UCSB in 2009. These materials, now archived as the "James Porter Moffett Papers, Mss 243," are being systematically and reverently reviewed by Damian Koshnick, a doctoral student in Language Literacy and Composition in the Graduate School of Education at UCSB. Damian has generously reported to me on his findings in the Moffett archive and occasionally has been able on the basis of his archival research to confirm or elaborate on details of the brief professional biography I have been drafting for this essay. Scholars interested in the Moffett archive may correspond with Damian Koshnick at koshnick@umail.ucsb.edu or contact the Department of Special Collections, Davidson Library at UCSB.

2. With an essay drawn from his thesis, Moffett won the prestigious undergraduate Bowdoin Essay Prize, whose prior and more recent winners have included Ralph Waldo Emerson, Jones Very, Henry Adams, Walter Jackson Bate, Delmore Schwartz, John Updike, and the current U.S. Chief Justice of the Supreme Court, John Roberts.

3. In the introduction to *Active Voice*, where Moffett (1981a) explains its origins in his Exeter experiments, he also explains that he hadn't intended to publish his experimental sequence of assignments but felt forced to do so by the fact that photocopies of his assignments made from the mimeographed version he had produced for himself and his Exeter colleagues in the 1960s were circulating ten and fifteen years later mainly throughout the National Writing Project and eventually got into the hands of other teachers who misused his assignments and sometimes offered public criticism of what was initially produced as part of an experiment in progress and was written up only for private circulation to continue the experimentation. (It came to my own writing project site in 1979 from someone in the Bay Area Writing Project where Moffett himself must have given out one of his original mimeographed copies: We copied it for all of our teachers and many of them copied it for their colleagues.) To avoid such continuing misunderstandings and a number of misuses of his work, he felt obliged to produce a revised version with an explanatory apparatus and publish it for the profession at large.

4. Muller's book, *The Uses of English: Guidelines for the Teaching of English from the Anglo-American Conference at Dartmouth College* (1967), was commissioned by the conference organizers as the "report on the proceedings at the seminar designed for the general reader." Muller was at the conference to observe and write about its proceedings from his perspective as an American professor of English with no particular expertise in the teaching of English in elementary and secondary schools. John Dixon, a British scholar who was an expert on teaching English to precollege students, was commissioned to write a report addressed to "the professional community." What is frustratingly clear to any sophisticated reader of Muller's report is how much this representative American professor of English could recount ideas (advanced mainly by the British representatives, but clearly by some Americans as well, including Moffett, Wallace Douglas, James Squire, and Benjamin DeMott, among others) about a student-centered approach to learning language and literature without understanding in any deep or meaningful way what he was talking about. He possessed what Moffett liked dismissively to call "recitational knowledge." From the time I read the book in 1967, I have assumed that it typifies the way the MLA wing of the profession of English (with notable exceptions like DeMott) generally understands the discourse of the field of English education, and I have had abundant evidence in the intervening years to confirm that prejudice, though there are numerous recent signs of a more enlightened consciousness in some important precincts of the organization.

5. A notable example of how the academic community is inclined in its most prestigious precincts to ignore or dismiss important contributions to theory that are offered largely for the improvement of instruction in K–12 education is found in the reception among the professoriate in English to Louise Rosenblatt's revolutionary and now classic volume of 1938, *Literature as Exploration.* Rosenblatt's book offered a pedagogically and philosophically sophisticated theory of literary reading and its transformative applications to instruction, introducing to the field of English education a transactional, reader response pedagogy for secondary English classes that dominated English teacher education courses in universities (if not most secondary classrooms themselves) throughout the period during which the New Criticism was virtually the only theory of criticism and teaching practice recognized by most college and university English professors (aside from the few who were professionally committed to the preparation of English teachers). Yet, Rosenblatt's work remained virtually unknown to the mainstream literary community until some years after the emergence of a reader response theory instigated by Stanley Fish (1967) and such continental theorists as Wolfgang Iser in the late 1960s and early 1970s. Hence, Jane Tompkins does not include Rosenblatt among the response theorists whose work she collects in her 1980 edited volume, *Reader-Response Criticism: From Formalism to Post-Structuralism,* but does list Rosenblatt's work in her bibliography. Then in 1983 the MLA finally acknowledged Rosenblatt's importance to the discourse of literary theory and pedagogy, when they published a new edition of her 1938 volume with a foreword by Wayne Booth.

That her groundbreaking book had been ignored for forty years by university English professors and the profession of English as represented by the MLA continued to humiliate and anger Rosenblatt until her death at the age of 100 in 2005, and she often spoke in private of the fact that she was denied the attention of the literary community by virtue of the attention she gave in her book to questions about the teaching of literature and especially teaching literature to high school students.

6. Gray tells the compelling and historically important story of the founding and early years of the Bay Area and National Writing Projects in *Teachers at the Center: A Memoir of the Early Years of the National Writing Project* (2000).

7. As if to second my final point and confirm a number of the claims I make about Moffett's powerful influence on English education and composition in Great Britain as well as in the United States, there appeared, as this essay was about to go to press, a collection of articles "rereading James Moffett," written mostly by British and Australian scholars in the September 2010 issue of the British journal *Changing English.*

Works Cited

Applebee, Arthur N. 1974. *Tradition and Reform in the Teaching of English: A History.* Urbana IL: NCTE.

Axelrod, Rise, and Charles Cooper. 1990/2010. *The St. Martin's Guide to Writing* (now in its ninth edition). New York: Bedford/St. Martin's.

Bazerman, Charles. 1994. "System of Genres and the Enactment of Social Intentions." In *Genre and the New Rhetoric*, edited by A. Freedman and P. Medway, 79–101. London: Taylor and Francis.

Bitzer, Lloyd. 1968. "The Rhetorical Situation." *Philosophy and Rhetoric* 1 (January): 1–14.

Blau, Sheridan. 1983. "Invisible Writing: Investigating Cognitive Processes in Composition." *College Composition and Communication,* 297–312.

Blau, S., P. Elbow, R. Caplan, et al. 1993. *The Writer's Craft (Grades 6–12).* Evanston, IL: McDougal Littell.

Britton, James, Tony Burgess, Nancy Martin, Aex McLeod, and Harold Rosen. 1975. *The Development of Writing Abilities in Children (11–18).* London: Macmillan Education.

Bryan, Jonathan R. 1974. "A Lively and a Rigorous English: Reflections on Teaching English in Great Britain." *College Composition and Communication* 25(2) (May): 160–65.

D'Angelo, Frank. 1975. *A Conceptual Theory of Rhetoric.* Cambridge, MA: Winthrop.

Dixon, John. 1967/1969. *Growth Through English.* London: Oxford University Press.

———. 1975. *Growth Through English: Set in the Perspective of the Seventies.* London: Oxford University Press.

Fish, Stanley. 1967. *Surprised by Sin: The Reader in Paradise Lost.* Cambridge, MA: Harvard University Press.

Foehr, Regina, et al. 1997–1998. "A Tribute to James Moffett." *Journal of the Assembly for Expanded Perspectives on Learning* 3: 1–12.

Freedman, Avivia, and Peter Medway. 1994. *Genre and the New Rhetoric.* New York: Taylor and Francis.

Gray, James. 1997. "James Moffett, 1929–1996: An Appreciation." *The Quarterly* 19(1): 33–34.

———. 2000. *Teachers at the Center: A Memoir of the Early Years of the National Writing Project.* Berkeley, CA: National Writing Project.

Gray, James, and Betty Jane Wagner. 1997. "Reflective Tributes to James Moffett's Influence on English Education." *English Education* 29(2) (May): 147–50.

Green, Judith, and Carol Dixon. 1993. "Talking Knowledge into Being: Discursive and Social Practices in Classrooms." *Linguistics in Education* 5: 231–39.

Harris, Joseph. 1997. *A Teaching Subject: Composition Since 1966.* Upper Saddle River, NJ: Prentice Hall.

Hirsch, E. D. 1977. *The Philosophy of Composition.* Chicago: University of Chicago Press.

Kinneavy, James. 1971. *A Theory of Discourse: The Aims of Discourse.* New York: Norton.

Lave, Jean, and Etienne Wenger. 1991. *Situated Learning: Legitimate Peripheral Participation.* Cambridge, MA: Cambridge University Press.

McClelland, Ben, and Timothy Donovan. 1985. *Perspectives on Research and Scholarship in Composition.* New York: MLA.

Miller, Carolyn. 1984. "Genre as Social Action." *Quarterly Journal of Speech* 70: 151–67.

Moffett, James. 1967. *Drama: What Is Happening.* NCTE Monograph. Urbana, IL: NCTE.

———. 1968. *A Student-Centered Language Arts Curriculum, Grades K–13: A Handbook for Teachers.* Boston: Houghton Mifflin. (Reissued by Boynton/Cook–Heinemann in 1992.)

———. 1968. *Teaching the Universe of Discourse.* Boston: Houghton Mifflin. (Reissued by Boynton/Cook–Heinemann in 1983).

———. 1973. *Interaction.* Boston: Houghton/Mifflin.

———. 1981a. *Active Voice: A Writing Program Across the Curriculum.* Portsmouth, NH: Boynton/Cook–Heinemann.

———. 1981b. *Coming on Center: English Education in Evolution.* Portsmouth, NH: Boynton/Cook–Heinemann.

Moffett, James, and Kenneth McElheny. 1966. *Points of View: An Anthology of Short Stories.* New York: Mentor.

Muller, Herbert. 1967. *The Uses of English: Guidelines for the Teaching of English from the Anglo-American Conference at Dartmouth College.* New York: Holt, Rinehart, Winston.

Myers, Miles. 1997–1998. "Remembering Jim." In "A Tribute to James Moffett." *Journal of the Assembly for Expanded Perspectives on Learning* 3: 1–12.

North, Stephen. 1987. *The Making of Knowledge in Composition: Portrait of an Emerging Field.* Portsmouth, NH: Boynton/Cook–Heinemann.

O'Connors, Robert. 1997. *Composition-Rhetoric: Backgrounds, Theory, and Pedagogy.* Pittsburgh, PA: University of Pittsburgh Press.

Rosenblatt, Louise. 1938. *Literature as Exploration.* New York: Appleton-Century (5th ed. published by MLA in 1995).

Russell, David. 1997. "Rethinking Genre in School and Society: An Activity Theory Analysis." *Written Communication* 14: 504–54.

Tompkins, Jane, ed. 1980. *Reader-Response Criticism: From Formalism to Post-Structuralism.* Baltimore: Johns Hopkins University Press.

Villanueva, Victor. 2003. *Cross Talk in Comp Theory: A Reader.* 2d ed. Urbana, IL: NCTE.

Warnock, John. 2000. "James Moffett." In *Twentieth Century Rhetorics and Rhetoricians: Critical Studies and Sources,* edited by Michael Moran and Michelle Ballif. Westport, CT: Greenwood Press.

6

A Stand in Time and Space
New Hampshire and the Teaching of Writing

Bonnie S. Sunstein

> How does the writer write? We must be able to answer this question
> to teach writing effectively. But we cannot discover how the writer
> works merely by studying what he has left on the page. We must
> observe the act of writing itself to expose to our students the process
> of writing as it is performed by the successful writer.
> —Donald M. Murray, *A Writer Teaches Writing*

In 1968, Don Murray named the task that became the scholarly project of
composition studies: "We must observe the act of writing itself. . . ." (1) In
1968, Murray, a writer who was less sure of himself as a teacher, reminded us
to observe the act of writing itself for the purpose of exposing students to "the
process of writing as it is performed by the successful writer." (1) Since then,
composition studies, a body of knowledge now recognized as a field of study
by the National Research Council, has broadened our attention on the products
of writing to include the processes by which they are created. Murray's was
not the only call for studies of the writing process in the middle of the twentieth century, but his was an extraordinarily influential voice as our attention
shifted from the study of professional writers' finished texts to the study of
student texts in the process of development.

In 1968, I was a high school teacher, less sure of myself as a writer, with
Murray's book on my desk and his suggestions embedded in my courses.
Since then, both for our profession and for me, it's been an era of convergences. Like autumn in New England, a time of contextual convergence—sea
and air, soil and leaf, foggy unreality and crisp reality—our profession has

experienced a season of shifting understandings and companion ironies. In this chapter, I consider the convergences of people and ideas, papers and books, time and space that marked this particularly fertile period at the University of New Hampshire (UNH). I was lucky to figure in the story, which itself figures significantly in the establishment of composition studies.

The Dons: Donald Murray and Donald Graves

During the second half of the twentieth century, conversations about the "writing process" found energy in scholarly colloquies like the 1966 Anglo-American Seminar on the Teaching of English held at Dartmouth College—in which British educators' emphasis on process and American educators' interest in product inspired curricular and instructional change in the teaching of writing. Although neither of them attended that conference, Don Murray and Don Graves, whose names are often associated with the term *process*, became New Hampshire professors whose scholarship and practice led to an explosion of interest in concepts such as *voice, audience, conference, workshop, response, revision.*

Murray was a Pulitzer Prize–winning author and career journalist hired to direct the UNH's composition program. He had written a lot. His family was young, and he often quipped that he took the job for career stability and health insurance. "I never wanted to teach," he told me. "I should have written a book called *A Writer Teaches Himself Teaching*" (personal communication, October 2006).

> I could be a hired assassin, or a garbage collector or all sorts of things that were higher on my list than teaching. . . . I liked the mentoring. . . . I didn't like the power of teaching. I didn't like the fact that people took me so seriously. I don't like to give criticism. I saw myself as continuing to learn, and so I tried to create class situations where I could be a fellow learner. I didn't like pouring information into people's heads, because I didn't think I had the information. (Unpublished transcript of a personal interview at Poynter Institute, January, 1997)

Murray never could, and never would, separate his writing from his teaching. He taught world affairs at Boston University and taught engineers at MIT to write scientific proposals and reports. He coached journalists at the *Boston Globe* and the *Providence Journal*. In 1966, the rural Hollis, New Hampshire schools hired him to teach a professional development course in writing for K–12 teachers, which became the first edition of his book, *A Writer Teaches Writing*.

All these years later, a few months before his death, I asked Murray why he continued teaching and writing about teaching writing. "Because I wanted to learn." One of his last columns for the *Globe* echoed the theme that guided so many for so long. "Friends wonder why I do not take it easy, why I don't play golf or walk through cathedrals in Italy," he'd written that week.

> I have an obsession. I write. I draw. I try to capture a fragment of life and reveal its wonder to you. I never get it quite right, but there is a joy in the trying that makes me young at 82. My New Year's wish for you, old and young, is that you find in the year ahead something you can't do. (2006)

Murray didn't care who you were or what you knew, as long as you were a writer wanting to learn something, willing to try by writing. He responded to third graders and doctoral students and published writers with equal enthusiasm. His gentle cynicism was a constant reminder that "composition studies" meant, simply, learning about and talking about people learning to write—and continuing to write.

A few years after Murray came to UNH, Graves arrived for his first job as a professor. He reminded us, again and again in his research seminars, "You've got to learn where something stands in time and space." Like some of us, he had been a doctoral student in his forties, having found his way to State University of New York–Buffalo after a career teaching and administering K–6 schools. Graves' dissertation research, conducted during 1972–1973, was about seven-year-olds' writing. His influential *Writing: Teachers and Children at Work* (1983) was the result of both his dissertation and his early research in New Hampshire. Here are the book's first words:

> Children want to write. They want to write the first day they attend school. This is no accident. Before they went to school they marked up walls, pavements, newspapers with crayons, chalk, pens or pencils. Anything that makes a mark. The child's marks say, "I am." "No you aren't," say most school approaches to the teaching of writing. (1983, 1)

Graves' research scheme was deceptively simple, opening a door to the qualitative and ethnographic research that has produced groundbreaking research in the fields of English education and composition studies. As a father of five and a longtime teacher, he knew that the best way to find out about children's thinking was, simply, *to ask them*. His exhaustive data documented kids as they wrote—how they moved, what they said, what they read, what they said about what they thought and read, what their teachers and peers did, the conditions in their classrooms, and of course, what they wrote—as they wrote it.

Blurring academic boundaries as well as research methods, Graves' work was, and still is, revolutionary, as it monitored how students, one at a time, bump up against a behemoth institution. Graves' major act of resistance was simplicity. Once, during one of his many public speeches, our classmate Mary Comstock Chase whispered, "I get it. He's Che Guevara masked as Mr. Rogers."

Like Murray's, Graves' motivation was curiosity. An intuitive researcher, he remembered keeping records at nine years old, about wood ticks, timing them to see which one was fastest on its tracks. He filled pads of paper with that data: "It's just the notion of finding out patterns . . . you just enjoy the trip and ask questions. You're always looking for the one big question—the one that will make the connections." (personal communication, 1988)

Graves' teaching of writing was not limited to children. His work with Ph.D. students was precise, courageous, and comprehensive. At our morning research seminars in his home study, the work was intense, consuming, puzzling, as thick as the forest outside his windows. But the wood stove was stoked and warm, the coffee was robust, and so was the company. With a bottomless sense of inquiry, he taught us how to observe. One Monday in January 1988, long before GPS devices and Doppler radar weather, he wrote this to us:

> Everyone does research. I plan to drive to Buffalo, NY, so I consult my driving log for previous trips (data source) and note that in January several weather systems are encountered between Boston and Buffalo. The trip is 480 miles, takes about 9½ hours, and some part of the journey will include snow; the question is, how much. I look at a national weather map to notice any fronts crossing from Chicago to the East, as the nine and one half hour trip will mean Chicago weather in Buffalo by the time I arrive. I call the New York Thruway report. . . . I am sympathetic to the cynic who says, "Why on earth do you need all that information? Why not just get in the car and drive? When you get there, you get there." A tough argument.
>
> I'll admit that data gathering can become so much a way of life that it is sometimes hard to tell whether the data exist to be used, or are enjoyable ends in themselves. Do I study to live, or do I live to study? I'd like to think that if I ask tough questions and work hard enough at the answers, my information will help others. (personal communication, 1988)

Graves was as insistent with us as he was with himself. We studied intricate detail, shared writing, responded for revision. We were English educators teaching writing to people of all ages, in and out of schools. His school-based research teams met weekly to share their data and begin to give shape to their findings. We wrote constantly, read our own and each other's writing. "Jeeze, we used to work at our 'one-pagers' for Graves' class," writes Lorri Neilsen, "and tune them up and tune them up so that they'd induce 'ah' or 'wow' from the audience." His meetings, undergraduate classes, and seminars were flurries of exchanging papers. His assignments ensured that we wrote for readers, another signature practice that some see as among UNH's contributions to composition studies in the late twentieth century.

We wrote "weekly reflections," which were not the same as the "one-pagers." Then, at the end of each month, we synthesized what we'd just finished in a monthly meta-reflection. With our dot-matrix printers and three-ring binders, we generated and responded to mounds of paper. Each week, each of us received a private page of writing from him and a collective one meant for all of us.

Graves hated the orthodoxies that came from categorizing, the very terms that made him famous, but he respected and followed the classroom conditions his "process" approach described:

1. time
2. choice
3. community
4. response.

In an early essay called "The Enemy Is Orthodoxy" collected in his 1984 *A Researcher Learns to Write*, he considers his own growing influence in the field, and warns against misunderstanding:

> The Writing Process Movement has been responsible for a new vitality in both writing and education. But orthodoxies are creeping in that may lead to premature old age. They are a natural part of any aging process . . . some are the result of early problems in research (my own included); others come from people who try to take shortcuts with very complex processes. These orthodoxies are substitutes for thinking. They clog our ears. We cease to listen to each other, clouding the issues with jargon in place of simple, direct prose about actual children. (1984, 182)

And then, predictably, he confronts, names, and discusses nine of the orthodoxies he's observed. I asked him to describe his position again, only a few years ago:

> The product is important but only after a long dance about the process. . . . When someone walks in, we take them as they are and then start asking questions, "What did you have in mind here? Teach me about what you are doing." (personal communication, 2006)

Doug Kaufmann has this to say:

> I've written . . . about the importance of living a literate life publicly in front of my students. . . . One word bubbles forth to me, out of favor because of its overuse and potential for vagueness and misinterpretation. . . . The word is *authentic*. With brilliant consistency, the program's principle figures lived what they taught. In a place where *process* was paramount, they modeled it by sharing their own writing, reading, teaching, and learning lives publicly. . . . They understood its power. (personal communication, 2006)

The power sat in one deceptively simple idea: Teaching writing demands the control of two crafts—teaching and writing. Murray and Graves learned it from each other and practiced it daily. They created the conditions for us, quite consciously, knowing that we would, in turn, set those conditions for our students.

Moving constantly between teaching and writing was part of the deal, as much as the fluidity between English and education. "They can neither be avoided, nor separated," Graves wrote in his first book (1982, 5). And Murray, in an earlier article about teaching, wrote:

> How do you motivate your student to pass through this process, perhaps even pass through it again and again in the same piece of writing? First, by shutting up. When you are talking, he isn't writing . . . you don't learn a process by talking about it, but by doing it. Next, by placing opportunity for discovery in your students' hands. . . . To be a teacher of a process like this takes qualities too few of us have, but which most of us can develop. We have to be quiet, to listen to respond. We are not the initiator or the motivator; we are the reader, the recipient. (1972, 5)

Murray was in the English department and Graves, across a vast lawn, six or seven buildings away, was in the education department. Writers and learners, first and foremost, they were constant good friends. "Murray helped me find my voice," remembers Graves, "and it came in an opening line, something about machine fire. 'Now that's your voice,' Murray told me, 'Write like that.'" (personal communication, 2006)

Sociocultural Conditions: Why Those Particular Years?

The pedagogical conditions in this small subculture were a remarkable convergence of separate fields, English education, and the developing fields of composition and literacy studies that were being influenced by Murray and Graves. But it was the late 1960s, early 1970s era, and powerful sociocultural conditions were already in place. As the 1967 song told us, "the dawning of the Age of Aquarius" was a recognizable signal (at least to astrologers) of individual, social, cultural, scientific, technological development, a peek at the globalization and intellectual, spiritual improvement we might be able to expect in the world by the end of one millennium and the beginning of another.

We're well into the new millennium now, and we remain on the cusp of change. The moon entered the seventh house, perhaps, at Jupiter aligned with Mars, but peace neither guided the planets nor love steered the stars. So far, not much mystic crystal revelation of the mind's true liberation. The "dawning," not the actual "age," the astrologers warned, would take a few hundred more years. If your astrological faith is as skeptical as mine, and you're remembering the song's romantic predictions and anachronistic words, I know you'll agree on one thing about the cultural climate into which this UNH program was born. Ideas and conventions were changing in every academic discipline, along with politics, popular psychology, premarital relationships, hem lengths, physics, food, footwear, and hairstyles.

Thomas Kuhn, professor of the history of science at the University of Chicago, used the term *paradigm shift* in his 1963/1970 *The Structure of*

Scientific Revolutions, paving one highway on a busy network of roads toward postmodern thinking. University of Texas rhetorician Maxine Hairston brought Kuhn closer to home for teachers of writing in her *College Composition and Communication* speech and now classic article, "The Winds of Change: Thomas Kuhn and the Revolution in the Teaching of Writing" (1982). Recognizing our own disciplinary paradigm shift, Hairston observes that "If [teachers of writing] teach from the traditional paradigm, they are frequently emphasizing techniques that the research has largely discredited." She asks, "What is the flaw in the traditional paradigm for teaching writing? Why doesn't it work?" Summarizing her observations, Hairston cites Don Murray as well as many seminal writing researchers like Sondra Perl and Nancy Sommers, both of whom hold degrees in English education:

> What are we finding out? One point becoming clear is that writing is an act of discovery for both skilled and unskilled writers; most writers have only a partial notion of what they want to say when they begin to write, and their ideas develop in the process of writing. . . . Another truth is that usually the writing process is not linear, moving smoothly in one direction from start to finish. It is messy, recursive, convoluted, and uneven. Writers write, plan, revise, anticipate, and review throughout the writing process, moving back and forth among the different operations involved in writing without any apparent plan. No practicing writer will be surprised at these findings: nevertheless, they seriously contradict the traditional paradigm that has dominated textbooks for years. . . .
>
> No revolution brings the millennium nor a guarantee of salvation, and we must remember that the new paradigm is sketchy and leaves many problems about teaching writing unsolved. (12–14)

Indeed, the paradigm was shifting, but as we know in hindsight, it's been slow. Ten years after Kuhn's article, but ten years before Hairston's words, I'd been teaching for several years and found myself at my first national conference. The National Council of Teachers of English sponsored an all-day workshop on writing research at its 1973 Philadelphia convention. Its leaders were three teachers from different grade levels engaged in current research projects: elementary researcher Donald Graves, secondary writing researcher Janet Emig, and college writing researcher Mina Shaughnessy. Sixty or so brave teachers spent much of the day reading paragraphs written by fourth, eighth, tenth graders, and college freshmen—on the same topics—and trying to identify which was which. Few could.

As a secondary English teacher, the day's work stunned me and sparked my thinking about student writing. Within a short time, those three workshop leaders would publish three important texts (Graves 1984; Emig 1971; Shaughnessy 1977) that changed the thinking of many other teachers, shifting our research paradigms in the study of composing. Certainly, as Kuhn had described earlier and Hairston confirmed later, our field was moving ever so slowly in a gradual process of destabilizing the very assumptions and beliefs our mainstream had carried about student writers and teaching writing. And like the process of writing itself, the paradigm shift proved to be recursive, messy, and full of revisions. It was, and still is, a very long "dawning."

Political-Economic Conditions: Why New Hampshire?

Why New Hampshire? When I lived and worked there, I liked to joke about the reason so much authentic, real-world writing and reading, and attention to their processes, happened in the "Live Free or Die" state. There was little tax money for school materials or statewide mandates. Budgets were frugal and curricula were spare. Town meetings regularly nixed school spending. Few schools, only those in the high-property tax towns, had full "class sets" of books. Textbooks were too expensive. And so teachers used available curriculum materials: pencils, paper, closets full of partial "class sets" of old books; hence, a lot of writing and documentation of independent reading, conditions that translate into a spirit of independence.

My now outdated joke was funny—at least I thought so—because of its poignant irony. Only in a state in which there were no mandated choices, no rules to break, and little public monies, a state that claims fierce allegiance to the individual, could there be such revolutionary educational activity. No mandates or large expenditures stood in the way. With pencils and papers and little piles of trade books, single students, small groups of students, and thoughtful passionate teachers were free to read, write, talk, listen, respond, revise, and most important, choose topics and genres for themselves according to what they wanted to learn.

"Live Free or Die" is the state's official motto, a motif in local jokes, an odd moniker on license plates, and a symbol of the independence inherent in the stereotypical New Englander as well as the American dream. It was written by General John Stark, New Hampshire's most famous Revolutionary War veteran, on July 31, 1809. Stark was in bad health and had to decline an invitation for a battle reunion. He sent his absentee toast by letter: "Live free or die: Death is not the worst of evils." (1809)

How did General Stark's attitude translate over the course of three centuries? Fierce independence, among other things, came to mean few taxes. Few taxes meant a paucity of public services. Although I taught in Massachusetts, I'd moved across the border to New Hampshire in 1968. My town had neither kindergarten nor trash collection. Tuition at the university was (and still is) among the highest in the country. New Hampshire's public revenue came from tourists' road tolls and residents' property taxes. Although the state legislature was (and still is) a gargantuan body of four hundred, it meets only forty-five days per year and pays each legislator $200 for a two-year term. Not much to motivate long conversations about education.

I generalize for effect, but the ironies smack of reality. For everyone to be free, students and teachers must enjoy equity and assume responsibility. Throughout the years I lived there, the governors would brag about New Hampshire's high SAT scores, but not mention that fewer students than in most other states could afford, either educationally or financially, to take the tests at all. Because families of five-year-olds had to pay for private kindergarten, the "tracking system" was all too clear, way too early. Throughout that period when UNH's writing programs flourished, there were many schools in New Hampshire with confused, underprepared, undersupported students and teachers. Schools in which no one was writing at all.

The Ph.D. Program

To fund his research on children's writing, Don Graves had received a grant from the Ford Foundation. Eventually that research led to university approval for a small interdisciplinary Ph.D. program that was called, simply, the "Ph.D. in Reading and Writing Instruction"; ten years later, the "Ph.D. in Literacy and Culture." We came from New York and Hawaii, Ohio and Colorado, Canada and China. We were English educators interested in the processes of reading, writing, listening, and speaking—for high school students, preschool and elementary children, college freshmen, adults, and second language learners. UNH admitted a first class in 1983. Others who taught college composition and English at area schools began to take classes regularly. I joined the cohort four years (and seven Ph.D. students) later.

Our program complemented the English Department's Ph.D. Program in Literature and Composition, and our classes blended. Instead of competition between programs, there was sincere and deliberate collaboration. Cohorts and committees converged and connected across disciplines. Among those who worked together: professors Tom Newkirk, Robert Connors, Tom Carnicelli, Lester Fisher, Burt Feintuch, Pat Sullivan in English; Jane Hansen, Tom Schramm, Susan Francosa, Ann Diller, Bill Wansart, and Sharon Oja in education. Interested others joined as associated faculty from psychology, sociolinguistics, anthropology, folklore, and history.

Courses came and went; scholarship was fluid and interdisciplinary, allowing for the ebbs and flows of people's academic schedules and interests. Our mentors worked hard to practice what they preached. As doctoral students, we had only two required research seminars. There were very few of us at a time, and we received financial support in exchange for a full time, three-year, on-campus commitment. We were each responsible for building a consistent profile of scholarship and determining cognate areas with appropriate choices. We consulted with both mentors and classmates. Unlike many Ph.D. programs, our advisors did not *own* us; we chose and switched mentors depending on what we wanted to learn at a given time. Whom we taught and what we wrote was not as important as *that* we taught and *that* we wrote.

Donna Qualley had taught high school English in Australia. She was an adjunct English composition instructor in 1983 and became a doctoral student nine years later in Education in 1992. Over twelve years, Donna developed her commitment to the relationship "between learning and knowing":

> We were learners rather than knowledge-acquirers. Our seminars were exploratory—what can we learn about creativity, writing, learning, about portfolios? Our teachers modeled this learning stance. . . . They didn't just teach what they knew. They taught us what they wanted to know. (personal communication, 2008)

Elizabeth Chiseri-Strater, high school teacher in New York City and college composition instructor, writes:

> We had a writer (Murray), a researcher (Graves), a rhet/comp person with roots in English education (Newkirk), a rhetorical historian (Connors) and an elementary reading specialist (Hansen). Combined, they helped us consider "literacy," not just "writing," not just "rhetoric," not just "educationese." They didn't mark their territories, but they had them. Graves taught us to be researchers. Connors taught us about the roots of literacy study and "composing." All of them, especially Jane Hansen and Tom Newkirk, taught us to be reflective about what we were learning while we were learning it. (personal communication, 2007)

Our teachers considered us *their* teachers, as well as their responsibilities. Our most sustainable resource was their confidence in our work. I was insecure and obsessively worried, like many middle-aged Ph.D. students, especially about conducting ethnographic research. While I was collecting dissertation data, Graves wrote me this note: "So you are deep in your own data now, Bonnie. You swim in the depths. Don't forget your snorkel. You have the knack of showing important details. . . ." (personal communications, August 15, 1990). Don understood my worries as well as my strengths. I stayed in the water.

The Legacy of Tradition Bearers

The Dons are not the whole story in the UNH's influence on composition. Scholars who study cultures look carefully for what we call "tradition bearers," the people whom a community recognizes as experts, ones whose artistic skills within that culture are broad and difficult to pinpoint. In addition to Graves and Murray, among the tradition bearers in the UNH community and beyond is Tom Newkirk, though he would be the last person to identify himself that way. As you'll see in his own chapter in this book, Tom's expertise spans English education and composition studies, and represents their interconnection. His thinking and writing provoke ideas and histories in both fields. For Tom, there are no canonical texts, no splits between disciplines. His eclectic publications reveal broad interests and influences drawn from an entomologist-academic father, adolescent restlessness, a lifelong fascination with Plato, Montaigne, the pragmatists, and American sports. Most important, he taught us—by his own example—to apply academic, scholarly rigor (some would call "objective") to our writing without losing a personal essayistic (some would call "subjective") voice.

Tom has published a wide range of studies, including investigations of the rhetoric of children, young boys' learning behaviors, the performances of students' writing and teachers' reading student papers, English education and composition studies' cognitive roots in ancient and European scholarship, the history of student essays and teachers' expectations in composition classes, contemporary practices and foibles in composition and English education, and the narrative elements of the educational case study. Quietly, steadily, with personality and humor, he pushes against whatever seems currently common-place in literacy education. His questions are legendary: Where's the tension? What's not working? What complicates it? His work models courage, enthusiasm, and creativity of thought.

Since 1982, Tom has held a biennial conference on teaching and writing for one intense October weekend, always inviting at least four concurrent speakers and packing two days full of carefully selected panels. The conference has been the scene of controversy and energetic discussion that has resulted in major books and arguments in the field of composition studies, but most important, in K–university teachers' reflection and examination of our professional practices. For many of us involved in the blend of English education and composition studies, every two years this conference offers us quick liminality, complete with teachable moments, a reflective pause in our publishing and teaching lives. For those of us lucky enough to have studied with him, Tom's influence is ever present in our intellectual courage to write through our hunches.

Of course there are others, each of whom contributed to the collective study of English education and composition studies in UNH. Vera John-Steiner, in her *Notebooks of the Mind*, distinguishes between "live mentors" and "distant teachers," our mentors-on-the-page. As writing teachers, we credit many from the theory and philosophy of education (John Dewey, Jerome Bruner, Maxine Greene, Paulo Freire), reading research (Rex Brown, Frank Smith, Patrick Shannon), rhetoric (Aristotle, Plato, Quintilian, through Fred Genung and Barrett Wendell).

Our legacy includes, too, the people with whom our encounters become instructive and equip us with the ability to "pay it forward." Here, the lines between tradition bearers and apprentices blur. There are the classroom teacher-writers whose work and colleagueship we enjoyed as classmates, colleagues, students, fellow researchers, and more widely through their own books, among them: Linda Rief, Susan Stires, Nancie Atwell, Pat McLure, Ellen Karelitz, Jack Wilde, Maureen Barbieri, Mary Ellen Giacobbe, Lucy Calkins, Carol Avery. Our fellow doctoral students have blurred these boundaries, too, in their work over the years, all professors of literacy studies and composition: Elizabeth Chiseri-Strater, Ruth Hubbard, Brenda Miller-Power,

Tom Romano, Peg Murray, Meg Peterson, Lad Tobin, Cinthia Gannett, Lorri Neilson, JoAnn Portalupi, Danling Fu, Peg Voss, Doug Kaufmann, Megan Fulwiler, Kate Tirabassi, Mike Michaud, Christina Ortmeier-Hooper.

Anthropological Clues

Anthropologists look for clues to a group's self-definition by collecting and interpreting artifacts and verbal art material and linguistic evidence of shared practices, common traditions, and language familiar within a culture. Each has common features, yet every member of the group adds a unique version. I share here a few examples that have become commonplace traditions in the teaching of writing.

The Writing Conference

The writing conference is a legendary practice. Of course, no one invented it, but Don Murray's work as a coach for journalists and as a working writer himself examined and redefined its behaviors. Murray came from a tradition of writing coaching; his own college writing teachers impressed him with this strategy. He refined it, practiced, and wrote about it (Tirabassi, unpublished dissertation written at the University of New Hampshire, 2007). Don Graves' research, talking to school-aged children about their writing, added an important dimension. No matter what a writer's age, shaping a text for an audience means imagining the shift between writer and reader. A writing conference allows teachers to enact that process. Lad Tobin writes of his work with Murray:

> In our weekly one-to-one conferences, Don would read my writing in a very different way from how I was reading my students' work: while I sat across from him in his basement home office, he would read my essay very quickly, without a pen in his hand, and then ask me questions that, amazingly, suggested that he was enjoying himself, that he was willing and even eager to be instructed by what I had to say, and that he felt my writing could be interpreted in all sorts of ways. (2008)

Specific questions and behaviors might seem rigid or inauthentic—ritualistic, in fact, but those of us who hold hundreds of writing conferences a year know that the questions are markers for the hard work a student writer needs to do—and for the teacher, as Tobin points out, to sense a students' idea, to enjoy the writing, to be instructed by it.

Framing a writer-centered writing conference with questions is a legacy we've each taken away. Here are a few questions I like to ask:

Of summary: Tell me about your paper in one or two sentences. What's the most important thing you want to say? What surprised you?

Of organization: Can you tell me more about . . . ? At what stage is your paper? Might you use the end at the beginning?

Of revision: How many different papers could you write from this one draft? How do you invite your reader into the paper? What kind of lead will you use?

And the most important question: What will you do next?

The One-Pager

The "one-pager," written and read aloud to trigger discussion, is a nod to the value of one person's response to a reading or a complex idea. Its ritualistic quality is part of its value in a classroom. To this day, I like to begin and end my classes with a formal one-pager, photocopied or e-posted for each person, which features one person's thinking at a time. While the writer reads aloud, we circle, underline, respond, extend or challenge thinking it provokes (or doesn't provoke). I keep a record, organized by topic and student and date, so I know who's written, what they've written about, and when they've written it. And, because teachers ought to want to do what they ask their students to do, I try to make sure I'm one of the first to write—and share—my own. Here is a quote from one I wrote for my students:

> Albert Camus wrote "An intellectual is someone whose mind watches itself." A little existential? Yeah. Maybe. But isn't this the very business of teaching students to learn? . . . [A] one-pager is . . . a way to watch my mind and invite others to watch it with me. It's an opportunity to lead a discussion with a pre-thought, written response to the hard collaborative work of a course. It's a once- or twice-in-a semester chance to foreground one person's thinking and share it with others. A one-pager ought to be a single reader's formalized synthesis, analysis, focus. One mind, frozen for one moment, in a public act of watching itself. (Sunstein unpublished class handout, University of Iowa; 1997)

The Portfolio

I've kept a portfolio for over twenty years, which I started as a student in Don Graves' class. I've edited three collections of teachers' essays and projects about portfolios, the first one with Don (1992, 1996, 1999). I've spent a lot of those years researching, talking, and thinking about portfolios, working with students from preschool through graduate school, from California to Maine, North Dakota to Texas, and teachers from places like Hawaii, Indonesia, Finland, and Bulgaria. Portfolios are not alternatives to assessment; they are complements. Portfolios, as we define them, take time, identity, and community for sustenance, as well as a sense of history, acts of choice, and moments of sincere collaboration. Portfolios highlight difference; how a person is unique. Work with portfolios is an act of rigorous qualitative research: it involves historical archiving, critical analysis, interdisciplinary understanding, meticulous documentation, connecting internal learning with external standards. Portfolios move forward and look back simultaneously, a pragmatic move evocative of William James, a progressivist practice reminiscent of John Dewey.

Keeping a portfolio is an ongoing act of conserving culture. It becomes a natural place in which teachers and kids participate in research and writing processes, a place in which students learn to analyze their self-selected data. It's no wonder that we developed these definitions together as students in Don Graves' seminar. "After enough whats, you see a how. . . . After a fair amount of hows, you get a sniff of a why," he wrote to us once in a one-pager. "The danger of the 'why' is that you can't watch direct evidence easily enough. But portfolios give us direct evidence, the artifacts, of learning. Students become their own researchers—about their own learning. Portfolios ARE research!" (personal communication, 1989)

A Proverb

Don Murray loved to use this metaphor, an argument about the processes of writing: "It's Hard to Infer a Pig from a Sausage." Many of us know this line. It's a conundrum, full of irony, humor, and wisdom. We can't pinpoint where it first appears. Journalists and writing teachers quote it regularly. It shows up on Web searches in journalism, composition, and education. Bruce Ballenger mentions it in his article, "The Importance of Writing Badly" (2001, 88). Whether Murray coined this phrase or not, those of us who knew Murray associate it with him. Maureen Barbieri, longtime English teacher and author, now at New York University, wrote to me about Murray's line:

> I remember it, and then I remember how shocked I was when Newkirk argued against it in some article. He said, *"We do it all the time."* (this inferring the sausage from the pig, he meant.) What I love about Newkirk is the way he thinks against the grain and does it so gracefully and eloquently, the way he questions things that most of us just accept. . . . Tom *always* made me think. (personal communication)

After Maureen wrote this note to me, I asked Tom Newkirk. Where—and why—had he argued with Murray's metaphor? He answered:

> I can't remember where I challenged that metaphor. It is of course true that we can't infer the pig from the sausage, but *we can* infer a few things about sausage making. The end product—the text—may not be a sufficient element in learning how to write, but it is a necessary condition. We have mentor texts; we emulate models. (personal communication)

Tom's response illustrates the spirit of the continual, pragmatic, collegial conversation about English education and composition, the "verbal art" in the UNH community. He plays with Murray's metaphor, infuses it with some metaphorical juice ("sausage making" "end product") until there's a new meaning, enriching Murray's original idea with Newkirk's intellectual spin.

A Few New Clichés

Without realizing it, many of us have collected the wisdom of these teachers over the years—in person and on the page, whether we actually knew them or not. Graves' and Murray's sayings, their "verbal art," may sound like clichés to young teachers of writing and research, but many of us remember when the concepts behind them were new to our profession. I gather a few here.

Murray on Writing

"Nulla sine dies linea." Never a day without a line (Horace, 65–68 B.C.). "Expect the unexpected." "Find your own voice." "You're writing when you're not writing." "Rewrite to find out what you have to say."

Graves on Research

"There's nothing as practical as a good theory. . . . You can't get out of bed in the morning without a theory." "Record your complaints. A complaint is really a wish." "Boredom is a state of constant equilibrium. Search the edges, round the corner. . . . Boredom will eventually set you free." "You don't ever own research. You're just a temporary custodian." "Spread out your 'array' of things, reorganize, look for the tension, look for the gaps, list what the study is NOT about." "Data that doesn't make sense is worth pursuing; that's where the richness is."

Finally, Autumn in New England

During my years at UNH, as both teacher and student, the focus was on learning, whatever the subject. We asked complicated questions about people's interactions with all kinds of texts, even questioned what we meant by the term *text*. We explored the links between writing and reading, learning and teaching, literature and composition. We and our work represented contextual convergence, a stand in time and place in which we were able to contribute to the knowledge of our fields. The late Robert Connors wrote,

> Composition history, like rhetorical history, is only one channel of the knowledge we in composition studies must seek. Yet without it, we are cut off from information of vast usefulness. We are not here alone; others have come before us, and from their situations, their struggles, victories, and defeats we can build the context that will give our work as teachers and theorists background, substance, and originality. Only by understanding where we came from can we ascertain where we want to go. (1991, 70)

Christina Ortmeier-Hooper studied the program's history and pedagogical roots. She cautions that as the field expands, theory and practice "divorce," institutionally and disciplinarily, and asks us to re-examine the connections between teacher education and composition. "My own experiences at the

University of New Hampshire," she adds, "suggest that there are places where the study of composition and teacher education have historically been more closely aligned. We cannot lose sight of our history." She recognizes composition's roots in English education, the interweaving of theory and practice, and sees them as ongoing, living topics of study:

> This notion of theory and practice serves to revive and respect pedagogy as a field of study in its right, and to understand our histories within the context of those pedagogical theories, not simply the rhetorical ones. We have a deeper, richer history to explore. . . . As Composition leans further away from issues of learning and cognitive development, I can't help but wonder if we are suffering from a "been there, done that" attitude toward these areas in our field. ("Theory and Practice: A History of Composition and Teacher Education at the University of New Hampshire," unpublished paper, 2007)

Don Murray gave us not only pedagogical knowledge but practitioner knowledge. He was a practicing writer who taught. Bruce Ballenger observes that may also have changed a genre:

> [T]he power of his method may transcend Murray and be located in the personal essay itself and, especially, in what the genre demands of writers—to be carried on their shoulders through busy crossroads of thought, dodging and weaving through a swarm of voices, entertaining both wonder and doubt. While the slender "I" may be a narrow gap to look through, the essay rides on the assumption that there is much to learn from the peculiarities of one writer's experience. . . . (2008a, 301)

Lad Tobin identifies a fundamental question in writing instruction, one that only a combination of composition and education studies can answer: "In the end . . . the underlying philosophical assumptions still seem less significant to me than the way in which a writing teacher answers this question: should a writing course be organized around production or consumption? It is around this very basic question that (at least) two paths diverge, and how a teacher chooses usually makes all the difference." (2005, 15)

Indeed, an ironic choice for a writing teacher, having to choose between the diverging paths of production and consumption, if one thinks about the differences our choices make. It was only a few miles from UNH, one earlier autumn, where Robert Frost described that yellow wood in which two paths diverged. Although he was sorry he could not travel both, it was the paths in the yellow wood that made him realize he had a choice at all.

In New Hampshire's autumn, fog settles there almost daily, over bridges in the mornings; by noon it yields to bright tufts of purple, red, and orange, landscapes framed in green pine and blue ocean. We stoke wood stoves against the growing chill, in leather boots and flannel shirts. We pick apples from our own trees, or at an orchard. We harvest pumpkins, carve them, bake them into soups and cakes and casseroles. Outsiders, the "leaf peepers" flock to see us enact these autumn rituals, one person at a time.

But, on the other hand, cultural historians teach us that New England's special features were a nineteenth-century invention and a result of fervent tree planting; what are now blazing forests were once flat meadows and farmland (Ryden 2001). And botanists describe the natural process of autumn scientifically: Spring and summer's chlorophyll system breaks down in every single leaf. The green disappears and gives way to latent pigments, carotenes, and anthocyanins. As days shorten and evenings cool, the waxy pH of the cell sap yields to winter. Each leaf separates from its stem, and the trees shed for another year.

Autumn in New England gave us and our teachers and students plenty to write about, year after year. And although the subject is an old cliché, each writer's version becomes new with each writing. As English educators who have spent much of our careers teaching composition, we know this well. Once in a while we get lucky—time and space and context converge to encircle a community of like-minded people to encourage, voices in counterpoint and harmony, giving birth to a rich and productive intellectual moment that helps to shape a profession.

Works Cited

Applebee, Arthur. 1974. *Tradition and Reform in the Teaching of English: A History.* Urbana, IL: NCTE.

Ballenger, Bruce. 2001. "The Importance of Writing Badly." In *Genre by Example: Writing What We Teach*, edited by D. Starkey. Portsmouth, NH: Heinemann.

————. 2008a. "Reconsiderations: Donald Murray and the Pedagogy of Surprise." *College English* 70(3) (January): 296–303.

————. 2008b. "Our Mornings with Murray." *Writing on the Edge* 19(1) (Fall): 40–46.

Bruner, Jerome. 1996. *The Culture of Education.* Cambridge, MA: Harvard University Press.

Connors, Robert. 1991. "Writing the History of Our Discipline." In *An Introduction to Composition Studies*, edited by Gary Tate and Erica Lindemann, 49–71. New York: Oxford University Press.

Dewey, John. 1938. *Experience and Education.* New York: Macmillan.

Dixon, John. 1967/1969/1975. *Growth Through English.* London: Oxford University Press.

Elbow, Peter. 1990. *What Is English?* New York and Urbana, IL: MLA and NCTE.

Emig, Janet. 1971. *The Composing Processes of Twelfth Graders.* Urbana, IL: NCTE.

Fu, Danling. 1996. *My Trouble Is My English.* Portsmouth, NH: Heinemann.

John-Steiner, Vera. 1985. *Notebooks of the Mind.* Albuquerque: University of New Mexico Press.

Glassie, Henry. 1989. *The Spirit of Folk Art.* New York: Abrams.

Gradin, Sherrie. 1995. *Romancing Rhetorics: Social Expressivist Perspectives on the Teaching of Writing.* Portsmouth, NH: Heinemann.

Graves, Donald H. 1983. *Writing: Teachers and Children at Work*. Portsmouth, NH: Heinemann.

———. 1984. *A Researcher Learns to Write: Selected Articles and Monographs*. Portsmouth, NH: Heinemann.

Graves, Donald, and Sunstein, Bonnie S. 1992. *Portfolio Portraits*. Portsmouth, NH: Heinemann.

Hairston, Maxine. 1982. "The Winds of Change: Thomas Kuhn and the Revolution in the Teaching of Writing." *College Composition and Communication* 33 (February): 76–78.

Kuhn, Thomas. 1963/1970. *The Structure of Scientific Revolutions*. 2d ed. Chicago: University of Chicago Press.

Lloyd-Jones, Richard, and Andrea A. Lunsford. 1989. *The English Coalition Conference: Democracy Through Language*. Urbana, IL and New York: NCTE/MLA.

McLaren, Peter. 1988. "The Liminal Servant and the Ritual Roots of Critical Pedagogy." *Language Arts* 65(2): 1988.

Muller, Herbert J. 1967. *The Uses of English: Guidelines for the Teaching of English from the Anglo-American Conference at Dartmouth College*. New York: Holt, Rinehart and Winston.

Murray, Donald M. 1968. *A Writer Teaches Writing*. Boston: Houghton Mifflin.

———. 1972. "Teach Writing as a Process Not Product." *The Leaflet*. New England Association of Teachers of English.

———. 1982. *Learning by Teaching: Selected Articles on Writing and Teaching*. Portsmouth, NH: Heinemann.

———. 2006. "Finding Pleasure in the Challenge of a Blank Sheet." *Boston Globe* (December 26).

Newkirk, Thomas, ed. 1986. *Only Connect: Uniting Reading and Writing*. Portsmouth, NH: Boynton/Cook–Heinemann.

Newkirk, Thomas. 1989. *Critical Thinking and Writing: Reclaiming the Essay*. Urbana, IL: NCTE/ERIC monograph.

———. 1997. "Looking Back to Look Forward." In *Teaching the Neglected R: Rethinking Writing Instruction in the Secondary Classroom*, edited by Thomas Newkirk and Richard Kent. Portsmouth, NH: Heinemann.

———. 2008. "Donald Murray and 'The Other Self.'" *Writing on the Edge* 19(1) (Fall): 47–52.

Newkirk, Thomas, and Lad Tobin, eds. 1994. *Taking Stock: The Writing Process Movement in the 90's*. Portsmouth, NH: Boynton/Cook–Heinemann.

Qualley, Donna. 2008. "Murray and the Process of Internal Revision: A Think-Piece." *Writing on the Edge* 19(1) (Fall): 31–39.

Rado, James, and Gerome Ragni. 1967. *Hair: The American Tribal Love-Rock Musical*. Music by Galt MacDermot. New York: Public Theater.

Romano, Tom. 2008. *Zig Zag: A Life of Reading, Writing, Teaching, and Learning*. Portsmouth, NH: Heinemann.

Rosenblatt, Louise. 1938/1978/1995. *Literature as Exploration*. 5th ed. New York: Modern Language Association of America.

———. 1978/1994. *The Reader, the Text, the Poem: The Transactional Theory of the Literary Work*. Carbondale, IL: Southern Illinois University Press.

Ryden, Kent. 2001. *Landscape with Figures: Nature and Culture in New England.* Iowa City, IA: University of Iowa Press.

Squire, James R., ed. 1977. *The Teaching of English: Seventy-Seventh Yearbook of the National Society for the Study of Education.* Chicago: University of Chicago Press.

Shaughnessy, Mina. 1977. *Errors and Expectations: A Guide for the Teacher of Basic Writing.* New York: Oxford University Press.

Stark, General John. 1809. Written toast, July 31, 1809. http://www.nh.gov/nhinfo/emblem.html.

Sunstein, Bonnie S. 1994. *Composing a Culture: Inside a Summer Writing Program with High School Teachers.* Portsmouth, NH: Boynton/Cook–Heinemann.

Tate, Gary, and Edward P. J. Corbett, eds. 1988. *The Writing Teacher's Sourcebook.* New York: Oxford University Press.

Tobin, Lad. 2005. "O Brave New World." *College Composition and Communication.*

———. 2008. "Why Murray Matters." *Writing on the Edge* 19(1) (Fall): 29–30.

Turner, Victor. 1967. *The Forest of Symbols: Aspects of Ndembu Ritual.* New York: Cornell University Press.

———. 1982. *From Ritual to Theater: The Human Seriousness of Play.* New York: PAJ Press.

Consulting Colleague/Classmates

Ballenger, Bruce. English, Boise State University, Boise, ID

Barbieri, Maureen. Education, New York University, New York, NY

Chase, Mary. Education, Seattle, WA

Chiseri-Strater, Elizabeth. English, University of North Carolina, Greensboro, NC

Fu, Danling. Education, University of Florida, Gainesville, FL

Gannett, Cinthia. English, Fairfield University, Fairfield, CT

Gradin, Sherrie. English, Ohio University, Athens, OH

Kaufmann, Doug. Education, University of Connecticut, Storrs, CT

Michaud, Mike. English, Rhode Island College, Providence, RI

Neilsen, Lorri. Education, Mt. St. Vincent University, Halifax, Nova Scotia

Newkirk, Tom. English, University of New Hampshire, Durham, NH

Ortmeier-Hooper, Christina. English, University of New Hampshire, Durham, NH

Qualley, Donna. English, Western Washington University, Bellingham, WA

Romano, Tom. Education, Miami University of Ohio, Oxford, OH

Stires, Susan. Education, Bank Street College, New York, NY

Tirabassi, Kate. English, University of New Hampshire at Keene, Keene, NH

Tobin, Lad. English, Boston College, Boston, MA

7

Robert Boynton and the Making of Composition
English Educator, Editor, and Publisher

Lil Brannon and Cy Knoblauch

If you were in graduate school in the 1970s, like we were, it wasn't hard to keep up with the latest books in composition. The entire lot wouldn't have filled a bookshelf. Except for an occasional university press book like Walker Gibson's *Tough, Sweet and Stuffy* (1966) or Martin Joos' *The Five Clocks* (1961), there was little else to read in book form, except from an obscure press called Hayden, a press known more for its books in science and law than its interest in teaching. Yet books like Ken Macrorie's *Telling Writing* (1985), Stephen Tchudi's *Teaching English: Reflections on the State of the Art* (1979), and Ann E. Berthoff's *Forming/Thinking/Writing* (1978) were circulating with the Hayden imprint, and if you stopped by the Hayden booth at National Council of Teachers of English (NCTE), you could pick up a poster picturing a wise owl, all decked out in mortar board and gown, with the caption "Whom?" The responsible party was Robert Boynton, a teacher and headmaster at Germantown Friends' Academy, a position he gave up in 1970 to go full-time into editing. Bob Boynton's books were finding their way into the hands of teachers who were hungry for professional conversation on the teaching of writing.

For those of us who came to composition during the 1970s, there was much energy and excitement about the possibilities of teaching writing. Stephen M. North in his Boynton/Cook volume *The Making of Knowledge in Composition* (1987) constructs a vivid "portrait" of this "emerging field." North describes how difficult it was during that time to make sense of the professional conversation of composition, because there were competing paradigms of knowledge-making happening at once. North argues that the field emerged from little *c*, a loosely affiliated group of writing teachers to Composition (big *C*), a professional, scholarly field, during the 1970s and 1980s. He notes, citing Arthur Applebee's history *Tradition and Reform in the Teaching of English* (1974), that even though the Conference on College Composition and Communication (CCCC) began in 1949, the work and scholarship of composition before 1970 was done primarily by teachers. North goes on to note that Kitzhaber's *Themes, Theories and Therapy* (1963) is, arguably, the first book published on composition, and even there its roots are in the practices of teaching. Unlike any other arts and science field in higher education, composition began through the work of practitioners, and this work was sustained and kept vital through the efforts of the publisher, Robert Boynton.

Today, when attendance at CCCCs is in the thousands, it is difficult to imagine the convention in the 1970s when the numbers were in the low hundreds. Like North, we remember how intense and exciting those meetings were. North recollects the heated political debates over students' right to their own language at the 1976 CCCC in Philadelphia, standing in that sweaty ballroom with the energy of a revival meeting, when Carl Klaus of Iowa held out the invitation that there were no "professional teachers of writing." North, like many other new scholars in the field, knew he wanted to take up that challenge—to see himself as a teacher of writing, and not "merely" a scholar. He notes Klaus's concern that there were "no professional teachers" was more a comment on the state of higher education and the socialization of scholars in the 1970s than on the status of practitioners. In the 1970s, one was prepared as a scholar of literature, and taught writing only enough to finish graduate school and find a real job teaching in one's literary specialty area. The scholarship and research in composition happened in cubicles shared by four or five graduate students and was circulated through word of mouth in the hallways of NCTE's annual convention.

If one views the published work in composition before the 1970s, the greater number of essays are testimonials about "what worked" in a classroom. The few research studies attempt to compare one teaching strategy with another, with the aim of proving one as superior, without first exploring whether or not any one intervention assists the development of writers at all (Braddock). It wasn't until 1971, with Janet Emig's well-known study, *The Composing Processes of Twelfth Graders*, that any one questioned whether the theory of composing that had been promulgated in textbooks and imposed by traditional practices bore any relation to how children actually compose.

A few years later, we can remember a banner that used to hang over the Hayden and then Boynton/Cook exhibits at meetings of NCTE and CCCC. Or at least, we think we remember a banner—the image retains a mythic vitality whatever its status as history. In our memory, it is surrounded by balloons, and the message on it is flanked by two of Sandy Boynton's radiant piglets. The message announces, with charming effrontery, that these books are "Not the Usual Hogwash." What a thing to say, in a convention center filled with buttoned-down, mostly predictable textbook publishers' booths! And what a challenge to all those aspiring scholars, wandering from one exhibit to the next, who could hardly claim to be enjoying meaningful careers if they had not yet measured up to the judgment emblazoned on that mischievous sign. It would be a pity if the scene never happened. And so we prefer to believe that the banner was there, its comic artistry vintage Sandy Boynton, and the irreverent sensibility pure Bob Boynton. It was there even if we were the only ones who saw it. And we will argue, it was in Bob Boynton's vision of teaching that composition retained its roots in the classroom and developed its conversation.

For Bob, congenial irreverence leavened a gently determined seriousness of purpose. He began his own company with his good friend Bill Cook in 1980, bringing with him the titles he had developed through Hayden. When Bill died unexpectedly, Boynton/Cook became virtually a one-man show, save for a writer/editor sidekick, Peter Stillman, who worked with Bob on many projects. We wouldn't care to imagine the miles Bob and Pete traveled, the book exhibit in the trunk of Bob's car, to attend National Writing Project meetings, summer institutes, and local conferences across the United States, whenever Bob thought that his books could support the conversation of teachers of writing who shared his commitments. The groups were generally small, and he had few textbooks promising big sales, so his tireless trekking must have had to do with those commitments. Although he would have scoffed heartily at the suggestion, Bob was, in his way, on a mission—one inspired largely by his own experience as a teacher and writer, and one given special impetus, no doubt, by the always plentiful hogwash available in the publishing world he saw around him. The press he founded, and that prospered under his editorial leadership, set a different standard from that of other houses— in the quality of its engagement with the educational public—interested in teachers and teaching; it sought to serve. Engagement was the mission. The Boynton/Cook that we remember, as long as Bob was editor, stood for certain things. We doubt that one could argue that Prentice-Hall or Little, Brown, Macmillan or Oxford, or even NCTE stood (or stands) for an articulate ideal across its entire list. But Boynton/Cook was more than a conduit for publication; it was a shaping influence on what writers should wish to write and what readers should wish to read. In fact, we argue that Bob Boynton, through his commitment to teaching and learning, was instrumental in making the field of composition, and his books keep alive the memory that composition's roots were in English education, in the hands of practitioners. He was one of the few publishers, back in those days, who would even consider work on the teaching of writing, and his list was more extensive than any other in the making of the field of composition.

What Boynton/Cook stood for had little to do with the intellectual debates of the early 1980s—the tussles in *College Composition and Communication* and *College English* among sundry rhetorical and pedagogical theories as scholars and researchers scrambled to stake claims in the new territory of composition studies. It wasn't that Boynton was uninterested in historical, empirical, or theoretical work. To the contrary—Boynton sought out any scholarship that offered possibilities for teachers; he was interested primarily in the thinking and learning that was going on as teachers of writing prekindergarten through university engaged in meaningful work. He made available *fforum*, a local publication at the University of Michigan that explored issues in the teaching of writing. *fforum*'s short essays on teaching connected the interests of university instructors with teachers of writing on all levels. *fforum*'s editor, the editor of this collection, invited work from Donald Graves and Jim Moffett, James Britton and Mike Torbe, as well as work from Janice Lauer, Lee Odell, David Bartholomae, and Peter Elbow.

Boynton/Cook published James Britton, Nancy Martin, and Pat D'Arcy from England and made many of their colleagues' books both in England and Australia available in the United States. These English education scholars from the University of London and the London area schools researched the writing of young children and theorized about how children could be taught more effectively. The depth of their insight sparked continued interest in issues of literacy and learning and greater intellectual exploration of these concepts in the United States. James Britton and Nancy Martin's work in writing across the curriculum arguably provided the intellectual underpinnings to the writing across the curriculum movement in the United States. And Bob Boynton published the work of many of its leaders, particularly Toby Fulwiler's *Teaching with Writing* (1986) and *The Journal Book* (Fulwiler and Gardner 1999); Art Young and Toby Fulwiler's *Programs That Work* (1989) and *Writing Across the Disciplines* (1986); Parker and Goodkin's *The Consequences of Writing* (1987); Siegel and Olson's *Writing Talks* (1983); and Mary Barr, Mary K. Healy, and Pat D'Arcy's *What's Going On* (1982).

The authors who wrote for Bob in those days cannot be homogenized as a school or camp representing some unified disciplinary perspective. No evident conceptual starting point links Ann Berthoff with Jim Moffett, or Nancie Atwell with Garth Boomer, or Janet Emig with Steve North, or Dixie Goswami with Jay Robinson. But they are linked in a distinctive way. Boynton/Cook gave voice to the scholarship of teaching—to teachers who see their classrooms, in Ann Berthoff's terms, as philosophical laboratories. In giving voice to teachers, Bob simultaneously gave voice to an emerging field, those who were interested in rhetoric and composition. His vision of English education extended beyond the preparation of K–12 teachers, and in publishing work in composition he was able to keep the conversation of teaching alive in universities' colleges of arts and sciences, where "teaching" as a topic had been seen as trivial—something akin to "How does one erase the blackboard or adjust the Venetian blinds?"

Prior to Boynton/Cook, the textbook industry dominated the conversation about teaching writing. Textbooks were used, as they are in many places today, to teach teachers about how to teach writing, even as they prescribed lessons on writing to students. Although the problems with textbooks are quite notable—that they are based on Freire's banking concept of education (1993, 61)—textbooks are particularly problematic when it comes to writing instruction. Rhetoric and grammar textbooks of the 1970s and 1980s implied that learning to write was a matter of learning the rules and text formats in the sequence prescribed by the textbook writer. Rhetoric readers, used as supporting material to grammar workbooks and rhetoric texts, also deceived students into thinking that some famous writer, say George Orwell, set out to write a compare/contract essay. The criterion used to select material for these readers had more to do with its organizational pattern than with anything provocative that the piece had to say. As the professional conversation critiqued these conventional practices and offered, instead, a different understanding of how to teach composing, the textbook industry was still producing the same old hogwash. Textbook writers, who were also contributing scholarship to the field in the professional journals, felt caught in a bind. They could make plenty of money producing every two years another edition of their writing textbook, yet they knew that what they were producing was at odds with the theory informing this new field. They would rationalize their choice to continue producing these worn-out ideas by believing that their publishers would not accept material that was too unlike the competitor's top-selling textbook. It was the "market"—the schools and colleges that bought the books and the testing industry that tested children and adults based on the books—that kept best practices out of the hands of teachers. Robert Boynton, however, knew hogwash when he saw it, and he found a publishing niche by believing in teachers.

Two kinds of hogwash reliably captured Bob's attention. One was this formulaic lore of textbooks, each one pointlessly replicating the half truths of a dozen others, all working with tedious inefficiency to propagate the mechanical view of literacy that Janet Emig famously called "magical thinking" (136). The other was the self-important pontifications of a scholarship about teaching in the language arts that was uninterested in the experience of teachers yet comfortable about directing their practice. Pompous research and boring textbooks talked about teachers, or at them, or even past them rather than to and with them. Such books framed the teacher as an object rather than a subject, at best an intermediary through which the convictions of a textbook are passed to students (ideally with as little interference from the teacher as possible) and at worst merely a topic of other people's learned conversation about what teachers should or shouldn't be doing. What made Boynton/Cook distinctive, separating it from mainstream commercial publishing and academic houses alike, was the implied reader in its books, the reader whose presence Bob sensed in manuscripts that appealed to him, and the one he helped writers to construct in their prose through his editorial advice. The reader written into Bob's books is the thoughtful teacher, not an academic scholar but a mature and curious citizen-scholar, aware of current knowledge, competent to apply it, but also competent to judge and reconceive it amid the practical necessities of the school world. The teacher as intellectual values new learning for the sake of reformed practice. The teacher as citizen, engaged in challenging public work, understands that the competing demands of students, parents, administrators, politicians, and taxpayers require mediations that are often unacknowledged in scholarship and undreamed of in the tidy, taxonomic world of textbooks.

Anyone who wrote for Bob understood that this was the reader you worked to construct and to address collegially in your prose. It meant you sought to write like a human being speaking to other human beings, professional equals with common interests, the way Ken Macrorie did, the way Nancy Martin did. Scholastic debate, oracular rhetoric, were objects of scorn—a big part of the hogwash. Some passion, some humor, a colloquial style, some timbre in the voice are important to that human interchange. More specifically, it meant respecting the professionalism of teachers, appreciating the stresses of the public forum in which they practice their complex art. Most importantly, it meant legitimizing the distinctive lens that teaching provides for viewing issues of language and literacy. The validation of what teachers know is the indispensible starting point for the forming of new knowledge and the changing of practice. Boynton/Cook made it a priority for scholars of composition to keep teachers in the conversation and to remember their own roots as well in the classroom.

Berthoff, an accomplished literary critic and teacher of writing, in *Reclaiming the Imagination* (1984) wrote of her concern with how the field of composition in the early 1980s was losing focus because of the rush of researchers and scholars who were beginning to dominate the conversation in the journals of the field. Berthoff argued that these scholars had no clue about the needs and interests of children and teachers who were doing the work of teaching and learning. Her concern was that composition might go either the way that "reading" did, becoming a pseudo-science and the province of cognitive psychologists whose interests were far away from the work of the classroom, or, just as problematic, as literary studies has, away from the classroom altogether, yet both feeling perfectly entitled to tell teachers what to do. Berthoff writes:

> Practice is often considered trivial, tiresome, not worth thinking about; indeed, the perennial complaint about composition classes is the almost intolerable boredom of what is going on, to say nothing of the resultant writing. And theory is often considered elusive or "abstract." Most current research is a travesty of both theory and practice because it almost never has anything to do with method, with pedagogy, with the way we teach. But theory and practice need one another and when they are brought to bear on one another—and that nexus is method—we stand a good chance of making our classrooms real philosophic laboratories. (1984, Preface)

The governing fiction that informs hers as well as other Boynton/Cook books is that she is writing as a teacher writing to, with, and for other teachers, where both writer and reader accept, as a given, the presumption that teaching is intellectual labor and that teachers are citizen intellectuals competently engaged in serious and demanding cultural work. The subtitle of Ann E. Berthoff's *The Making of Meaning* (1981) is, after all, *Metaphors, Models, and Maxims for Writing Teachers*. She says in her preface that the work she has collected in this volume was originally written for "school teachers, college teachers, and teachers of teachers." And she speaks directly to them:

> It is often said that people learn to write by writing—and this is true, if it's said in rejection of the idea that people learn to write by drilling for skill or by reading what rhetoricians have to say about invention, arrangement, style; surface features and deep structure, narration, definition, description; problems solving, tagnemic heuristics, getting into your left hemisphere and getting out again. But writing can't teach writing unless it is understood as a nonlinear, dialectical process in which the writer continually circles back, reviewing and rewriting. . . . Students, when they have been taught anything at all about writing, have often been taught some very wrongheaded things, such as outlining as the first step; not writing at all "until you know what you want to say"; . . . casting so-called thesis statements in the form of simple assertions. (3)

Indeed, for all of those writing for Boynton/Cook, their ethos was that of a philosopher, constructing their classrooms as a site for reflection, action, and change. They wrote as teachers for an audience of teachers, their work with students their driving force. Steven North, for instance, whose scholarly contributions began in the 1980s, with writing one of the first dissertations on writing centers and continuing with his first book *The Making of Knowledge in Composition* (1987), constructs himself as a teacher and champions the work that teachers do. In *The Making of Knowledge in Composition*, a volume that surveys all the competing research paradigms in composition, he develops teachers' knowledge—lore—as a particular kind of knowledge made by teachers, among whom he counts himself. He describes this knowledge as a pragmatic blend of classroom experience, book learning, and thoughtful efforts to bring the two together. North's book also explores how knowledge gets made in composition by scholars and researchers, and he explains that world in the way only an insider knows them. But this book found its way onto the Boynton/Cook list because it also acknowledged and championed teachers and made claims to the importance of teachers to how knowledge gets made and practiced.

Boynton's own scholarly credentials not withstanding—his undergraduate degree was from Princeton, his master's in education was from Harvard, and he completed coursework for the Ph.D. at Teachers College, Columbia University—he understood that for scholarship to be purposeful, to make real changes in people's lives, it needed to connect with teachers. It was also through his own educational experiences that he made friends with and later published the work of other teacher educators—Ken Macrorie and James Moffett. Macrorie certainly shared Boynton's disdain for pompous academic puffery, shamelessly calling cramped academic style and formulaic writing, *Engfish* (1985, 1). His books document how students should speak from their everyday voices, speak gracefully and purposefully, but speak to the world— not just to academics, but to their communities, families, and friends. In *Searching Writing*, Macrorie helps students understand that research, too, is connected to one's need to know the world rather than some boring exercise concocted by teachers called *the* research paper.

Reading early Boynton/Cook books from today's vantage point gives one a sense of what people interested in composition were up against in the early days of the field. Moffett's *Coming on Center: English Education in Evo-lution* (1981), for example, chronicles Moffett's experiences as an English educator, interested in the teaching of the English language arts. He writes of being asked to a meeting of faculty representatives from Purdue, Illinois, and Indiana universities who had received a two-year grant from the U.S. Office of Education to produce "A Catalogue of Representative Behavioral Objectives in English, Grades 9–12." Moffett writes:

> Posing as child-centered while actually generating a very destructive "con-stant focus on the child" struck me as exactly parallel to the fraudulent double speak claims of programmed instruction to be "individualized." No one has ever tried to measure the incalculable negative effects of keeping chil-dren perpetually under this kind of spotlight and of regarding them as score-sources while they are trying to grow up. This is not education but child molestation. . . . My purpose in relating this is not to embarrass these well-intentioned people but to point out what we very much need to face in the future—that it's better to do without funding than to become enslaved to its source. Schooling in the United States is supposed to be a function of munici-pal or county government, not of state or federal government. (11–12)

Along with these essays (which could have been written in today's cli-mate of "No Child Left Behind" and "Race to the Top"), Moffett also writes of teaching literacy and integrity in the teaching of writing. Not only do his essays give an image of the scene of language learning in the United States during the decade of the 1970s, but Moffett also argues for a view of teaching writing that begins as he says "with teachers, not government, and spreads in grassroots fashion from the bottom up instead of from the top down" (81). He shows how "traditional schooling has shown no respect for writing, exploiting composition instruction as a way to service its testing system and as a way to spawn the pencil pushers required to stock all those clerical jobs in indus-try and government, where you do not want thinkers. You just want people who have passed minimal standards—can read just well enough to follow directions and write just well enough to take dictation" (128). Moffett also rebukes teachers who "themselves have practiced writing so little that they fall back on hopelessly irrelevant procedures. Many simply don't know how real writing takes place" (128). He goes on to advocate for groups like the National Writing Project and notes its success as being based on the idea that the Writing Project makes "teachers practitioners instead of mere preachers" (128–29).

Others in English education through Boynton/Cook were also speaking about literacy and learning. In *Fair Dinkum Teaching and Learning*, Garth Boomer (1985) chronicles the journey of a teacher, himself, toward becoming a classroom researcher and an agent for change in schools. He notes that English education, particularly curriculum development and inservice education, is a "natural" progression for one who is interested in language "because talking language inevitably leads one to consider learning, and learning is at the heart of all education" (133). He calls for teachers to become researchers and learn along with their students. He rewrites one of his theoretical arguments about the development of writing abilities, showing explicitly how theory has implications for the classroom and how it can inform teachers' daily lives.

John Mayher's *Uncommon Sense* (1989) documents how "common-sense" curriculum has dominated English teaching as he calls for a new vision of "uncommon" sense. His vision of language and learning forms much of the conceptual base for writing theory that came from scholars who finished the Ph.D. program in language education at New York University: Sondra Perl, Joseph Harris, John Clifford, and Cynthia Onore and Nancy Lester (also contributors to Boynton/Cook), to name a few.

By training, Mayher, Moffett, and Boomer were teacher educators. And their larger work on the preparation of teachers included a thread on the teaching of writing. Although she too worked in teacher education, Janet Emig's major contribution was arguably to the teaching of writing. The *Web of Meaning* (1983), a collection of her writings that had been published elsewhere, had dramatic impact on how language was theorized and taught in writing classrooms. Like Moffett's work, mentioned earlier, her essays give us a glimpse at traditional practices that she was arguing were not based on sound theory or on evidence of how children learn. Her essay "The Tacit Tradition: The Inevitability of a Multi-Disciplinary Approach to Writing Research " set the terms for how this emerging field called composition could itself become a discipline, and how interdisciplinary research could be promoted and judged. Emig formed the conscience of this new endeavor called "composition" by arguing that "literacy is not worth teaching if it doesn't provide access; if it doesn't sponsor learning; if it doesn't unleash literal power; if it doesn't activate the greatest power of all—the imagination" (178–79).

In the concluding essay of *Prospect and Retrospect* (Britton and Pradl 1982), a 1980 lecture originally delivered in Sydney, Australia, Jimmy Britton proposes raising a glass and drinking a toast to what he calls, hopefully, the "decade of the teacher," an enlightened moment born of the realization that "what the teacher can't do in the classroom can't be achieved by any other means." His toast may have been premature, but it precisely expresses the informing spirit of Boynton/Cook. Bob's would have been the first glass raised. We like to think in the same way about Bob standing with his books under that banner and Jimmy making his toast—complementary moments outside of time, emblematic of a vision that these remarkable educators shared and summoned the rest of us to pursue. We can see the two of them lifting tall glasses to the merciful demise of hogwash, and to the decade of the teacher, as often as it may occur. We have a suspicion that neither of them is drinking tea.

Works Cited

Applebee, Arthur. 1974. *Tradition and Reform in the Teaching of English*. Urbana, IL: NCTE.

Barr, Mary, Mary K. Healy, and Pat D'Arcy. 1982. *What's Going On: Language/ Learning Episodes in British and American Classrooms, Grades 4–13*. Portsmouth, NH: Boynton/Cook–Heinemann.

Berthoff, Ann E. 1978. *Forming/Thinking/Writing*. Hayden.

———. 1981. *The Making of Meaning: Metaphors, Models, and Maxims for Writing Teachers*. Portsmouth, NH: Boynton/Cook–Heinemann.

———. 1984. *Reclaiming the Imagination*. Portsmouth, NH: Boynton/Cook– Heinemann.

Boomer, Garth. 1985. *Fair Dinkum Teaching and Learning: Reflections on Literacy and Power*. Portsmouth, NH: Boynton/Cook–Heinemann.

Britton, James, and Gordon Pradl. 1982. *Prospect and Retrospect*. Portsmouth, NH: Boynton/Cook–Heinemann.

D'arcy, Pat. 1989. *Making Sense, Shaping Meaning: Writing in the Context of a Capacity-Based Approach to Learning*. Portsmouth, NH: Boynton/Cook–Heinemann.

Emig, Janet. 1971. *The Composing Processes of Twelfth Graders*. Urbana, IL: NCTE.

———. 1983. *The Web of Meaning*. Portsmouth, NH: Boynton/Cook–Heinemann.

Freire, P. 1993. *Pedagogy of the Oppressed*. New York: Continuum.

Fulwiler, Toby. 1986. *Teaching with Writing*. Portsmouth, NH: Boynton/Cook– Heinemann.

Fulwiler, Toby, and Susan Gardner, eds. 1999. *The Journal Book*. Portsmouth, NH: Boynton/Cook–Heinemann.

Fulwiler, Toby, and Art Young, eds. 1986. *Writing Across the Disciplines: Research into Practice*. Portsmouth, NH: Boynton/Cook–Heinemann.

———. 1989. *Programs That Work*. Portsmouth, NH: Boynton/Cook–Heinemann.

Gibson, Walker. 1966. *Tough, Sweet and Stuffy*. Bloomington, IN: Indiana University Press.

Joos, Martin. 1967. *The Five Clocks*. Boston, MA: Harcourt.

Kitzhaber, A. 1963. *Themes, Theories, and Therapy.* New York: McGraw-Hill.

Lloyd-Jones, R., L. Schoer, and R. Braddock. 1963. *Research in Written Composition.* Urbana, IL: NCTE.

Macrorie, Ken. 1985. *Telling Writing.* Portsmouth, NH: Boynton/Cook–Heinemann.

———. 1988. *The I-Search Paper: Revised Edition of Searching Writing.* Portsmouth, NH: Boynton/Cook–Heinemann.

Martin, Nancy. 1983. *Mostly About Writing: Selected Essay of Nancy Martin.* Portsmouth, NH: Boynton/Cook–Heinemann.

Mayher, John. 1989. *Uncommon Sense: Theoretical Practice in Language Education.* Portsmouth, NH: Boynton/Cook–Heinemann.

Moffett, James. 1988. *Coming on Center: English Education in Evolution.* Portsmouth, NH: Boynton/Cook–Heinemann.

North, Stephen M. 1987. *The Making of Knowledge in Composition.* Portsmouth, NH: Boynton/Cook–Heinemann.

Onore, C., and Lester, N. 1990. *Learning Change: One School District Meets Writing Across the Curriculum.* Portsmouth, NH: Boynton/Cook–Heinemann.

Parker, R., and V. Goodkin. 1986. *The Consequences of Writing: Enhancing Learning in the Disciplines.* Portsmouth, NH: Boynton/Cook–Heinemann.

Siegel, M., and T. Olson. 1983. *Writing Talks.* Portsmouth, NH: Boynton/Cook–Heinemann.

Stock, Patricia L. ed. 1983. *fforum.* Portsmouth, NH: Boynton/Cook–Heinemann.

Tchudi, Stephen. 1979. *Teaching English: Reflections on the State of the Art.* Hayden Book Company.

8

Education
The E-Word in Composition Studies
Charles Moran

The relationship between English and education has been close and symbiotic in my life and in the life of what I'll call "composition studies." Yet the "education" piece has largely disappeared from view—from my own view of my profession and my history, and from our professional literature. I take as my professional homes the College Composition and Communication Conference and its journal, the Computers and Composition conference and its journal, and the National Writing Project. The first two of these have become very "English," closer to contemporary critical theory than to learning theory, despite the fact that what we principally do is teach in and administer first-year college writing programs, most of which include substantial teacher-training programs. In composition studies, we are less proud of our connection to schools of education, and more proud of our connections to English. In this chapter, I'll open with an account of some aspects of my personal, professional history, a history that enacts at an individual level our profession's move away from the field of education and its move toward the field of English. In so doing, we will be watching the operation of ideology at what Foucault would call "the capillary level" (1980, 39). As Foucault describes the process, an ideology expresses itself in the actions of individuals, and by these same actions of individuals it reproduces itself. Power is thus not exerted by an "evil other" upon us, but is constituted and reproduced through our actions as individuals.

By *ideology*, I mean a constellation of assumptions that travel together, that form a belief structure that shapes a group's values and behavior. The group in question, of which I am proud to be part, is the profession of the teaching of English and the language arts in America. Although I'm too fully immersed in the ideology of my profession to see it entirely or, perhaps, clearly, I want to focus on what I see to be a central professional assumption: that research is more valuable than teaching. From this assumption, it follows that "higher" education is better than "secondary" or "elementary," because research is understood to happen at universities and not at elementary schools, practitioner research notwithstanding. From this assumption, it also follows that the most important work of English is literary research and criticism, and not teaching or thinking about teaching. From this assumption, it follows as well that at research universities English and education should be separate entities and that English should have more prestige power and seem more central to the university's mission. From this assumption, it follows, finally, that activities considered "English education" will have less prestige and power in English departments than literary study and research.

Working within value systems constituted by this ideology, a person entering our profession would tend to want to migrate from low-prestige institutions to higher-prestige institutions—from K–12 teaching to research at a four-year, Ph.D.-granting university. In the process of making this transition, the person would move, in English, toward research, the study of literature, and away from teaching: toward "English" and away from "education." And so it has been with me. The pieces of a history that follow will illustrate Foucault's understanding of the ways in which power functions in society:

> Power is employed and exercised through a net-like organization. And not only do individuals circulate between its threads; they are always in the position of simultaneously undergoing and exercising this power. They are not only its inert or consenting target; they are always also the elements of its articulation. In other words, individuals are the vehicles of power, not its points of application. (1980, 98)

Through these scraps of history, I hope to contribute to what Foucault terms "an *ascending* analysis of power, starting, that is, from its infinitesimal mechanisms, which each have their own history, their own trajectory, their own techniques and tactics" (99).

I began my working life as a teacher—well, there were summer jobs in a machine shop, on a farm, as paid crew on other peoples' sailboats—but given my background I never considered these jobs preprofessional. They were summer jobs, and they clearly were not the first steps in anything I could imagine to be a career. I believe, however, that I learned more from my summer in the machine shop than I learned in any other comparable period in my life: about race relations, about labor/management relations, about the difficulty and complexity of the machinist's trade. My boss, Alex, was a master machinist, someone who could instantly and intuitively translate a set of blueprints into a work schedule, routing the piece through the machine shop, from milling machine to lathe to grinder and back. He taught me to grind cutting tools for my lathe—different cutting angles for different metals. I learned to sharpen drill bits freehand. I still consider the work of a machinist a metaphor and a standard: tremendous intelligence, complex knowledge, and a finished product, a piece of metal fabricated within two thousandths of an inch of the specified dimensions.

But my real working life began when in the spring of 1958 I was hired as an English teacher by St. George's School, in Newport, Rhode Island, where I had been a student only four years before. After six months in this first job, I knew two things: I wanted to teach English for the rest of my life, if the world would permit me to do so; and I did not want to teach forever at this boy's prep school. I had discovered that the literature I taught had transformative value for me and occasionally for my students. It had not had this value for me as a college student, but it certainly did now that I'd begun to read as a teacher. My student work in English had been desultory, at best, and as a result I felt that I needed to know more about English and American literature if I wanted to continue on as a teacher. I had in mind at this point teaching English in public high schools or, perhaps, at a really good prep school.

So, following the advice of a friend, John Rowe Workman, a classics professor at nearby Brown University, I applied for the Master of Arts in Teaching program in English at Brown and was accepted. When I arrived there in the fall of 1961, I could not find the building that housed the Education department, and did not therefore sign up for any education courses. I did find the English department, housed with seeming prominence in a building next to the library, and went there and registered for a full slate of English courses, one of which was an MAT English course taught by Barbara Lewalski on the metaphysical poets. I loved the readings and the coursework, so different now from my undergraduate experience of English, the difference due entirely, I believe, to my sense that I was learning for a purpose: learning English and American literature so that I could return to the classroom and teach these literatures to high school students. I received A's in all my courses (for the first time in my life) and praise from my teachers. Barbara Lewalski asked me to sign up for her Milton seminar in spring, and George Anderson, the chair of the department, stopped me in the hall and told me that I really should become part of the Ph.D. program in English. Flattered, I did.

I want to reflect for a moment on what happened here: on the forces that were in play in this piece of my personal history. Foucault tells us that we individually enact and reproduce at the capillary level the ideologies that inform our culture. "The individual which power has constituted is at the same time its vehicle" (1980, 98). I went to Brown to learn to teach; I could not find the education building but did find the English building. Was this because the education building was more obscure than the English building? Less well marked on the campus map? More difficult to find, and further from the perceived center of the campus? Probably. If so, the design of the university enacted and reproduced that university's value system. Or was my inability to find the education building caused by my own preference? Did I want to find the English building more than I wanted to find the education building? Probably. If so, my choice reflected my own value system, which enacted and reproduced the value system of the culture I was working in. I had been brought back to St. George's by a mentor, Norry Hoyt, sailor, raconteur, photographer, chair of the English department, and a Ph.D. in English from Yale. He'd written his dissertation on Trollope, captained the swimming team, and was now teaching at St. George's, the only Ph.D. on the faculty, a bright blue gown in the otherwise dreary academic processions that accompanied graduations and official school events. His Ph.D. was in English, and he was a teacher. The contours of his life seemed something to shoot for. He'd never had a methods course himself, and his mentoring of me as a new teacher presumed that literature taught itself, somehow, in the presence of a good teacher.

I need to say that any action is the result of what the environmental biologists would call "a cocktail of agents," but for our purposes here I want to isolate two likely principal causes for my inability to find the Education building at Brown: my value system and Brown University's value system. I can't attempt the machinist's precision here and assign a ratio between the two or even say which was the more powerful in "hiding" the education building and giving the English building prominence. But certainly my inability to find the education building was not an innocent act. The building was there; it was on the campus map; the office had a telephone number. I could have found it. The pair of us, the University and I, each enacting the ideology of my chosen profession, moved me toward English and away from education. The English department faculty, in asking me to join their ranks, had told me explicitly that I had a fine mind, but implicitly that fine minds should be applied to important work: the study of English and American literature. By implication, teaching was less important work, work perfectly well accomplished by less-fine minds.

The choice that I made, to pursue the Ph.D. in English, at times seemed disastrous. I often felt that I was working against my own grain. As I realized while studying for my comprehensive examinations, I had left teaching far behind, and with it the motive, the energy—the potential classroom application of what I was learning—that had brought me to graduate school in the first place. At Brown I'd done well as a teacher of first-year writing, so well that my dissertation advisor, Edward Bloom, to whom I owe an everlasting debt for staying with me through my dissertation and helping me through the job search, advised me to stay clear of what was then called "freshman English" because, he told me, it had been the death of many a good scholar. The last stages of the Ph.D. program were, for me, a real grind, something I had to finish because not to finish would have been failure. I had followed not my bent, but the siren calls of perceived power and prestige. I know this now, and understood it then, though not with the post-Foucauldian vocabulary available to me today. As a number of my St. George's colleagues told me, I had made a mistake—had wasted five years on Ph.D. study, years that could have better been spent in the classroom.

Yet a decade ago, when our son was in the middle of his Ph.D. program in geophysics and wanted to drop out and teach, I advised him to continue with his degree, telling him that he could always teach, but that there was power and prestige attached to research, and that if he set up as a teacher in the present political and economic climate, he'd not have access to the same power that he'd have if he established himself as a researcher. With the Ph.D., I told him, he could always choose to teach; without the degree, he'd have to teach, and probably five classes per day. If what you really believe is what you advise your children to do, then I still believe, way down deep, that education is a dangerous place to go. I'm reminded of a recent conversation I had with a diplomat in Washington, D.C., about his son's work as an elementary teacher in the D.C. schools. I praised the work, saying that this was the most valuable work his son could be doing. The diplomat replied, "Well, he can't do this forever. The glass ceiling, you know." By "glass ceiling," it turned out, he meant salary. Teachers were paid poorly; as a teacher the son could not have the affluent life envisioned for him by his father. I was appalled, but then remembered what I had said to my son. This father and I were of one mind. We both wanted power and prestige for our children, and we believed that teaching was not the place where these were to be found.

I pushed on with my dissertation, and, in the spring of 1967, faced a choice: I could return to secondary school teaching, or I could go on the college job market as what I'd been trained to be: a scholar in the literature of eighteenth-century England. Kay and I now had a son, so the economic imperative was there: At that time and place, university work would pay more than secondary school teaching. The pay differential is not only an economic imperative. It did and does create and reflect a vertical metaphor: higher education is better than lower; and, within the world of "higher" education, the four-year research institution is at the top of the heap. If I were to go to a four-year research institution, I'd be paid more and, not coincidentally, teach less. Reasoning that I could always choose to move down the scales of pay and prestige, but that I'd find it practically impossible to move up those same scales, I chose to enter the postsecondary job market and was hugely fortunate to be hired by the English Department at the University of Massachusetts at Amherst. My contract said that if I had my dissertation completed by September 1, I'd come on as an assistant professor, teach three courses per semester, and be paid $9,500/year. If my dissertation were not complete, I'd come on as an instructor, would teach four courses per semester, and would be paid $8,500/year. There it was again: the inverse correlation between teaching/rank and earning power. The more you teach, the lower your rank and the less you get paid. And still in our department we speak of the reduced teaching loads that we get for doing departmental administration or, less frequently, research, as an award of "released time"—we are "released" from teaching. No one has yet imagined an equally prestigious "release" from research and publication that might support one's teaching.

Once in my job, despite the fact that I'd been hired, and would be evaluated, as a specialist in literary research, I gravitated toward work that we'd call "English education." I served on our department's undergraduate studies committee and helped build a new curriculum for the English major. I served on our English education committee, which was the only contact we had with our School of Education, and it was a tenuous connection at best: five English and one education faculty. This committee worked with area secondary school teachers preparing to teach English. We developed a methods course that included work in local schools, and through this and through our supervisory work, we developed close ties with secondary English teachers in our area. All of this was deeply engaging, and it was working against the departmental grain. Had I not kept a hand in literary study, I'd not have been rehired. And had not the department's situation changed drastically, I might not have been granted tenure and promoted. I was permitted to move into work that I'd call English education because our English department was in trouble, and felt that it needed to move into areas other than literary research if it were to survive.

And here's how that happened. In the late 1960s and early 1970s, our English department had grown substantially, hiring ten or more new teachers every year over a five-year period, more than doubling the size of the department. It had done so because the University of Massachusetts at Amherst was growing rapidly, and because the English Department had four semester-long courses that every university student had to take: two semesters of first-year English and two semesters of a sophomore-level Masterpieces of Western Literature sequence. The masterpieces courses were entirely faculty taught; each of us taught two sections of this course each semester, and one course in our specialty. In the political and curricular turmoil of the early 1970s, however, these requirements went by the board. The department gladly allowed Walker Gibson to take what we called "freshman English" out of English and into a pan-disciplinary rhetoric program; and within the department we broadened the canon of the Western civilization course as we realized how limiting this canon was. Finally, the requirement that we had, for principled reasons, sabotaged, became untenable as a university requirement. The result was that in the space of two years, we had lost all of our required courses and were in a free-market situation. We had lost our entitlement, much as English has lost its entitlement nationwide, and we were forced to sell our goods, and, if these goods did not sell, to find new and different goods to take to market.

It is in this context that our then-chair Joe Frank encouraged us in the work of English education, in part because he believed in it, and in part because he now had a large department, some one hundred faculty members, with too little to do. He encouraged us to connect with area high schools, to develop our department's MAT program, and to do inservice work with paraprofessionals in New York City. He was aided and abetted in this by Walker Gibson, a distinguished new hire, a poet and a rhetorician, fresh from New York University and "sunrise semester," who soon became president of the National Council of Teachers of English and encouraged us in this new direction, far from the literary scholarship I'd been trained to do, but close to the work I really wanted to do. Gibson encouraged us to propose to the National Endowment for the Humanities (NEH) an "institute for the teaching of writing," designed for inservice secondary English teachers, which was funded and held on our campus in 1978 and again in 1980. He and Joe Frank had been reading Tom Wilcox's 1973 study, *The Anatomy of College English*, in which Wilcox argued persuasively that English departments should become, as he termed it, less "pure":

> College English teachers are not, then, a very venturesome lot. Although they tell themselves they should, they seldom leave the relatively safe grounds of their own preserve, and what innovation they contemplate or accomplish is limited, in most cases, to the confines of their own discipline or their own language. Perhaps this inclination to stay at home is a perfectly proper impulse to avoid overextending themselves as they did earlier in the century; it may also be a heritage of the New Criticism of the thirties and forties, with its emphasis on attention to literature as literature. What then seemed an admirable purity may now seem mere timidity, however; and the time for excursions out of "English" into neighboring academic domains may once again be at hand. (110)

Wilcox went on to scold English departments for designing inadequate teacher-preparation programs: only 34 percent required a methods course, just 60 percent required a course in the study of language, only 55 percent required a course in advanced composition (114). These statistics suggested to Wilcox that "schools of education, to whom the English faculty has sometimes been reluctant to entrust the training of the teachers who will prepare its undergraduates, may now be doing a better job at that task than they themselves can or will do when it is left to them" (115).

So the winds, at least locally, had begun to change; in our department, the work of English education was beginning to be respected. NEH funded our Institute for the Teaching of Writing, which for three years immersed me and three colleagues in the work of English Education. One of our group, Joe Skerrett, brought me to James Moffett, a person I'd not heard of in my Ph.D. training. Another colleague, Jim Leheny, arranged to have Nancy Martin spend a day at our institute, and through this connection, introduced me to the work of the London Schools Council projects, which was just becoming available here through Ward Lock and Boynton/Cook: Nancy Martin's *Writing and Learning Across the Curriculum 11–16* (1976), James Britton et al.'s *The Development of Writing Abilities (11–18)* (1975), and Britton's *Language and Learning* (1970). Together we read James Dixon's *Growth Through English* (1967), which emanated from the Dartmouth Conference, Mina Shaughnessy's *Errors and Expectations* (1977), Richard (Jix) Lloyd-Jones, Richard Braddock, and Lowell Schoer's *Research in Written Composition* (1963), and Janet Emig's *The Composing Processes of Twelfth Graders* (1971). We read Don Murray's *A Writer Teaches Writing* (1968), and, though I'd not want to characterize Murray's work as "English education," we found in his appendix, "A Writing Teacher's Library," the works of John Dixon, Daniel Fader, John Holt, David Holbrook, Herbert Kohl, James Moffett, and publications of the London Association for the Teaching of English.

The education that we had given ourselves in our work in these NEH institutes led us into English education in two rather different ways: toward our department's sponsorship of a National Writing Project site, and toward the establishment within English of a new university writing program. First, the institutes led to the establishment of the Western Massachusetts Writing Project as a part of our English department. The 1978–1980 institutes created a corps of teachers who wanted to continue the connections established by these programs. This group pushed for the establishment of a UMass-Amherst Writing Project, with regular summer programs for area K–12 teachers and fall and spring conferences. The programs were sponsored not by our English department or by the university, but by the Five College Consortium: the University of Massachusetts, Amherst, Hampshire, Mount Holyoke, and Smith colleges. Under this sponsorship, the programs continued to grow until, in 1990, the governing board, chiefly composed of K–12 teachers, determined that we should apply to become a National Writing Project site affiliated with the English department at the university. As I write this, the Western Massachusetts Writing Project site is a vibrant and active site, directed by my colleague Anne Herrington.

Second, our work in the NEH institutes gave us the confidence to propose a new university writing program that would return the first-year writing program to the English department. This program came into being in 1982, just two years after the completion of the second NEH institute. The university writing program employed some ninety teaching assistants, and a good piece of the program's work was the training of teachers—roughly thirty of whom were new to the program in any given year. Our writing program included a substantial writing across the curriculum component, so we found ourselves in the business of inservice staff development for university faculty. This is, within English, the work of English education: training new teachers (preservice) and training experienced teachers (inservice). This pedagogical emphasis is reflected in our Ph.D. program as well, where we now have a strong concentration in composition and rhetoric, one that has a fine placement record and national reputation. Our university writing program has been cited by *U.S. News and World Report* as one of the best writing-in-the-disciplines programs in the country. The program is alive and well.

Yet the ideology that has obscured English education—the assumptions that teaching is less important than research and "higher" education better than "lower"—still finds itself expressed in the community that I think of as "mine," loosely defined by the journal *CCC*. We have become increasingly "professional," and by that I mean that we have adopted the values of English at the four-year research university. As Joe Harris puts it in *A Teaching Sub-*

ject, "I do not want that professionalization to come at the cost of the close ties to teaching that are what give so much work in the field its political and intellectual edge" (1997, xi). How many of us, senior persons in our field, really teach first-year writing courses? Along with the "close ties to teaching" that we may be losing—and I think here of the arguments that regularly surface in our discourse that we should eliminate first-year writing courses and become more-pure writing researchers—we have lost sight of a piece of our history, the close ties to the work in English education that is a substantial piece of our intellectual and social foundation.

To conclude this chapter, I want to illustrate—perhaps not prove to everyone's satisfaction, but illustrate—this point with three recent episodes drawn from my professional reading life. In each of these, we see subjects constituted by, and through their actions reproducing, our professional ideology.

1. I am reading in Jane Maher's (1997) biography of Mina Shaughnessy, one of my professional heroes. As I read, I am surprised at how "English" Shaughnessy is. I met her in the context of her work at City College, and imagined then that her situation there, which involved a lot of teacher and tutor training, was "home" for her. Yet although this is not a conspicuous part of her legend, according to her biographer she desperately wanted to be English. She was an undergraduate speech major, and a theater minor, at Northwestern (Maher 1997, 21). She took a Master's degree in English at Columbia University. The title of her Master's thesis was "An Annotated Bibliography of Masters' Theses Written at Columbia University: 1930–39 on Seventeenth-Century English Literature" (Maher 1997, 37). I can't imagine a more narrowly scholarly project— even a bit mind-killing. I wonder why her advisor set her to this project? Some lines of inquiry are best not pursued. But she did it. She badly wanted an English position at Hunter (Maher 1997, 86–87) but could not get one without the Ph.D. Yet, when she was working on *Errors and Expectations*, Shaughnessy drew on the English education community: Janet Emig, James Britton, Nancy Martin (1977, 130). In her list of suggested readings, there is the occasional person from the world of literary criticism, but most of her suggestions are from the world of English education. For instance, under the heading of "Writing and the Writing Process," she cites Jacques Barzun, but also Tony Burgess, Janet Emig, and Lev Vygotsky. Under "The Learner's Situation," the readings are entirely English education: Britton, Bruner, Cazden, a book on Piaget, and *Letters to a Teacher*, by the Schoolboys of Barbiana. It's tempting to think that Shaughnessy came to her intellectual home in her work with basic writers; but it's also tempting to think that she was heard in our profession because she was, at heart, someone who so wanted to be English. If she had set out to get her MAT at Brown University, as I did, would she have found the Education building?

2. In 1980, I published an article in *CCC*, "Teaching Writing/Teaching Literature"; and in 1990, a book chapter, "Reading Like a Writer," in both arguing that in teaching literature we should structure our curriculum so that students write before they read. In that way, I argued, our students will read like writers, becoming insiders, something like fans who know the game. Both the article and the chapter felt new to me, and the argument must have seemed new to those who accepted the articles for publication. Now it is almost thirty years later and I am rereading James Moffett's *Teaching the Universe of Discourse* (1968), which I have assigned for my graduate seminar, "Writing and the Teaching of Writing." I come across this on page 110: "When you yourself invent, you see all the choices, make decisions; the arbitrariness and inevitability of what professionals do disappears. It all begins to make sense. You are on the inside of the game, and it is more fun to play this way." There it is: that's what I'd said, but long before I'd said it. Now certainly I had read this in my first trip through the book, in 1978. But I had forgotten that it was there. This forgetting has its source, certainly, in our need as researchers to be finding the new; and it may have its source as well in what Harold Bloom termed "the anxiety of influence." But I believe that it had its principal source in my profession's ideology, a belief system that minimizes the contributions of those in English education. If we reread Moffett carefully, we find that his influence on composition studies has been profound, but is largely unacknowledged: his careful work with genre, with freewriting, with audience, and, in this particular case, with a way of integrating writing with the study of literature. So too with Janet Emig, James Britton, Nancy Martin—and the list could go on for another page or two. Todd Taylor's *CCC* citation index tells us that in the period 1991–1998 Moffett's work was cited ten times; Foucault's, twenty-one; and Elbow's, more than fifty. Like Shelley's poet, Moffett is an unacknowledged legislator of our time.

3. I'm working my way through an essay-in-manuscript in which the writer sets out to deconstruct the literature/composition divide in English, an admirable and important project. Appropriately resisting that binary, the writer nevertheless accepts as axiomatic that English *is* a binary. In this writer's view, there is literature, and there is composition, but there's no English education. The writer invokes Louise Rosenblatt without noting her critical contributions to English education, and cites Don Murray and Peter Elbow but not James Britton or Nancy Martin or Janet Emig. The writer cites Elbow's essays, which chronicle "the war between reading and writing" and refer to the "two cultures" of English: literature and composition. Both the "war" metaphor and the "two cultures" metaphor map a Manichaean universe with two great powers: literature and composition. In this worldview education, let alone English education, has no place at all. If there's a battle being fought, education is a bystander.

The writer goes on to cite Maxine Hairston's call to separate composition from literature, another important statement of the prevailing view of English as composed of two territories, literature and composition. In my comments to the editor who has sent me the manuscript for review, I say that the writer is wrong to exclude education, and English education, from English—but that the writer is, alas, one of us. This writing enacts and reproduces the prevailing ideology, as expressed in Elbow's essay, in Jim Berlin's and Steve North's histories of the field, and as expressed in my career choices and in my advice to my son, "at the capillary level."

Forgetting is necessary to the writing of history, as it is necessary to life. To include is to exclude; to remember is to forget. As a late-career teacher just now retired, I am beginning to clean house: to put into the blue recycling box papers that have piled up in too many places and to prune my library, both at home and at my office. This housecleaning is a species of forgetting. It is a necessary act. If I am to be able to function, I have to houseclean. Yet this housecleaning, this forgetting, is never innocent. What gets thrown away? Who is forgotten? And by whom? Jeanne Gerlach and Virginia Monseau, in *Missing Chapters: Ten Pioneering Women in NCTE and English Education*, argue that "scholars in the past have largely ignored the place of women in the history of English Education" (1991, xiv). Clearly the forgetting of English education has much to do with the forgetting of women's work: teaching, like cooking, seems to leave no history. But as I hope I've illustrated, this forgetting is not simply the work of "scholars." It is too easy to blame a seemingly unitary entity for what is clearly an unjust and undesirable result. As Foucault shows us, the distribution of power is the work of individuals, as they make choices in their daily lives, enacting, and thereby reproducing, the values of the culture. About this situation there is nothing to be "done" at the macro-level. But at the level of the individual, we can see and understand our own choices and look carefully at the ways in which they may reinscribe and reproduce values that, in principle, we do not hold.

Works Cited

Alsup, Janet. 1999. "Seeking Connection: An English Educator Speaks Across a Disciplinary 'Contact Zone.'" *English Education* 34(1): 31–49.

Blaustein, Andrew R., and Pieter T. J. Johnson. 2003. "Explaining Frog Deformities." *Scientific American* 288(2) (February): 65.

Braddock, Richard, Richard Lloyd-Jones, and Lowell Schoer. 1963. *Research in Written Composition*. Urbana, IL: NCTE.

Britton, James. 1970. *Language and Learning*. London: Penguin.

Britton, James, et al. 1975. *The Development of Writing Abilities (11–18)*. London: Macmillan.

Dixon, John. 1967. *Growth Through English*. London: Oxford University Press.

Emig, Janet. 1971. *The Composing Professes of Twelfth Graders*. Urbana, IL: NCTE.

Foucault, Michel. 1980. *Power/Knowledge: Selected Interviews and Other Writings, 1972–1977*, edited by Colin Gordon, translated by Colin Gordon, Leo Marshall, John Mepham, and Kate Soper. New York: Pantheon Books.

Gerlach, Jeanne Marcum, and Virginia R. Monseau. 1991. "Introduction." In *Missing Chapters: Ten Pioneering Women in NCTE and English Education*, xiv. Urbana, IL: NCTE.

Harris, Joseph. 1997. *A Teaching Subject: Composition Since 1966*. Saddle River, NJ: Prentice Hall.

Maher, Jane. 1997. *Mina P. Shaughnessy: Her Life and Work*. Urbana, IL: NCTE.

Martin, Nancy, et al. 1976. *Writing and Learning Across the Curriculum 11–16*. London: Ward Lock.

Moffett, James. 1968. *Teaching the Universe of Discourse*. Boston: Houghton Mifflin.

Moran, Charles. 1980. "Teaching Writing/Teaching Literature." *College Composition and Communication* 32: 21–30.

———. 1990. "Reading Like a Writer." In *Vital Signs: Bringing Together Reading and Writing*, edited by James L. Collins, 60–70. Portsmouth, NH: Boynton/Cook–Heinemann.

Murray, Donald M. 1968. *A Writer Teaches Writing*. Boston: Houghton Mifflin.

Shaughnessy, Mina P. 1977. *Errors and Expectations*. New York: Oxford University Press.

Taylor, Todd. *CCC Citation Index*. Available at: www.ncte.org/ccc/5/. Data drawn 3/5/03.

Wilcox, Thomas W. 1973. *The Anatomy of College English*. San Francisco: Jossey-Bass.

9

On My Disciplinary Birth

Keith Gilyard

A commonplace circulates that rhetoric is the mother of composition. Situated high enough up the ladder of abstraction or far enough back in time, the premise is true, I suppose, sort of like Lucy, that fully upright *Australopithecus afarensis*, being the mother of all the people now inhabiting the planet Earth. But at the level of our very real, immediate, biological lives, we each have a mother who is not Lucy. And to extend the metaphor, insofar as it can hold, my disciplinary mother is not rhetoric but English education. In 1981, my old intellectual self embraced the English education program at New York University (NYU). Two years later, well before graduation, I was a living, breathing, sometimes hollering, compositionist.

Here's the remix. In January 1980, I began tutoring in the writing center at LaGuardia Community College. I was one of the few tutors who held a Master's degree, so later that year I was given an opportunity to teach basic writing courses as an adjunct instructor. I had no discipline, either in the sense of being systematic or in the sense of having a field of study I called a professional home. I did possess some fairly decent teaching proclivities given my experiences as a creative writer and M.F.A. student, and my prior involvement with literacy efforts in my community. I had been a pretty restless, inquiring, active, politically engaged student on my own. Moreover, I was led by fellow community activists to read parts of Paulo Freire's *Pedagogy of the Oppressed* (1970) when I was a teenager. So I was never going to be satisfied simply with skilling and drilling students no matter their classification. I knew that student intention and input needed to be taken seriously. However, I have to admit that, because my neointuitive sense did not always save me, nor did Freire, I sometimes operated, mainly as a concession to department mandates, very much within the current-traditional paradigm.[1] I spent more time pacing students through decontextualized grammar exercises than I wish to reveal. The absence of a reliable theoretical scale meant the absence of a specific ethical mechanism by which I could (and would) eschew pedagogical practices in which I did not believe. If questions had been ethical for me, mandates would have been immaterial. But, as I said, I had no discipline.

Professor Marian Arkin came to the rescue. I suppose she saw a flash of talent and suggested that I pursue further graduate study with the aim of teaching English full-time. I rejected the idea instantly. To me, doctoral study meant reading a slew of books about which I was unlikely to care very much. The only doctoral program I had ever applied to promptly returned my application fee. The brochure for that program had advertised an innovative, interdisciplinary course of study, one open to student design. So in my application letter, I described the left-nationalist political framework that I was interested in relative to African American literature and how coursework and independent study of that sort could connect to other work I would do as a writer of fiction and poetry. But those folks weren't ready for all of that in the mid 1970s. At least I got my money back, which I regarded as a sign of the school's integrity. At any rate, Professor Arkin explained that NYU was the program she had in mind. The more she talked, the more I softened my objection, and eventually I decided to investigate. I would have no job security as an adjunct. LaGuardia Community College proved that to me quite soon. And who knew if or when I would hit as a writer?

Shortly thereafter, I intently perused the program description: "While most universities offer English courses in one college, and education courses in another, from our point of view, theory, content, and method are inseparable, and our courses and approaches reflect this philosophy. Our faculty focus on interactive processes between reader/viewer and work, writer and audience, speaker and listener, teacher and student, school and community. And throughout our courses we emphasize the development, application, and evaluation of teaching materials and strategies" (Doctoral Program in English Education, ca. 1980, 1). A promising start, I surmised. I didn't fear theory, had done plenty in activist study groups. I certainly needed method so that I could systematically follow the best of my inclinations. I sensed the content would be cool. Further on in the document, I spotted my intended specialization, Curriculum #711A, Composition Education: "Focuses on writing as a process of learning; analyzes relationships among audience, function of writing, and theories of discourse; offers implications and strategies for integrating writing in all areas of the curriculum with special emphasis on the problems faced by the basic writer" (2). English education at NYU sounded like the play for me. I enrolled like Marvin, as in Gaye, meaning let's get it on.

In the 1981 spring semester, I joined a tradition fashioned primarily by pioneers Louise Rosenblatt and Lou LaBrandt and being managed and modified at that time by the likes of John Mayher, Marilyn Sobelman, Harold Vine, Mitchell Leaska, Roger Cayer, and Gordon Pradl. Transactional educational theory reigned, and the political emphasis, though hardly ever stated explicitly, was the development of critical, meaning-making language users as an essential component of a functional democracy. The notion was progressive, and you could take it more radical, more Marxian like Freire, if so disposed. After all, Richard Ohmann's far-left *English in America* (1976) was on the reading list given to all students upon entry. The environment seemed inviting. In this context, I tackled the mélange of philosophy, psychology, history, sociology, anthropology, literary criticism, research methodology, linguistics, and pedagogy through which I was supposed to become a better writing teacher.

That first semester I took two seminars: Linguistics, Society, and the Teacher, taught by Roger Cayer, and Prose Style in English, offered by Mitchell Leaska. In the first course, I was introduced to various principles of sociolinguistics, including *linguistic equality, communicative competence*, and *code switching*. I already possessed, in fact lived, an essential insight: The variety of English one speaks cannot alone account for much in terms of explaining school failure or success. The sociolinguists immediately became my allies, providing bountiful language that I could use to argue my case. Dell Hymes' lengthy introduction to the collection *Functions of Language in the Classroom* (1972) particularly spoke to me. Because Hymes encouraged teacher research and stressed the idea of provisional knowledge, he both spurred me to conduct formal experiments in the classes I would teach and spared me from the excessive claims of theoretical linguistics. I would view transformational grammar, for example, interesting as it sometimes was, as still just grammar—and no grammar model alone can be a sufficient pedagogy.

John Gumperz and Eduardo Hernández-Chavez (1972), in "Bilingualism, Bidialectalism, and Classroom Interaction," their contribution to that anthology, pointed in a specific pedagogical direction. They suggested that students and teachers discuss course goals with the aim of arriving at a common understanding concerning communicative effectiveness. Texts then would be assessed, with students working in groups taking the lead, based on the established norm. In their own research, Gumperz and Hernández-Chavez found that this approach led to improvements in both student motivation and technical proficiency. I drew an asterisk in the margin along with the notation, "Can use this in class."

An additional agenda item came from Leaska's course. The focus was on comparing natural narratives of the type described by William Labov (1972, 354–96) as "the transformation of experience in narrative syntax" with portions of fictional narratives such as Daniel Defoe's *Moll Flanders* (1722), Charles Dickens' *David Copperfield* (1850), Mark Twain's *Huckleberry Finn* (1885), and William Faulkner's *The Sound and the Fury* (1929). This represented a worthwhile look at how literary narrative is constituted linguistically, but right away I became more interested in the application of natural narrative to the teaching of composition. Mary Louise Pratt (1977), long before the profession heard her espouse the arts of the contact zone (1991), nudged me along the way, for it was through her *Toward a Speech Act Theory of Literary Discourse* that I became familiar with Labov. Pratt explained, following Labov, that a fully formed natural narrative contains *abstract, orientation, complicating action, evaluation, resolution,* and *coda.* After discussing at length the similarities between literary narrative and natural narrative, she concluded, "All the problems of coherence, chronology, causality, foregrounding, plausibility, selection of detail, tense, point of view, and emotional intensity exist for the natural narrator just as they do for the novelist, and they are confronted and solved (with greater or lesser success) by speakers of the language every day. These are not rhetorical problems that literary narrators have had to solve by inventing a poetic language; they are problems whose solutions can readily be adapted from spoken to written discourse" (1977, 66–67).

I didn't aim for my students to write novels, but I figured that if I could demonstrate to them through a study of natural narrative that they already commanded many of the rhetorical resources needed to write successfully, whether the task was fiction, narrative essay, or thesis-support work, then they could see the value of a descriptive method based on their output. I could dispense with the old, often inadequate prescription of *introduction, supporting paragraphs,* and *conclusion.* I wrote in my notebook, "Respect the students' work and get the students to respect their own work."

Can the study of natural narrative really make a difference? In retrospect, I would say yes. We read some of them, wrote some of them, edited our own and those of others—all to good effect. But I never wanted to develop a natural-narrative fetish or become stuck in any particular routine. I thought natural narrative, like the technique of employing student groups, was a good item for the toolbox. However, I looked for more tools. And new theories— which also are tools.

By the fall of 1981, the stakes had been raised. I landed a one-year, full-time appointment at Medgar Evers College, which is located in Brooklyn. The college, which always has been officially a four-year school, operated fiscally as a community college because of concessions made during the New York City budget crisis of the 1970s. I had five writing sections, approximately thirty students in each, all of whom were considered basic writers. Their collective optimism conveyed an overriding message to me: "We hope you good at this."

I took two more seminars (after classes in history and psychology over the summer): Introduction to Applied Linguistics and Doctoral Seminar in English Education. Gordon Pradl taught both. The first prompted more experimentation in my writing classes as I sought additional applications for linguistic theory. I had a specific interest in empirically testing claims about the influence of speech on composing, what many teachers termed *dialect interference.* This was their rationale for trying to "correct" speech as part of their writing pedagogy. I thought those teachers' efforts to be a dubious enterprise. It had been stressed to me, as I traveled some of the creative writing circles in New York City, including at Columbia University, that one had to read to write. It was axiomatic that the more you read, the better writer you would be. I became surer in my thinking when I read John Mayher's unpublished manuscript "Linguistics for Who-Never-Will-Be Linguists." I never sat in a classroom with Professor Mayher, but I might as well have done so given his massive manuscript, which was required reading for us. At any rate, Mayher argued clearly that to focus on speech–writing and, for that matter, speech–reading connections would be to miss the real action. The link that writing instructors should be most concerned with is the link between reading and writing. Would empirical work, even a rudimentary form, confirm my own sense and Mayher's reasoning? I formed my hypothesis (that the speech–writing link was weak), chose a special language feature to consider (-*ed* endings), collected writing samples, taped students, and involved fellow faculty members as readers and raters. I'll simply say of the study that I was satisfied with the results.

In the English education seminar, the talk was more global. We discussed texts that gave us a broad conception of how we fit as budding, NYU-style English educators within institutional and intellectual histories: Susanne Langer's *Philosophy in a New Key* (1942), George A. Kelly's *A Theory of Personality* (1963), David Holbrook's *English for the Rejected* (1964), Stephen Toulmin's *Human Understanding* (1972), Arthur Applebee's *Tradition and Reform in the Teaching of English* (1974), John Rouse's *The Completed Gesture* (1978), Jane Tompkins' edited collection *Reader-Response Criticism* (1980), Erich Auerbach's *Mimesis* (1953), Louise Rosenblatt's *The Reader, the Text, the Poem* (1978), and Roland Barthes' *Writing Degree Zero* (1968).

Kelly's ideas, his anticipatory, transactional psychology, have been enormously important in terms of my thinking about how belief systems operate for individuals and how people tend to resolve contradictions by assigning different status to competing propositions. There are several implications of Kellyan psychology. The most pertinent for that seminar was that it set the table for analyses of interpretation. As indicated, I had long felt reading to be an important funding source for writing. But I never thought much about how interpretation occurred or how it was a constructivist activity. In this regard, Tompkins' then-recent anthology was invaluable. As she characterized reader-response scholarship, "Reading and writing join hands, change places, and finally become distinguishable only as two names for the same activity" (Tompkins 1980, x). Contributors demonstrated, sometimes dazzlingly, that point, people like Stanley Fish, Wolfgang Iser, Norman Holland, and, to a lesser extent, Walker Gibson. But I came back most frequently to Gibson's republished 1950/1980 essay, "Authors, Speakers, Readers, and Mock Readers," because he identified as a writing teacher. He had been president of the National Council of Teachers of English and had chaired the Modern Language Association's Division on the Teaching of Writing. (In 2003, I delivered the Walker Gibson Lecture, with him seated in the audience, at the University of Massachusetts.)

Gibson theorized that readers adopt personas as authors do. To be a mock reader one had to be active, psychologically in motion as one sought to clarify values through reading. Gibson raised the question of what or who students want to be in relation to texts. Admittedly, as Tompkins pointed out, Gibson's notion was still text-centered and thus, though significant, not a radical statement among reader-response critics. The most productive analysis for me was Rosenblatt's *The Reader, the Text, the Poem* (1978). The *poem* not the *text* was the literary work, and only the *reader* could construct the *poem*. That particular insight wasn't new by the time we read Rosenblatt, though in real time she expressed such thinking long before anyone we read in the Tompkins book. Moreover, Rosenblatt explicitly proffered a vision, influenced by Walt Whitman, in which a truly democratic society necessitated a democratic view of the reader and the reader's role. This is the practical relevance for all students and language educators of her painstaking analysis.

Another text I return to is Toulmin's *Human Understanding* (1972). Toulmin takes it pretty deep, about five hundred pages deep, in his attack on rigid formalism regarding questions of rationality. He posits, instead, a notion of rationality that stresses historicism, empiricism, functionality, and adaptation. There is more than one Idea of the Good (or Idea of Good Grammar). In an undergraduate philosophy course, I had been briefly introduced to Plato and the debate about form versus objects. I never got the point somebody made about the chairs we were sitting in not being real. Only the idea of the chair was. Would the floor we hit also not be real if we fell out of the chairs that were not really real? That was my teenage grappling with the thing. Now I still admired Plato, mainly because of how he represented Socrates and incorporated all of that powerful verbal game in those dialogues. I had to pass on Platonist idealism, though, especially because there were some historical materialist escorts waiting for me just around the corner. The upshot is that I was predisposed to endorse Toulmin's project. In fact, I thought he took too long—eighty-five pages in—to make a key point for me: "In all our subsequent enquiries, therefore, our starting-point will be the living, historically-developing intellectual enterprises within which concepts find their collective use; and our results must be referred back for validation to our experience in those historical enterprises" (1972, 85). Always an experimenter anyway, I noted my impatience in the margins of my copy. Almost three hundred pages later, Toulmin still harped on the issue, and I still tracked him with my yellow highlighter: "The Practical Reason like the Pure Reason must have an eye, not to the Good or the Best, and still less to the Only-Coherently-Conceivable, but rather to the Better; and, the rationality of collective human enterprises being what it is, this means always the Better-for-the-Time-Being" (371). I truly thought I humanly understood the argument by then.

Although I didn't have the language at the time, looking back I realize that Toulmin lined up as an antifoundationalist, and I firmly with him, against proponents of philosophical rationalism. This debate would continue to unfold in the social sciences and humanities with all the ebbs and flows that big-idea debates tend to have. In those days, I did not presume that antifoundationalism, or antifoundationalist jargon, is what a writing teacher needed. I never mentioned Toulmin. However, I did know that his logic supported the idea that students were writers and not merely people learning to write, that they already had meaningful things to express, and that those gestures toward meaning had to take priority over the rigid, narrow, formal exercises laid out in many writing classrooms.

In Doctoral Seminar in English Education II, taught by Harold Vine the following semester, spring 1982, we continued an informative reading schedule, the most important book being James Britton's *Language and Learning* (1972). For one of our written assignments, Professor Vine asked us to identify major hypotheses and postulates in Britton's book. On March 15, I listed nine and considered the final one to be the most significant: "In order to maximally develop the skills of transactional reading, transactional speaking, and transactional writing, these uses of language must be required across the whole range of the curriculum at all levels. Only then can these particular uses of language fulfill the necessary function of allowing students to deepen their understanding concerning different aspects of life. Students required to use transactional language across the curriculum will show greater progress in thinking skills than those students who are not required to use such language across the curriculum."[2]

Vine next prodded us to think about research projects. About halfway through the semester, I scribbled a note on my syllabus: "Ask Vine about retrospective 'case study' of my own language development." By the end of the semester, I offered a five-page document, of which Vine was most supportive, describing my dissertation plans. As I contemplated the field—a combined English education–composition field in my view—and the contribution I thought I could begin to make, I asserted, "I will not be primarily concerned with explaining, per se, the writings of others. I want to see if they can explain me." The project wasn't focused enough at that point. I needed to take more courses, read more, attend National Council of Teachers of English and Conference on College Composition and Communication conventions, and meet Geneva Smitherman.

At the same time I was in Vine's course, I studied with Geoffrey Summerfield. He was an old-school hipster, British style, who had participated in the 1966 Dartmouth Conference[3] and had newly arrived to teach at NYU. Before the first class, I was hanging out with George Chapman, a friend from the old neighborhood who would later be an informant for my dissertation. I think we were trying to pretend we hadn't reached the age of thirty. I told George that he should come with me to class, Applied Linguistics in the Classroom. "You mean just walk up in there like how we do?" I immediately replied, "Just like that." So we sauntered in, a few minutes late, loose and angular, our flair coming from our where. Summerfield was crazy about us, became mildly upset when he found out that George was only visiting.

Through Summerfield's guidance, I took another look at Barthes (1977), this time his aphoristic book *Roland Barthes*. Summerfield was very interested in the notion of the *Doxa*, or the central beliefs of a people, what we might call the *superordinate construct* in Kelly's terms or sometimes term *dominant discourse* in our professional literature. Barthes himself described the *Doxa* as "Public Opinion, the mind of the majority, petit bourgeois Consensus, the Voice of Nature, the Violence of Prejudice" (47)—and also as a "wrong object" and "dead repetition" (70–71). In any case, Summerfield stressed that language is the most sensitive bearer of the *Doxa*. In addition, Summerfield pushed us, as other professors had done, to consider issues of language and society as directly connected to schooling. As a final assignment, he gave us a series of questions to answer. Two specifically related to the work I did at Medgar Evers College. The first: Give an account of any major linguistic principles that have affected, or are affecting, your view of your students' language, both oral and written.

I revised the question before answering, writing to Summerfield, "Chomsky, for one, argues convincingly that the study of language cannot be separated from the study of Mind.[4] So, first off, when you write 'linguistic principles,' I assume you mean psychological principles as well." Then I followed:

1. Along with George A. Kelly, I believe there are alternate ways of construing, of anticipating events in the world. A person's actions in any situation will depend on how he [still had some sexist language going on] perceives that particular situation. If a person perceives a certain body of knowledge as having no value, he will not choose to learn it. There is a curious tension in the remedial students [was also still trapped in some retrograde terminology about students] with whom I work. They want degrees so they can make it in the market place, but frequently they resist speaking and writing the language of the market place. There seems to be some conflict between different sets of expectations.

2. I believe in the self-fulfilling prophecy. If a student believes he can achieve very little, he will indeed achieve very little in terms of his potential.

3. Along with Joshua Fishman, I feel that the idea of "repertoire expansion" (77)[5] makes more sense than trying to suppress one language variety in order to impose another upon a student. The acquisition of Standard English on the part of Blacks would probably be made easier if the whole mood to eradicate the "vernacular" were not so popular among members of the dominant culture.

4. According to R. A. Hudson, "One of the most solid achievements of linguistics in the twentieth century has been to eliminate the idea (at least among professional linguists) that some languages or dialects are inherently better than others" (1980, 191–92). I agree with this concept of linguistic equality, and I make my convictions clear to my students. All languages I know of are rule governed and fully conceptual. None indicates cognitive deficiency on the part of the speaker. The doctrine of linguistic equality is crucial as it forces the rejection of any argument

that claims social inequality is based on inherent linguistic inequality. We have heard such nonsense far too long.

5. Britton has provided me with hypotheses concerning the functions of talk and writing in the classroom. I hope my paraphrasing does justice to the concepts he presented rather loosely in *Language and Learning*:

    a. Talk is important in that it allows us to negotiate for ourselves a position of strength in the world. Talk provides the feedback, which assures us of the reality and feasibility of our representations of the world, and of our place within them. This process of identification and modification must take place *in* school as well as in the outside world, so ample opportunity for talk should be an essential part of any curriculum. (1972, 134–41, 222–23)

    b. The value of writing lies in the shaping of experience, in exploring the possibilities of experience without the pressing demands of actual speaking and listening. Writing is to be seen as a tremendous aid to formal learning (thinking); thus, much writing should be required of students. (Britton 1972, 248–64)

I closed, "These, then, are some of the major principles affecting my view of both my students and their work."

The second question, actually an imperative, that Summerfield presented was this: Note any features of your students' language that (a) irritate you; (b) seem to you in need of change, improvement, or correction. I responded:

It should be obvious by now that any notions of "irritation" and "correction" are foreign and irrelevant to me. I do not deal in terms of annoyance and eradication. I do not even think, pedagogically, in terms of language per se. My concern is that my students, virtually all of whom speak some nonstandard dialect [more outdated terminology], can acquire the ability to produce the standard dialect in appropriate contexts, to indeed know which contexts are the appropriate ones. So again I am talking about communicative competence and repertoire expansion.

Language learning on the adult remedial level is as much a "buying into" proposition as anything else. Synchronic models of language may fit the needs of theoretical linguistics, but as social matrixes are embedded in all "live" languages, it is improper to speak of language learning without some consideration of the overall learning situation, or without a conception of the learner as an active participant in what is going on. I say all this to say that rather than think in terms of irritation and correctness, what teachers of nonstandard speakers [despite all of my studies, still slipped and conflated speaking with writing] ought to be prepared to do is praise and encourage the language they encounter. This may be the best and only start toward their students' acquisition of the standard dialect. For you can be sure, for the most part, that if you reject their tongue, they will reject yours.

At that point I was nearly a compositionist, I think, looking back. I was in the process of going public, at least public within professional circles, although sometimes in too zealous and fumbling a manner. In 1982, I spoke at a language symposium at Medgar Evers College (I had received another one-year appointment). In March 1983, I attended my first CCCC convention and served as an associate chair on the panel, "Strategies for Enabling Congenial Composing," featuring Geoffrey Summerfield, John Rouse, and Judith Fishman. Also, to hear some more of the composition conversation, I bounced around to a variety of sessions, including one that highlighted Smitherman, "Black Student Writers and Linguistic Implications for Social Change."

After CCCC, I felt I needed to have a go-to rap about composition to be all the way in the field. Practitioners and theorists must construct composition for themselves. The transactionalists at NYU certainly felt that way, and I do now. Obviously, I was stitching together some understandings in the context of their English education courses. I occasionally referred back to an essay I read in Pradl's applied linguistics course, Nan Elsasser and Vera P. John-Steiner's "An Interactionist Approach to Advancing Literacy" (1980). They kept the stress on social dimensions of literacy and grounded their educational experiments in Freirean and Vygotskian principles—prompting me to read Vygotsky (1962). But I didn't have the overview, the synthesizing spin. I picked that up later in the year when I read the just-released *Learning to Write/Writing to Learn*, written by John Mayher, Nancy Lester, and Gordon Pradl (1983). My transactions out of class with the scholarship of NYU folks (Nancy had been a student and would later teach there) would be the perfect complement to in-class activity. I figured they planned it that way just for me.

Many of the insights in *Learning to Write/Writing to Learn* have informed my work over my growing years (still growing). I habitually return to the distinction the authors make (51–55) between an analytic model of writing instruction (focus on error) and a development one (primary concern with learners in transition who build on existing strengths to expand verbal repertoires). This typology has proven to be a reliable way for me to sort proposals for writing pedagogy. Moreover, I probably repeat as much as anyone the teaching mantra: *fluency clarity correctness* (4). Sometimes, though, I translate the Mayher, Lester, and Pradl conception (got to have my own style) into *flow grow show*. Useful as well is the authors' concept of *matured fluency*, a display of literacy characterized by *flexibility*, *confidence*, and *voice* (60).

And so in 1983, I became a compositionist. I have been one ever since. I had more seminars to take, papers to write, teaching to do, and experiments to conduct. Graduation was still a couple of years away. But I was in the discipline.

I am not only in composition. Literary criticism long has been an identity for me. Rhetoric, in the strict disciplinary sense, has been a new beginning. But the phrase "new beginning" is, in the final analysis, an oxymoron. Some of my colleagues in rhetoric, fun bunch that they are, argue that at NYU I was studying the rhetoric of English education as an initial theoretical entry into composition. I have to grant them the truth of their statement, but we don't have to play every language game at home.

In 1990, I strode confidently into the lobby of the Palmer Hotel in Chicago. The place was abuzz with the chatter that one expects at a CCCC convention. My mother accompanied me because she wanted to visit a childhood friend from Georgia who lived in the city. I spotted Geoffrey Summerfield and immediately introduced my mother to him. He asked in a surprised tone, kidder that he often could be, "And you admit that you're his mother?" My mother laughed, a wisdom laugh that I knew so well, and replied, "Of course." Joke or no, she knew that you should not ever deny—or let anyone else ever deny—what is yours.

Notes

3. According to Richard Young (1978), features of the paradigm include "emphasis on the composed product rather than the composing process; the analysis of discourse into words, sentences, and paragraphs; . . . and the strong concern with usage (syntax, spelling, punctuation) and with style (economy, clarity, emphasis)" (31). John Clifford (1981) notes the "instructor is the sole teacher, audience, authority, and evaluator" (44).

4. Reference is to Britton (1972): "We have been considering transactional writing, and because an important point has to be made in this connexion, we shall add it here. It concerns the conditions necessary in school for the development of transactional writing, speaking and reading. The point is this: these uses of language are the joint responsibility of the teachers of all subjects on the curriculum. Children will learn to master transactional language by using it, and they will need to use it in every kind of lesson. It seems to me urgently necessary that this responsibility should be faced: and the first necessary step is that secondary school staffs should by consultation arrive at an agreed policy for language across the curriculum in the school in which they work" (263–64).

5. Held at Dartmouth College, the conference, funded by Carnegie Endowment and organized by the Modern Language Association and the National Council of Teachers of English, was a historic gathering of British and American educators.

6. Reference is to Noam Chomsky (*Language and Mind*, 1972).

7. The source is actually Joshua A. Fishman and Erika Lueders-Salmon (1972).

Works Cited

Applebee, A. 1974. *Tradition and Reform in the Teaching of English.* Urbana, IL: National Council of Teachers of English.

Auerbach, E. 1953. *Mimesis: The Representation of Reality in Western Literature.* Princeton, NJ: Princeton University Press.

Barthes, R. 1968. *Writing Degree Zero*, translated by A. Lavers and C. Smith. New York: Hill and Wang.

———. 1977. *Roland Barthes.* New York: Hill and Wang.

Britton, J. 1972. *Language and Learning*. Harmondsworth, UK: Penguin.

Chomsky, N. 1972. *Language and Mind*. Rev. edition. New York: Harcourt, Brace and Jovanovich.

Clifford, J. 1981. "Composing in Stages: The Effects of a Collaborative Strategy." *Research in the Teaching of English* 15(1): 37–53.

Defoe, D. 1722. *The Fortunes and Misfortunes of the Famous Moll Flanders*.

Dickens, C. 1850. *David Copperfield*.

Elsasser, N., and V. P. John-Steiner. 1980. "An Interactionist Approach to Advancing Literacy." In *Thought & Language/Language & Reading*, edited by M. Wolf, E. Radwin, and M. K. McQuillan, 451–65. Cambridge, MA: Harvard Educational Review.

Faulkner, W. 1929. *The Sound and the Fury*. New York: Jonathan Cape and Harrison Smith.

Fish, S. E. 1980. "Interpreting the *Variorum*." In *Reader-Response Criticism: From Formalism to Post-Structuralism*, edited by J. P. Tompkins, 164–84. Baltimore: Johns Hopkins University Press.

Fishman, J. A., and E. Lueders-Salmon. 1972. "What Has the Sociology of Language to Say to the Teacher? On Teaching the Standard Variety to Speakers of Dialectal or Sociolectal Varieties." In *Functions of Language in the Classroom*, edited by C. B. Cazden, V. P. John, and D. Hymes, 67–83. New York: Teachers College Press.

Freire, P. 1970. *Pedagogy of the Oppressed*, translated by M. B. Ramos. New York: Continuum.

Gibson, W. 1950/1980. "Authors, Speakers, Readers, and Mock Readers." In *Reader-Response Criticism: From Formalism to Post-Structuralism*, edited by J. P. Tompkins, 1–6. Baltimore: Johns Hopkins University Press.

Gumperz, J., and E. Hernández-Chavez. 1972. "Bilingualism, Bidialectalism, and Classroom Interaction." *Functions of Language in the Classroom*, 84–108. New York: Teachers College Press.

Holbrook, D. 1964. *English for the Rejected: Training Literacy in the Lower Streams of the Secondary School*. Cambridge, MA: Cambridge University Press.

Holland, N. 1980. "Unity identity text self." *Reader-Response Criticism: From Formalism to Post-Structuralism*, edited by J. P. Tompkins, 118–33. Baltimore: Johns Hopkins University Press.

Hudson, R. A. 1980. *Sociolinguistics*. Cambridge, MA: Cambridge University Press.

Hymes, D. 1972. "Introduction." In *Functions of Language in the Classroom*, edited by C. B. Cazden, V. P. John, and D. Hymes, xi–lvii. New York: Teachers College Press.

Iser, W. 1980. "The Reading Process: A Phenomenological Approach." In *Reader-Response Criticism: From Formalism to Post-Structuralism*, edited by J. P. Tompkins, 50–69. Baltimore: Johns Hopkins University Press.

Kelly, G. A. 1963. *A Theory of Personality: The Psychology of Personal Constructs*. New York: W. W. Norton.

Labov, W. 1972. *Language in the Inner City: Studies in the Black English Vernacular.* Philadelphia: University of Pennsylvania Press.

Langer, S. 1942. *Philosophy in a New Key: A Study in the Symbolism of Reason, Rite, and Art.* Cambridge, MA: Harvard University Press.

Mayher, J. S., N. Lester, and G. M. Pradl. 1983. *Learning to Write/Writing to Learn.* Portsmouth, NH: Boynton/Cook–Heinemann.

Ohmann, R. 1976. *English in America: A Radical View of the Profession.* New York: Oxford University Press.

Pratt, M. L. 1977. *Toward a Speech Act Theory of Literary Discourse.* Bloomington, IN: Indiana University Press.

———. 1991. "Arts of the Contact Zone." *Profession* 91: 33–40.

Rosenblatt, L. 1978. *The Reader, the Text, the Poem: The Transactional Theory of the Literary Work.* Carbondale, IL: Southern Illinois University Press.

Rouse, J. 1978. *The Completed Gesture: Myth, Character and Education.* New York: Skyline Books.

Tompkins, J. P. 1980. "An Introduction to Reader-Response Criticism." In *Reader-Response Criticism: From Formalism to Post-Structuralism*, edited by J. P. Tompkins, ix–xxvi. Baltimore: Johns Hopkins University Press.

———, ed. 1980. *Reader-Response Criticism: From Formalism to Post-Structuralism.* Baltimore: Johns Hopkins University Press.

Toulmin, S. 1972. *Human Understanding: The Collective Use and Evolution of Concepts.* Princeton, NJ: Princeton University Press.

Twain, M. 1885. *The Adventures of Huckleberry Finn.*

Vygotsky, L. 1962. *Thought and Language*, edited and translated by E. Hanfmann and G. Vakor. Cambridge, MA: The M.I.T. Press.

Young, R. 1978. "Paradigms and Problems: Needed Research in Rhetorical Invention." In *Research in Composing*, edited by C. R. Cooper and L. Odell, 29–47. Urbana, IL: National Council of Teachers of English.

Afterword

A Case for Collaboration: Intertwined Roots, Interwoven Futures

Last year I entered a conversation with smart and articulate colleagues across the country who came together because of our shared interest in the teaching of writing at the secondary and postsecondary levels and our shared concern over the direction taken by some of the so-called "reform initiatives" as they impact writing and writing instruction. Over the course of many months, we collaborated to create a document called the *Framework for Success in Postsecondary Writing*, a kind of guide to the habits of mind and experiences that are critical for college success. (See http://wpacouncil.org/framework for the full document and accompanying resources.) In this joint undertaking by the National Council of Teachers of English (NCTE), the National Writing Project (NWP), and the Council of Writing Program Administrators (CWPA), my role was to represent NCTE, chairing a small subcommittee of NCTE members composed of college-level English education professors and compositionists, many of us former high school teachers. In parallel fashion, the NWP group, led by Anne Marie Hall of the University of Arizona, included both secondary and college teachers and the CWPA group, led by Linda Adler-Kassner of the University of California at Santa Barbara, included mostly compositionists. The project's chair was Peggy O'Neill of Loyola University Maryland, an active member of the composition community and a former high school teacher. As we thought hard and discussed honestly our concerns with recent renditions of "college and career readiness," especially as that phrase impacts writing and writing pedagogy, we relied not only on each other's areas of disciplinary expertise, but also on the blurred boundaries of our knowledge and interests. We were all compositionists, we were all English educators—whether we lived in English departments, freestanding writing programs, colleges of education, or high schools. Our work together reflected the kind of interdisciplinary conversation that was part of all of our professional histories.

As I read and reread the essays in this book, I keep thinking about this experience of developing the *Framework* as emblematic of what many of these authors are talking about. As we did the research, the thinking, and the writing of the *Framework* and then took it out on the road to secondary and community college teachers for feedback (literally—as we created workshops surrounding draft renditions of the document and solicited response from those attending), we were exhilarated by both the variety of voices we heard and the shared understandings we discovered. In many ways, we were a contemporary example of the kind of collaboration that the authors of this book describe so well, living proof that these connections can, do, and should exist between composition and English education. In our case, these connections arose in part from our similar roots, but also from the recognition of our similar interests. What we saw was that the intersections are natural ones and that the end results—when we take care to recognize and celebrate these intersections—can be vitally important for literacy teaching and learning.

These intersections, what we used to refer to in my graduate school days as the "interdiscipline of composition," are what inspired me to do the work I do. I began my career as a high school English teacher, someone who had first found a passion in composition studies as I was immersed in the work for my M.Ed. in the Teaching of English at the University of Virginia. When I left high school teaching to pursue a Ph.D. at the University of Michigan in the late 1980s, I—like the authors of the essays in this volume—dove into the books and essays and research studies of those scholars and publishers who first brought issues of writing pedagogy to the attention of teachers everywhere. Like Sheridan Blau, I was captivated by the stance of James Moffet; like Anne Gere, I learned from the lessons of Richard Braddock; like Tom Newkirk, my eyes were opened by the words of James Kinneavy; like Charles Moran, I eagerly gobbled up the writings of Mina Shaughnessy; like Bonnie Sunstein, I found comfort in the ideas of "the Dons" (Graves and Murray); like Keith Gilyard, I stretched my thinking by reading James Britton; and like Cy Knoblauch and Lil Brannon, I found a home in the magic of Boynton-Cook publications. And because of the intimacy of the world of composition studies at that time, I was able to meet many of those scholars who were writing so thoughtfully about composition and teaching. I will never forget the conference organized by my mentor Jay Robinson, when I got a chance (as a graduate student!) to sit and talk with my academic heroes: Cy Knoblauch and Lil Brannon, Janet Emig, Anne Berthoff, and David Bartholome, among others.

At the same time, I read Vygotsky and Bakhtin, Robert Coles and Clifford Geertz, Paulo Freire, Sartre, and James Boyd White—thoughtful scholars across a variety of disciplines whose work informed my questions about writing theory and practice. Like the authors in this volume, I lived in a world in which the questions were big ones, in which the boundaries between English education and composition were seamless, in which the disciplines of anthropology and phenomenology and linguistics and sociology all connected, in which the voices of each group informed the others, in which the lines between secondary and college writing instruction were blurry, in which the readings we relied on and the practices we espoused were nuanced rather than separate. As the authors of the essays in this book so clearly demonstrate, we in composition and English education were in many ways united because of what has often been described as our second-class citizenship in the departments of English: We weren't literature specialists. Rather, we were united by our interest in how students learn to write and how a focus on pedagogy might impact how we in turn saw the bigger picture that theory provided us. In other words, for most of us, the beginning to understanding began in our teaching; where that took us depended on our lenses. And so we studied Derrida and Foucault, even as we read John Dewey and Maxine Greene and Nancie Atwell and Peter Elbow. And in our minds, so interconnected were the two fields that when many of us went on the job market in the late 1980s and early 1990s, we felt very comfortable applying for jobs as either compositionists (usually in English departments) or English educators (in either English or education departments), or sometimes both. My own path took me to a position in composition at Eastern Michigan University, but I was not surprised at all to find myself teaching a combination of first-year composition and methods courses; restarting an NWP site; regularly attending both Conference on College Composition and Communication and NCTE conventions; serving as a liaison with the College of Education and with the literature specialists in my own department. That this multipronged role should seem perfectly ordinary was what my academic training taught me; that it should seem fun and exciting was what my beliefs about writing and pedagogy made clear.

As several of the authors in this volume have noted, this vision of the interdiscipline of composition seems more out of favor these days. As Jim Zebroski explains in his essay, the reasons vary. Perhaps it is because of

> the passing or retiring of the first generation of compositionists, many of whom received degrees in colleges of education; turf battles; matters of funding; the emergence of poststructuralist theory and cultural studies critique; the decline of social science research—including, for example, sociology and anthropology—in composition and rhetoric; and the location in the 1980s of most of the new doctoral programs in composition and rhetoric within English departments. (46)

All those reasons make sense to me. As I've worked in a university for the last twenty-one years, I've watched these changes both locally and nationally and seen not only the resulting specializations that can occur, but, too often, a disinclination to understand and respect the work of each other. But it doesn't have to be that way. In fact, I want to argue why this separation does not serve us well in the long run.

Education is under fire. Literacy education is bearing the brunt of much of the heat. We need look no further than the emphasis on specified (and, I would argue, reductive) types of writing called for in the Common Core Standards, the increasing use of both high- and low-stakes standardized tests in the secondary writing curriculum, the limited input on decisions about how concepts (like college and career readiness) are defined, and the commercialization of standards and curriculum to know that we need to be a big tent in order to have a big voice. Increasingly, the practice of education is being mandated by legislators, publishing companies, and others who are neither scholars in the field nor teachers of actual students. If we have any hope of being heard, we need to be heard together: K–12 teachers who bring a vast knowledge of how writing is taught and learned, college instructors who focus on the teaching of writing as their main mission, English educators who work with preservice and practicing teachers, scholars who study the theorized practice of composition. And to be heard together, we have to begin by listening to each other, recognizing what each of us brings to the discussion and how the roles we currently occupy don't define or limit what we can bring to the table. We do share an interest; we do share knowledge. And together, perhaps, we can be heard.

English education and composition studies are rooted together in so many ways; our intertwined histories, as we learn from this volume, make this evident. At this juncture in history, our interests and our futures are interwoven as well. Right now we need to take advantage of our shared passions and expertise; right now is the time to bring to the table all of what we know and—in the company of smart and caring others—try to get this work, the literacy education of our students, done right.

Cathy Fleischer
Eastern Michigan University

coming together,
not dwelling on
distinctions

Contributors

Sheridan Blau is Distinguished Senior Lecturer in English Education and Coordinator of the English Education Program at Teachers College, Columbia University. He is also Professor of English and Education (Emeritus) at the University of California, Santa Barbara, where for thirty years he directed the South Coast Writing Project and Literature Institute for Teachers. He is a former President of the National Council of Teachers of English (NCTE) and recipient of NCTE's Distinguished Service Award. He has published widely on literary, pedagogical, and professional topics and authored a number of textbooks in composition and literature. His book for teachers and scholars, *The Literature Workshop: Teaching Texts and Their Readers* (Heinemann, 2003), won the NCTE/Conference on English Education (CEE) Richard Meade Award for outstanding research in English education. His most recent and forthcoming publications include articles on teaching *Paradise Lost*, on academic writing about literature, and on the nature of literary knowledge.

Lilian Brannon and Cy Knoblauch are professors of English at University of North Carolina–Charlotte. Among other books and articles, they have cowritten *Rhetorical Traditions and the Teaching of Writing* (Boynton/Cook, 1984) and *Critical Teaching and the Idea of Literacy* (Boynton/Cook, 1993). Robert Boynton served as their editor.

Janet Emig is University Professor Emerita of Rutgers, The State University of New Jersey. In 2006, she won the NCTE James R. Squire award for her "transforming influence on the profession." She is currently revising her poetry for publication.

Cathy Fleischer is Professor of English at Eastern Michigan University, where she teaches courses in English education and written communications and codirects the Eastern Michigan Writing Project. She also serves as Special Imprint Editor for the Principles in Practice series for the NCTE. Author of numerous books and articles about teachers and writing, her book *Writing Outside Your Comfort Zone* (coauthored with high school teacher Sarah Andrew-Vaughan; Heinemann, 2009) won the CEE's James Britton Award. Her recent work has focused on the ways teachers can reach out to others to help them better understand issues of literacy, codirecting the Family Literacy Initiative (a parent outreach program), and authoring *Reading & Writing & Teens: A Parent's Guide to Adolescent Literacy* (NCTE, 2010).

Anne Ruggles Gere is Arthur F. Thurnau Professor and Gertrude Buck Collegiate Professor at the University of Michigan where she directs the Sweetland Center for Writing and Cochairs the Joint Ph.D. Program in English and Education, the program from which she took her own Ph.D. Before entering graduate school, she was a high school English teacher, and her first academic position was at the University of Washington where she was the founding director of the Puget Sound Writing Program. A winner of the Richard Meade award for outstanding research in English education, she is a former president of NCTE and a former chair of College Composition and Communication. She has published a dozen books and over seventy articles; most recently, she published an article about directed self-placement in *Assessing Writing* and served as executive editor of an NCTE series titled Supporting Students in a Time of Common Core Standards.

Keith Gilyard has lectured widely on language, literature, education, and civic affairs. His books include the education memoir *Voices of the Self: A Study of Language Competence* (Wayne State University Press, 1991), for which he received an American Book Award; *Composition and Cornel West: Notes Toward a Deep Democracy* (Southern Illinois University Press, 2008); and *True to the Language Game: African American Discourse, Cultural Politics, and Pedagogy* (Routledge, 2011). Gilyard has served on the executive committees of the NCTE, the CEE, and the Conference on College Composition and Communication (CCCC). He is currently Distinguished Professor of English at The Pennsylvania State University, University Park.

Charles Moran is Emeritus Professor of English at the University of Massachusetts–Amherst. With Gail Hawisher, Paul LeBlanc, and Cynthia Selfe, he coauthored *Computers and the Teaching of Writing in American Higher Education, 1979–1994* (Ablex, 1996). With Anne Herrington, he has coedited *Genre Across the Curriculum* (Utah State University Press, 2005) and *Writing, Teaching, and Learning Across the Disciplines* (MLA). With Anne Herrington and Kevin Hodgson, he coedited *Teaching the New Writing: Technology, Change, and Assessment* (Teachers College Press, 2009). He was the founding director of the University's Writing Program and one of the founding directors of the Western Massachusetts Writing Project.

Thomas Newkirk is Professor of English at the University of New Hampshire where he founded the New Hampshire Literacy Institute, now in its thirty-second year. He is the author of numerous articles, op-ed pieces, and book chapters on literacy at all levels. In 2000, he won the David H. Russell Award from NCTE for his book, *The Performance of Self in Student Writing* (Boynton/Cook, 1997). He is currently completing *The Art of Slow Reading: Six Time-Honored Practices for Engagement* (Heinemann), scheduled for publication in late 2011.

Patricia Lambert Stock is Professor Emerita of English and of Writing, Rhetoric and American Cultures in Michigan State University. A former president of NCTE and recipient of the council's Distinguished Service Award, she has written books and articles about literacy teaching and learning, the scholarship of teaching, writing centers, and contingent faculty in higher education. Her published work has been recognized with the James Britton, Richard A. Meade, and Janet Emig Awards; with Hofstra University's National Research Award; and with the CCCC's Outstanding Book Award.

Bonnie Sunstein is Professor of English and Education at the University of Iowa where she directs undergraduate nonfiction writing in English, chairs English Education, and teaches courses in research, nonfiction writing, English education, and American folklore. She has taught in public schools and colleges throughout New England and at writing institutes across the country and abroad. Her books focus on portfolios, teacher research, and ethnographic research methods. Her chapters, articles, and poems appear in professional journals and anthologies. Her career testifies to composition's roots are in English education.

Kathleen Blake Yancey is Kellogg W. Hunt Professor of English and Distinguished Research Professor at Florida State University, where she directs the Graduate Program in Rhetoric and Composition. She has served as President of the NCTE; Chair of CCCC; and President of the Council of Writing Program Administrators. Currently Second Vice-President of South Atlantic Modern Language Association, she will assume the Presidency in 2013. Codirector of the Inter/National Coalition for Electronic Portfolio Research, she is also the editor of *College Composition and Communication*. She has authored, edited, or coedited eleven scholarly books and over seventy articles and book chapters. Her edited volume *Delivering College Composition: The Fifth Canon* (Boynton/Cook, 2006) won the Best Book Award from the Council of Writing Program Administrators, and in 2010 she was the recipient of the Florida State University Graduate Teaching Award.

James Zebroski, senior faculty member in rhetoric and composition at the University of Houston, has taught in a variety of settings including the public schools. At the University of Houston, he teaches freshman composition, advanced composition, creative nonfiction, gay literature, and graduate seminars on subjects including Vygotsky, critical theory, and pedagogy. Zebroski is author of *Thinking Through Theory: Vygotskian Perspectives on the Teaching of Writing* (Boynton/Cook, 1994), more than forty articles and chapters in books on wide-ranging topics, including the social formation of gay authorship, politics of writing instruction, ethnographic writing, post-Fordism and twenty-first-century composition, contemporary composition history, composition textbook advertisements, and response to student texts. Most recently he has published "Theory in the Diaspora" (2005), "Social Class as Discourse: Mapping the Landscape of Class in Rhetoric and Composition" (2006), and "Critical Theory, Critical Pedagogy, and the Re-conceptualization of Rhetoric and Composition" (2011)—all in the *Journal of Advanced Composition*. His current research interests include investigations into a "postmodern Lev Vygotsky," social class theory, and curriculum theory. He and his colleagues at the University of Houston have just put into place a new Ph.D. program in Rhetoric, Composition, and Pedagogy.

Index

Abstraction, 92–93
Abstractive amplitude, 92
Academic discourse, 35, 42
Academic presses, 67–68
Achebe, Chinua, 58
Acknowledgments, 52
Active Voice: A Writing Program Across the Curriculum (Moffett), 82, 96, 101*n*3
Adams, Anthony, 86, 101
Adams, Henry, 101
Adjunct pay, 64–65
Adler, Renata, 60
Adler-Kassner, Linda, 160
Advanced Placement test alternatives, 77
AEPL (Assembly for Expanded Perspectives on Learning), 99
African American History Museum, Smithsonian Institution, xiii
African American vernacular dialect, 154–55
Alfred, William, 58
Allen, Don Cameron, 20*n*7
Allerton Park Conference, 1962, 20*n*7
Alsup, Janet, 79
American Association of Teachers of Journalism, 9
American College and University, The (Rudolph), 8
American Indians, 72, 78, 79
Amherst College, 17, 142
Analogical thinking, 93
Analytical writing instruction model, 156
Anatomy of College English, The (Wilcox), 141
Anderson, George, 137

Angell, James B., 8, 11
Anglo-American Seminar on the Teaching and Learning of English (Dartmouth Conference), 30, 36–39, 65, 83, 85–88, 97, 106, 141, 153
drama study group, 86
"An Interactionist Approach to Advancing Literacy" (Elsasser and John-Steiner), 156
"Annotated Bibliography of Masters' Theses Written at Columbia University, An: 1930–1939 on Seventeenth-Century English Literature" (Maher), 143
Anthropology, 116
Antifoundationalists, 152–53
Applebee, Arthur, xi–xiv, 2, 83, 85, 125, 151
Applied linguistics, 150–51, 153–54
Aristotle, 45, 115
Arizona, University of, 160
Arkin, Marian, 148
Arnold, Matthew, 56
Articulation theory, 6–7
Assembly for Expanded Perspectives on Learning (AEPL), 99
Atwell, Nancie, 67, 68, 96, 115, 127, 162
Auden, W. H., 55
Auerbach, Erich, 151
Authoring a Discipline: Scholarly Journals and the Post-World War II Emergence of Rhetoric and Composition (Goggin), xi

"Authors, Speakers, Readers, and Mock Readers" (Gibson), 151
Authors, students as, 31, 32, 39–42
Authorship
defined, 31, 39
egalitarian change and, 39–42
process theory and, 42
Avery, Carol, 115
Axelrod, Rise, 94

Bailey, Richard W., 13, 17
Baker, Doug, 79
Baker, Franklin T., 9
Bakhtin, Mikhail, 68, 161
Ballenger, Bruce, 118, 120
Barbieri, Maureen, 115, 118
Barnes, Douglas, 86
Barr, Mary, 127
Barritt, Loren S., 18
Barthes, Roland, 31, 151, 153–54
Bartholomae, David, 17, 127, 161
Barzun, Jacques, 143
Basic writers, 147, 150–51, 155
Bate, Walter Jackson, 101
Bateman, Donald, 34
Bay Area Writing Project, 67, 89, 96, 97, 101*n*2, 102*n*6
Bazerman, Charles, 78, 96
Becker, Alton L., 9
Beer Picnic, The (Emig), 55
Beers, Kylene, 67
Belief systems, 151
Believing game, 52
Belles lettristic studies, 19
Benedict, Ruth, 54
Benjamin, Walter, 26
Berlin, James A., xi, 1, 7, 9, 27, 29, 59, 145